WWK7

FLEET HISTORIES

OF

THE MUNICIPALITIES OF TRANSVAAL PROVINCE, SOUTH AFRICA

ALBERTON MUNICIPALITY

BENONI MUNICIPALITY

BOKSBURG MUNICIPALITY

BRAKPAN MUNICIPALITY

EKURHULENI TRANSPORT

HERCULES MUNICIPALITY

JOHANNESBURG MUNICIPAL TRANSPORT
JOHANNESBURG METROPOLITAN BUS SERVICE

KEMPTON PARK MUNICIPALITY

KEMPTON PARK BUS SERVICE

NIGEL MUNICIPALITY

NORTHERN BUS SERVICE, JOHANNESBURG

ROODEPOORT MUNICIPALITY

SPRINGS MUNICIPALITY

PUBLISHED BY

THE PSV CIRCLE

DECEMBER 2013

FOREWORD

This publication lists known data for the municipal bus operators in Transvaal Province. Full histories are shown for Johannesburg Municipality and Ekurhuleni Transport. Other operators are included but with far more limited data. Official records do not appear to remain for these operators, all of whom ceased many years ago. Histories for several other operators have already been published in an earlier book and these are listed below in the contents. The other major operators in Transvaal Province are PUTCO and successors to United Transport. Future publications will cover them. Transvaal Province ceased to exist in 1994 and the towns and cities in this book became part of Gauteng Province.

This book is one of a series drafted by the late Andrew Johnson, following his extensive research in South Africa. It was completed by David Corke. It would not have been possible without the assistance of Johannesburg Metropolitan Bus Service and Ekurhuleni Transport. Valuable help was also given by John Herdman, Ron Phillips, David Powell, Graham Shields, John Shearman, Gavin Strachan and Peter Tulloch.

Photographs have kindly been supplied by Stewart J Brown, Andrew Johnson, Alan Mortimer, Stan Hughes, Jim Neale, Graham Shields and John Squier. Thanks are also offered to Mike Eyre for preparing the photographs for publication.

This is one of a range of publications produced by The PSV Circle primarily as a service to its members. The information contained herein has been taken from the range of sources indicated above; either from observation or other research and also includes information provided from other reputable sources. Considerable time and effort has been taken to ensure that the content of this publication is as complete and accurate as possible but no responsibility can be accepted for any errors or omissions.

The list of municipal bus companies and other major urban operators follows. This also serves as a contents.

Abbreviations Used:

AB&C	Africa Body & Coach	ECW	Eastern Coachworks
AMC	Afinta Motor Corporation	MCCW	Metro-Cammell
BBA	Bus Bodies (Port Elizabeth)	TMBB	Transvaal Motor Body Builders
BBL	Bus Bodies (Letaba)	VSA	V.S.A.
BMS	B.M.S. (British Mining Supplies)		

Layout:

Fleet No	Registration No	Chassis Type	Chassis No	Bodybuilder	Body No	Date New	Date In	Date Out

Any general comments on this publication may be sent to the Publications Manager, Unit GK, Leroy House, 436 Essex Road, London, N1 3QP or via email to **publications.manager@psv-circle.org.uk**. Details of how to join The PSV Circle and a list of all our publications can be obtained from The PSV Circle website - **www.psv-circle.org.uk**.

ISBN: 978-1-908953-20-9

Published by the PSV Circle.
© The PSV Circle December 2013

ALBERTON MUNICIPALITY

Alberton Municipality commenced in 1956. The fleet was at its maximum size in 1984 at 139 buses. Non-white services then passed to PUTCO in 1985. Operations ceased completely in 1993 by which time the fleet only totalled 32.

No	Reg	Make/Model	Chassis	Body		Type			
21	TDK 2722	Leyland ERT2/1	551931	BBA	117/5	B52F+13	2/56	2/56	-/--
22	TDK 2723	Leyland ERT2/1	551932	BBA	117/6	B52F+13	2/56	2/56	/
23	TDK 2724	Leyland ERT2/1	551980	BBA	117/7	B52F+13	2/56	2/56	-/--
24	TDK 2725	Leyland ERT2/1	551978	BBA	155/1	B52F+13	2/56	2/56	-/--
25	TDK 3878	Leyland ERT2/1	573506	BBA	270/9	B62F+16	4/58	4/58	-/--
26	TDK 3879	Leyland ERT2/1	572975	BBA	270/7	B62F+16	5/58	5/58	-/--
27	TDK 2720	Leyland ERT2/1	551929	BBA	117/3	B62F+16	2/56	2/56	-/--
28	TDL 3917	Leyland ERT2/1	573748	BBA	270/6	B62F+16	4/58	4/58	-/--
29	TDK 2721	Leyland ERT2/1	551930	BBA	117/4	B62F+16	2/56	2/56	-/--
30	TDK 3916	Leyland ERT2/1	580806	BBA	284/3	B62F+16	10/58	10/58	-/--
31	TDK 2726	Leyland ERT2/1	551979	BBA	155/2	B52F+13	2/56	2/56	-/--
32	TDK 2701	Leyland ECPO2/1R	575387	BBA	193/7	B42F+12	9/57	9/57	-/--
33	TDK 2719	Leyland ERT2/1	551928	BBA	117/2	B62F+15	2/56	2/56	-/--
34	TDK 3457	Leyland ERT2/1	573745	BBA	271/2	B62F+16	5/58	5/58	-/--
35	TDK 3456	Leyland ERT2/1	573744	BBA	271/1	B62F+16	5/58	5/58	-/--
36	TDK 2718	Leyland ERT2/1	551927	BBA	117/1	B62F+15	2/56	2/56	-/--
15	TDK 3801	Leyland ERT2/1	580651	BBA	313/1	B62F+16	12/58	12/58	-/--
16	TDK 3802	Leyland ERT2/1	580652	BBA	313/2	B62F+16	12/58	12/58	-/--
17	TDK 3803	Leyland ERT2/1	580876	BBA	320/1	B62F+16	3/59	3/59	-/--
18	TDK 3804	Leyland ERT2/1	580877	BBA	320/2	B62F+16	3/59	3/59	-/--
19	TDK 3805	Leyland ERT2/1	580878	BBA	320/3	B62F+16	3/59	3/59	-/--
20	TDK 3806	Leyland ERT2/1	580879	BBA	320/4	B62F+16	3/59	3/59	-/--
2	TDK 3906	AEC Regal IV	9825E2400	TMBB		B62F+15	7/59	7/59	-/--
3	TDK 3912	AEC Regal IV	9825E2404	TMBB		B62F+15	10/59	10/59	-/--
4	TDK 3913	AEC Regal IV	9825E2405	TMBB		B62F+15	10/59	10/59	-/--
5	TDK 4031	AEC Regal IV	9825E2192	TMBB		B62F+15	5/60	5/60	-/--
6	TDK 3907	AEC Regal IV	9825E2194	TMBB		B62F+15	7/59	7/59	-/--
7	TDK 3908	AEC Regal IV	9825E2401	TMBB		B62F+15	9/59	9/59	-/--
8	TDK 3909	AEC Regal IV	9825E2241	TMBB		B62F+15	9/59	9/59	-/--
9	TDK 3910	AEC Regal IV	9825E2193	TMBB		B62F+15	9/59	9/59	-/--
12	TDK 3911	AEC Regal IV	9825E2403	TMBB		B62F+15	9/59	9/59	-/--
13	TDK 4030	AEC Regal IV	9825E2514	TMBB		B62F+15	9/59	9/59	-/--
1	TDK 1938	Leyland ERT2/1	622582	Craftsman		B66F+16	-/63	-/63	-/--
10	TDK 2919	Leyland ERT2/1	622420	Craftsman		B66F+16	-/63	-/63	-/--
11	TDK 1591	Leyland ERT2/1	L01124	Craftsman		B66F+16	-/63	-/63	-/--
14	TDK 1592	Leyland ERT2/1	?	Craftsman		B66F+16	-/63	-/63	-/--
3	TDK 7305	AEC Kudu	2S2RA203	BBA	2195/2	B66F+16	2/66	2/66	-/--
6	TDK 2125	AEC Kudu	2S2RA204	BBA	2195/3	B66F+16	2/66	2/66	-/--
8	TDK 6402	AEC Kudu	2S2RA205	BBA	2195/4	B66F+16	3/66	3/66	-/--
9	TDK 6918	AEC Kudu	2S2RA202	BBA	2195/1	B66F+16	3/66	3/66	-/--
15	TDK 7690	Leyland ERT2/1	L40368	BBA	2194/1	B67F+16	6/66	6/66	-/--
16	TDK 7691	Leyland ERT2/1	L44436	BBA	2194/2	B67F+16	6/66	6/66	-/--
17	TDK 7692	Leyland ERT2/1	L44437	BBA	2194/3	B67F+16	6/66	6/66	-/--
18	TDK 7693	Leyland ERT2/1	L45003	BBA	2194/4	B67F+16	6/66	6/66	-/--
5	TDK 6284	Daimler SRC6	36165	BBA	2244/1	B65F+15	10/67	-/68	-/--
2	TDK 6726	Daimler SRC6	36287	AB&C		B65F+15	-/68	-/68	-/--
4	TDK 6964	Daimler SRC6	36284	AB&C		B65F+15	-/68	-/68	-/--
7	TDK 6727	Daimler SRC6	36286	AB&C		B65F+15	-/68	-/68	-/--
19	TDK 6285	Daimler SRC6	36167	AB&C		B65F+15	-/67	-/67	-/--
20	TDK 6963	Daimler SRC6	36201	AB&C		B65F+15	-/68	-/68	-/--
3	TDK 14191	Daimler SRC6	36321	Craftsman	CC-11-2	B65F+16	10/70	10/70	-/--
12	TDK 14190	Daimler SRC6	36322	Craftsman	CC-11-1	B65F+16	10/70	10/70	-/--
21	TDK 14192	Daimler SRC6	36320	Craftsman	CC-11-3	B65F+16	10/70	10/70	-/--
22	TDK 14193	Daimler SRC6	36323	Craftsman	CC-11-4	B65F+16	10/70	10/70	-/--
23	TDK 2398	Mercedes-Benz	007367	?		B61F+15	-/70	-/70	-/--
24	TDK 2400	Mercedes-Benz	000011	?		B61F+15	-/70	-/70	-/--
25	TDK 2404	Mercedes-Benz	000020	?		B61F+15	-/70	-/70	-/--

101	TDK 1911	Mercedes-Benz OH1517 000465	BBA	2653/1	B60F+21	10/70	10/70	-/--
102	TDK 1928	Mercedes-Benz OH1517 000466	BBA	2653/2	B60F+21	10/70	10/70	-/--
103	TDK 1933	Mercedes-Benz OH1517 000467	BBA	2653/3	B60F+21	10/70	10/70	-/--
104	TDK 2011	Mercedes-Benz OH1517 000102	BBA	2653/4	B60F+21	10/70	10/70	-/--
105	TDK 2035	Mercedes-Benz OH1517 000024	BBA	2653/5	B60F+21	10/70	10/70	-/--
106	TDK 10454	Mercedes-Benz OH1517 000468	BBA	2653/6	B60F+21	10/70	10/70	-/--
107	TDK 2048	Mercedes-Benz OH1517 000101	BBA	2653/7	B60F+21	10/70	10/70	-/--
108	TDK 2074	Mercedes-Benz OH1517 000801	BBA	2653/8	B60F+21	10/70	10/70	-/--
109	TDK 2077	Mercedes-Benz OH1517 000814	BBA	2653/9	B60F+21	10/70	10/70	-/--
110	TDK 2092	Mercedes-Benz OH1517 000815	BBA	2653/10	B60F+21	10/70	10/70	-/--
111	TDK 2097	Mercedes-Benz OH1517 000800	BBA	2653/11	B60F+21	10/70	10/70	-/--
		Mercedes-Benz OF1617/60 694449	BBA	2608/1	B60F+21	2/71	2/71	-/--
		Mercedes-Benz OF1617/60 677589	BBA	2608/2	B60F+21	2/71	2/71	-/--
		Mercedes-Benz OH1317 000875	BBA	2754/1	B---F	7/71	7/71	-/--
		Mercedes-Benz OH1317 000876	BBA	2754/2	B---F	7/71	7/71	-/--
		Mercedes-Benz OH1317 000881	BBA	2754/3	B---F	7/71	7/71	-/--
		Mercedes-Benz OH1317 000882	BBA	2754/4	B---F	7/71	7/71	-/--
3	TDK 17622	Leyland ERT2A/1	7102260	BBA	2821/1	B60F+16	4/72	4/72	-/--
8	TDK 17623	Leyland ERT2A/1	7102261	BBA	2821/2	B60F+16	4/72	4/72	-/--
9	TDK 17624	Leyland ERT2A/1	7102688	BBA	2821/3	B60F+16	4/72	4/72	-/--

Notes:

TDK 2722-5, 3878/9, 2720, 3917, 2721, 3916, 2726/01/19, 3457/6 (21-35) renumbered 47-59/62/1 -/70.

TDK 2718, 3801-6 (36, 15-20) renumbered 60, 41-6 -/70.

TDK 3906 (2) is quoted with chassis number 9825E2912, an incorrect number. The number shown above is allocated to Alberton and has been deduced by process of elimination.

TDK 3906/12/3, 4031, 3907-10 (2-9) renumbered 67/4, 70, 68/5/9/6/3 -/70.

A 1965 fleet list gives 1-36 as detailed above, 37-49 as trucks while 50-55 are light delivery vans.

TDK 7305, 2125, 6402, 6918 (3, 6, 8, 9) renumbered 74/1/3/2 -/70.

TDK 6284 (5) ex demonstrator as B53F.

		AEC Kudu	3S2RA953	BBA	2822/1	B---F	4/72	4/72	-/--
		AEC Kudu	3S2RA954	BBA	2822/2	B---F	4/72	4/72	-/--
		AEC Kudu	3S2RA955	BBA	2822/3	B---F	4/72	4/72	-/--
		AEC Kudu	3S2RA956	BBA	2822/4	B---F	4/72	4/72	-/--
120	TDK 8531	AEC Kudu	32SRA1003	BBA	2886/1	B63F+16	11/72	11/72	6/85
121		AEC Kudu	32SRA1002	BBA	2886/2	B63F+16	11/72	11/72	-/--
122	TDK 4364	AEC Kudu	32SRA1057	BBA	2886/3	B63F+16	11/72	11/72	6/85
123		AEC Kudu	32SRA1061	BBA	2886/4	B63F+16	11/72	11/72	6/85
		Leyland ERT2A/1	7105382	BBA	2888/1	B---F	2/73	2/73	-/--
		Leyland ERT2A/1	7105383	BBA	2888/2	B---F	2/73	2/73	-/--
		Leyland ERT2A/1	7105384	BBA	2888/3	B---F	2/73	2/73	-/--
		Leyland ERT2A/1	7105392	BBA	2933/1	B---F	8/73	8/73	-/--
		Leyland ERT2A/1	7105390	BBA	2933/2	B---F	8/73	8/73	-/--
		Leyland ERT2A/1	7105391	BBA	2933/3	B---F	8/73	8/73	-/--
		Leyland ERT2A/1	7200700	BBA	2933/4	B---F	9/73	9/73	-/--
		Leyland ERT2A/1	7200701	BBA	2933/5	B---F	9/73	9/73	-/--

196	TDK 19319	AEC Kudu	3S2RA1053	BBA	2934/2	B63F+16	7/73	7/73	6/85
197	TDK 19316	AEC Kudu	3S2RA1052	BBA	2934/1	B63F+16	7/73	7/73	6/85
198	TDK 19318	AEC Kudu	3S2RA1054	BBA	2934/3	B63F+16	7/73	7/73	6/85
199	TDK 19315	AEC Kudu	3S2RA1065	BBA	2934/4	B63F+16	9/73	9/73	6/85
200	TDK 19320	AEC Kudu	3S2RA1060	BBA	2934/5	B63F+16	7/73	7/73	6/85
35		Foden 4XB6/16	?	Brockhouse		DP59F	by 12/74	by 12/74	by 12/89
36	TDK 7419	Foden 4XB6/16	77994	Brockhouse		DP59F	5/74	5/74	6/85
37	TDK 21928	Foden 4XB6/16	?	Brockhouse		DP59F	by 12/74	by 12/74	by 12/89
00	TDK 7400	Foden 4XB0/10	?	Brockhouse		DP59F	by 12/74	by 12/74	by 12/89
39	TDK 7431	Foden 4XB6/16	77990	Brockhouse		DP59F	10/74	10/74	6/85
40		Foden 4XB6/16	?	Brockhouse		DP59F	by 12/74	by 12/74	by 12/89
134	TDK 23754	Mercedes-Benz	980268	BBA	3099/1	B63F+16	4/75	4/75	6/85
135	TDK 23753	Mercedes-Benz	980269	BBA	3099/2	B63F+16	4/75	4/75	6/85
136	TDK 23751	Mercedes-Benz	980270	BBA	3099/3	B63F+16	4/75	4/75	6/85
137		Mercedes-Benz	987535	BBA	3099/4	B63F+16	4/75	4/75	6/85
138	TDK 23752	Mercedes-Benz	987536	BBA	3099/5	B63F+16	4/75	4/75	6/85
		Mercedes-Benz	987537	BBA	3100/1	B63F+16	4/75	4/75	-/-
4	KZH 531T	Mercedes-Benz	987803	BBA	3100/2	B63F+16	4/75	4/75	-/94
5	KYN 096T	Mercedes-Benz	981045	BBA	3100/3	B63F+16	4/75	4/75	-/94
6	KYN 094T	Mercedes-Benz	988082	BBA	3100/4	B63F+16	4/75	4/75	-/-
7	KYN 093T	Mercedes-Benz	990413	BBA	3100/5	B63F+16	4/75	4/75	-/94
10	KYN 092T	Mercedes-Benz	990414	BBA	3100/6	B63F+16	4/75	4/75	-/94
		Mercedes-Benz	102725	BBA	3100/7	B63F+16	5/75	5/75	-/-
		Nissan CB20N	0041	BBA	3188/1	B64F+16	4/76	4/76	-/-
		Nissan CB20N	0045	BBA	3188/2	B64F+16	4/76	4/76	6/85
303	TDK 7791	Nissan CB20N	0077	BBA	3188/5	B64F+16	4/76	4/76	6/85
304	TDK 8897	Nissan CB20N	0049	BBA	3188/3	B64F+16	4/76	4/76	6/85
305	TDK 3664	Nissan CB20N	0072	BBA	3188/4	B64F+16	4/76	4/76	6/85
306	TDK 5422	Nissan CB20N	0078	BBA	3188/6	B64F+16	4/76	4/76	6/85
163	TDK 25707	Nissan CB20N	0076	BBA	3188/7	B64F+16	4/76	4/76	6/85
164	TDK 25708	Nissan CB20N	0079	BBA	3188/8	B64F+16	4/76	4/76	6/85
165	TDK 25709	Nissan CB20N	0074	BBA	3188/9	B64F+16	4/76	4/76	6/85
175	TDK 25710	Nissan CB20N	0080	BBA	3188/10	B64F+16	4/76	4/76	6/85
176	TDK 25711	Nissan CB20N	0081	BBA	3188/11	B64F+16	4/76	4/76	6/85
177	TDK 25712	Nissan CB20N	0082	BBA	3188/12	B64F+16	4/76	4/76	6/85
		Nissan CK10	11224	BBA	3189/1	B40F+12	5/76	5/76	-/-
		Nissan CK10	11446	BBA	3189/2	B40F+12	5/76	5/76	-/-
		Nissan CK10	11453	BBA	3189/3	B40F+12	5/76	5/76	-/-
		Nissan CK10	11666	BBA	3189/4	B40F+12	5/76	5/76	-/-
		Nissan CB20	00234	BBA	3285/1	B63F+16	5/77	5/77	-/94
		Nissan CB20	00246	BBA	3285/2	B63F+16	5/77	5/77	-/94
109	TDK 31142	Nissan CB20	00231	BBA	3286/1	B63F+16	5/77	5/77	6/85
131	TDK 31143	Nissan CB20	00233	BBA	3286/2	B63F+16	5/77	5/77	6/85
141	TDK 31144	Nissan CB20	00243	BBA	3286/3	B63F+16	5/77	5/77	6/85
145	TDK 31145	Nissan CB20	00235	BBA	3286/4	B63F+16	5/77	5/77	6/85
146	TDK 31146	Nissan CB20	00232	BBA	3286/5	B63F+16	5/77	5/77	6/85
148	TDK 31147	Nissan CB20	00236	BBA	3286/6	B63F+16	5/77	5/77	6/85
307	TDK 31148	Nissan CB20	00247	BBA	3286/7	B63F+16	5/77	5/77	6/85
308	TDK 31149	Nissan CB20	00240	BBA	3286/8	B63F+16	5/77	5/77	6/85
26	TDK 665	?	?	?		B—F	by 11/77	by 11/77	-/-
130	TDK 13908	Nissan CB20N	00320	?		B76F+28	5/78	5/78	6/85
132	TDK 14335	Nissan CB20N	00328	?		B76F+28	5/78	5/78	6/85
133	TDK 14417	Nissan CB20N	00347	?		B76F+28	5/78	5/78	6/85
139	TDK 14644	Nissan CB20N	00348	?		B76F+28	6/78	6/78	6/85
143	TDK 14669	Nissan CB20N	00343	De Haan		B76F+28	6/78	6/78	6/85
144	TDK 14677	Nissan CB20N	00338	?		B76F+28	6/78	6/78	6/85
150	TDK 15132	Nissan CB20N	00336	De Haan		B76F+28	6/78	6/78	6/85
158	TDK 15238	Nissan CB20N	00322	?		B76F+28	6/78	6/78	6/85
309	TDK 15706	Nissan CB20N	00344	?		B76F+28	6/78	6/78	6/85
310	TDK 15930	Nissan CB20N	00319	?		B76F+28	6/78	6/78	6/85

Notes:

The 4 1972 AEC Kudu with body numbers 2822/1-4 were registered TDK 17618-21, order unknown. TDK 17619 was numbered 117.

One of the 1973 Leyland ERT2A/1 was TDK 15743 (191)
TDK 19319/6/8/5/20 (196-200) had 3 axles.
TDK ?, 7419, 21928, 7430/1/? (35-40) were used on 'whites-only' services and were probably completed to
    a higher standard, hence DP59F. The registration TDK 7429 was carried by one of the
    Fodens, which also had chassis number 77996. 35/?/39 were later renumbered 209/210/211;
    the unknown bus was the one registered TDK 7429. The others may have been renumbered,
    but if so, their new numbers are not known.
TDK 23754/3/1/?/2, ?, KZH 531T, KYN 096/4/3/2/?T (134-8, ?, 4-7, 10) were Mercedes-Benz OF1617/60
    with chassis numbers prefixed 355098.20 (10 prefixed 355098.24).
The registrations shown for 4-7 and 10 are not the original ones.
Two 1976 Nissan CB20N are quoted as 12, 13. These were latterly registered KZN 439T, KTG 469T
    respectively and survived till 1993. They may have been those with body numbers 3188/1, 2.
Two of the 1976 Nissans CK10 were 9, 11, latterly registered KTG 488T, KYH 119T.
The 1977 Nissan CB20 with body numbers 3285/1, 2 were 16, 17, order unknown. These were latterly
    registered LVN 637T, LYM 538T respectively
2 Nissan CB20 have been reported rebodied (no further details) by -/89.

Disposals:

TDK 8531, 4364, ?, ?, 19319/6/8/5/20 (120/2/3/96-200): PUTCO 268-75.
TDK 7419/29/31 (209-11): PUTCO 1097-9.
TDK 23754/3/1/?/2 (134-8): PUTCO 3718-22.
KZH 531T (4): Concordia Tours, Honeydew 21.
KYN 096/3/2T (5/7, 10): Highway Bus Lines, thence to Concordia Tours, Honeydew 22/3/4.
? (?) (Nissan CB20N 0045): PUTCO 4505.
TDK 7791, 8897, 3664, 5422, 25707-12 (303-6, 163-5/75-7): PUTCO 4504/6-14.
TDK 31142-9 (109/31/41/5/6/8, 307/8): PUTCO 4515-22.
TDK 13908, 14335/417/644/69/77, 15132/238/706/930 (130/2/3/9/43/4/50/8, 309/10): PUTCO 4523-32.

174	BWN 785T	Nissan CB20N	00512	?			B80F+28	3/79	3/79	6/85
178	BWN 775T	Nissan CB20N	00513	?			B80F+28	3/79	3/79	6/85
179	BWN 767T	Nissan CB20N	00555	?			B80F+28	3/79	3/79	6/85
180	BWN 763T	Nissan CB20N	00517	?			B80F+28	3/79	3/79	6/85
181	BWN 752T	Nissan CB20N	00526	?			B80F+28	3/79	3/79	6/85
182	BWN 739T	Nissan CB20N	00544	?			B80F+28	3/79	3/79	6/85
183	BWN 729T	Nissan CB20N	00511	?			B80F+28	3/79	3/79	6/85
184	BWN 715T	Nissan CB20N	00506	?			B80F+28	3/79	3/79	6/85
185	BWN 708T	Nissan CB20N	00516	?			B80F+28	3/79	3/79	6/85
186	BWN 698T	Nissan CB20N	00519	?			B80F+28	3/79	3/79	6/85
187	BWN 684T	Nissan CB20N	00502	?			B80F+28	3/79	3/79	6/85
188	BVH 017T	Nissan CB20N	00504	?			B80F+28	3/79	3/79	6/85
189	BVH 054T	Nissan CB20N	00492	?			B80F+28	3/79	3/79	6/85
192	BVH 076T	Nissan CB20N	00441	?			B80F+28	3/79	3/79	6/85
193	BVH 094T	Nissan CB20N	00491	?			B80F+28	3/79	3/79	6/85
194	BWN 793T	Nissan CB20N	00505	?			B80F+28	3/79	3/79	6/85
18	BWN 796T	Nissan CB20N	?	?			B63F+17	-/79	-/79	-/94
19	BWN 816T	Nissan CB20N	?	?			AB107F+50	-/79	-/79	-/94
20	BVC 589T	Nissan CB20N	?	?			AB107F+50	-/79	-/79	-/94
21	BWN 811T	Nissan CB20N	?	?			B65F+15	-/79	-/79	-/94
201	FVM 525T	Nissan CB20N	01881	?			B65F+15	-/81	-/81	6/85
202	FVM 519T	Nissan CB20N	01882	?			B65F+15	-/81	-/81	6/85
203	FVM 480T	Nissan CB20N	01883	?			B65F+15	-/81	-/81	6/85
204	FVM 563T	Nissan CB20N	01901	?			B65F+15	-/81	-/81	6/85
205	FVM 544T	Nissan CB20N	01908	?			B65F+15	-/81	-/81	6/85
206	FVM 529T	Nissan CB20N	01902	?			B65F+15	-/81	-/81	6/85
207	FVM 503T	Nissan CB20N	01998	?			B65F+15	-/81	-/81	6/85
208	FVM 556T	Nissan CB20N	01990	?			B65F+15	-/81	-/81	6/85
14	FND 126T	Nissan CB20N	01899	BBL	567/1		B68F+16	-/81	-/81	-/94
15	FND 141T	Nissan CB20N	?	?			B75F+20	-/81	-/81	-/--
24	GWT 267T	Leyland Victory	JVTB971000	BBL	665/1		B56F+21	-/82	-/82	-/94
25	GWT 253T	Leyland Victory	JVTB970914	BBL	664/2 (?)		B56F+21	-/82	-/82	-/94
26	GWT 329T	Leyland Victory	JVTB800264	BBL	664/1		B60F+15	-/82	-/82	-/94
27	GWT 284T	Leyland Victory	JVTB971002	BBL	664/3		B60F+15	-/82	-/82	-/94
28	GWT 377T	Leyland Victory	JVTB971001	BBL	665/2		B65F+16	-/82	-/82	-/94
1	JGF 248T	Mercedes-Benz	937318	BBL	?		B65F+16	-/83	-/83	-/94

2	JGF 237T	Mercedes-Benz	937319	BBL	?	B65F+25	-/83	-/83	-/94
101	HGX 934T	Mercedes-Benz	913583	?		B62F+16	-/83	-/83	6/85
103	HGX 935T	Mercedes-Benz	913584	?		B62F+30	-/83	-/83	6/85
104	HGX 931T	Mercedes-Benz	913585	?		B62F+30	-/83	-/83	6/85
105	HGX 936T	Mercedes-Benz	913586	?		B62F+30	-/83	-/83	6/85
106	HGX 937T	Mercedes-Benz	913973	?		B62F+30	-/83	-/83	6/85
107	HGX 938T	Mercedes-Benz	913974	?		B62F+30	-/83	-/83	6/85
110	HGX 932T	Mercedes-Benz	913975	?		B62F+29	-/83	-/83	6/85
111	HCX 040T	Mercedes-Benz	913976	?		B62F+29	-/83	-/83	6/85
113	HGX 927T	Mercedes-Benz	914472	?		B62F+30	-/83	-/83	6/85
115	HGX 926T	Mercedes-Benz	922345	?		B62F+30	-/83	-/83	6/85
161	JDV 201T	Mercedes-Benz	966566	?		B62F+30	-/83	-/83	6/85
162	JDV 202T	Mercedes-Benz	966966	?		B62F+30	-/83	-/83	6/85
166	JDV 203T	Mercedes-Benz	966769	?		B62F+30	-/83	-/83	6/85
167	JDV 204T	Mercedes-Benz	966763	?		B62F+30	-/83	-/83	6/85
168	JDV 206T	Mercedes-Benz	966764	?		B62F+30	-/83	-/83	6/85
169	JDV 205T	Mercedes-Benz	966765	?		B62F+30	-/83	-/83	6/85
170	JDV 207T	Mercedes-Benz	966968	?		B62F+30	-/83	-/83	6/85
171	JDV 208T	Mercedes-Benz	966565	?		B62F+30	-/83	-/83	6/85
172	JDV 209T	Mercedes-Benz	?	?		B62F+30	-/83	-/83	6/85
173	JDV 210T	Mercedes-Benz	967763	?		B62F+30	-/83	-/83	6/85
22	LBD 608T	Nissan CB20N	02496	BBL	929/1	B64F+20	-/86	-/86	-/94
23	LBD 614T	Nissan CB20N	02503	BBL	929/2	B65F+16	-/86	-/86	-/94
32	MBS 154T	Mercedes-Benz L613	004701	BBA	4359/1	B21F	9/87	9/87	-/94
		Nissan CB20N	00495	BBA	4390/1	AB---	-/79	3/88	-/--
		Nissan CB20N	00494	BBA	4390/2	AB---	-/79	3/88	-/--
29	NGD 932T	ERF Super Trailblazer	57884	Santini		B60F+20	3/89	3/89	-/94
30	NGD 936T	ERF Super Trailblazer	60375	BBL	1170/2	B60F+20	3/89	3/89	-/94
31	NHP 980T	Isuzu Kombi	?	?		M--	-/89	-/89	-/94
8	RVP 935T	ERF Trailblazer E6RE	70931	BBL	1603/1	B61F+15	4/93	4/93	6/95
3	RVP 934T	ERF Trailblazer E6RE	70932	BBL	1603/2	B61F+15	4/93	4/93	6/95

Notes:
The 1979 Nissans with 80 seats has 3 axles.
GWT 267/53, 329, 284, 377T (24-8) were Leyland Victory 2. GWT 377T (28) later renumbered 302.
JGF 248/37T (1/2) were Mercedes-Benz OF1624 with chassis numbers prefixed 397047-65-.
HGX 934/5/1/6-8/2/40/27/6T (101/3-7/10/1/3/5) were Mercedes-Benz OF1624 with chassis numbers
    prefixed 397047-65-.
JDV 201-4/6/5/7-10T (161/2/6-73) were Mercedes-Benz OF1624 with chassis numbers prefixed 397047-65-.
Nissan CB20N 00495/4 may have operated for Alberton from 1979 and were rebuilt to AB-- in 3/88.

Disposals:
BWN 785/75/67/3/52/39/29/15/08, 698/84T, BVH 017/54/76/94T (174/8-89/92/3): PUTCO 4533-47.
BWN 793T, FVM 525/19, 480, 563/44/29/03/56T (194, 201-8): PUTCO 4548-56.
FND 126T, GWT 267/53, 329, 284T (14, 24-7): Concordia Tours, Honeydew 28, 7-10.
GWT 377T (28): Highway Bus Lines, thence to Concordia Tours 11.
JGF 248/37T (1/2): Concordia Tours, Honeydew 19, 20.
HGX 934/5/1/6-8/2/40/27/6T (101/3-7/10/1/3/5): PUTCO 3723-32.
JDV 201-4/6/5/7-10T, RVP 935/4T (161/2/6-73, 8,3): PUTCO 3733-42, 602/1.
LBD 608/14T, NGD 932/6T (22/3/9/30): Concordia Tours, Honeydew 36/7, 43/4.

BENONI MUNICIPALITY

Benoni Municipality started operating buses in the 1930s. The fleet total had reached 98 buses when services
were abandoned in 1990. Some operations appear to have remained – or been resurrected - as one vehicle
passed to the new Ekurhuleni Transport in 2000.

	Albion PKA26	5098F			11/31	11/31	-/--
	Albion PKA26	5098G			11/31	11/31	-/--
	Albion SpPW65	16028B			12/33	12/33	-/--

		Albion SpPW65	16028C				12/33	12/33	-/--
		Albion SpPW67	16206I		B30-		11/34	11/34	-/--
		Albion SpPW67	16206J		B30-		11/34	11/34	-/--
		Albion SpPW67	16207A		B30-		11/34	11/34	-/--
		Albion SpPW67	16207C		B30-		11/34	11/34	-/--
		Albion SpPW67	16207D		B30-		11/34	11/34	-/--
7	TA 12	(one of above)							
		Albion SpPV71 5LW	11604H				1/36	1/36	-/--
		Albion SpPV71 5LW	11604I				1/36	1/36	-/--
		Leyland TS7	9307				-/36	-/36	-/--
		Leyland RTS8	16914	Park Royal		B39F	3/38	3/38	-/--
		Leyland RTS8	16915	Park Royal		B39F	3/38	3/38	-/--
8		(one of above two)							
19		Daimler COG5	8469	Park Royal		B39F	12/38	12/38	by-/48
20		Daimler COG5	8470	Park Royal		B39F	12/38	12/38	by-/55
21		Daimler COG5	8487	Park Royal	B5642	B39F	7/39	7/39	by-/54
36	TA 814	Bristol LL5G (?)	W4.012	Welfitt Ody		B39F	2/47	2/47	-/56
37	TA 141	Bristol LL5G	61.033	Welfitt Ody		B39F	-/47	-/47	-/56
38	TA 146	Bristol LL5G (?)	W4.024	Welfitt Ody		B39F	5/47	5/47	-/56
39	TA 481	Bristol LL5G (?)	W4.023	Welfitt Ody		B39F	6/47	6/47	6/58
34	TA 39	Leyland OPS1	461478	BMS		B35F	8/47	8/47	6/58
14	TA 922	Leyland OPS1	461501	BMS		B35F	8/47	8/47	6/58
23	TA 406	Daimler CVG5X	13349	BMS		B39F	9/47	9/47	-/57
24	TA 442	Daimler CVG5X	13356	BMS		B39F	10/47	10/47	6/58
25	TA 354	Daimler CVG5X	13353	BMS		B39F	10/47	10/47	6/58
35	TA 211	Daimler CVG5X	13345	BMS		B39F	1/48	1/48	6/58
1	TA 763	Bristol LWL6G	67166	ECW	2362	B39F	8/48	8/48	2/63
6	TA 795	Bristol LWL6G	77003	ECW	2367	B39F	8/48	8/48	2/63
11	TA 810	Bristol LWL6G	67167	ECW	2363	B39F	8/48	8/48	2/63
13	TA 817	Bristol LWL6G	77005	ECW	2368	B39F	9/48	9/48	-/58
15	TA 865	Bristol LWL6G	77009	ECW	2370	B39F	9/48	9/48	-/58
19	TA 869	Bristol LWL6G	77010	ECW	2371	B39F	9/48	9/48	2/63
27	TA 7076	Bristol LWL6G	77042	ECW	2399	B39F	12/48	12/48	2/63
40	TA 7079	Bristol LWL6G	77038	ECW	2404	B39F	12/48	12/48	2/63
2	TA 8212	Bristol LWL6G	77056	ECW	2409	B39F	12/48	12/48	-/58
8	TA 8213	Bristol LWL6G	77036	ECW	2397	B39F	12/48	12/48	-/58
26	TA 8214	Bristol LWL6G	77031	ECW	2393	B39F	12/48	12/48	2/63
28	TA 8215	Bristol LWL6G	77018	ECW	2383	B39F	12/48	12/48	2/63
30	TA 8216	Bristol LWL6G	77015	ECW	2382	B39F	12/48	12/48	-/--
31	TA 8217	Bristol LWL6G	77026	ECW	2387	B39F	12/48	12/48	2/63
17	TA 7068	Bristol LWL6G	77045	ECW	2402	B39F	7/49	7/49	2/63
5	TA 9695	Leyland HR44	504429	BBA	M616	B44F	1/52	1/52	-/65
7	TA 9696	Leyland HR44	504430	BBA	M617	B44F	1/52	1/52	-/65
32	TA 9697	Leyland HR44	504431	BBA	M618	B44F	2/52	2/52	-/66
9	TA 5208	Leyland HR44	520715	BBA	M695	B45F	2/53	2/53	-/--
10	TA 9840	Leyland OPSU2/1	514844	BBA	M654	B53F	8/52	8/52	9/66
12	TA 9841	Leyland OPSU2/1	514847	BBA	M657	B53F	8/52	8/52	8/66
18	TA 9842	Leyland OPSU2/1	514846	BBA	M656	B53F	8/52	8/52	-/66
29	TA 9843	Leyland OPSU2/1	514845	BBA	M655	B53F	8/52	8/52	-/64
21	TA 10904	Leyland OPSU2/1	540247	BBA	M1112	B67F	5/54	5/54	11/59
22	TA 10911	Leyland OPSU2/1	540448	BBA	M1113	B67F	6/54	6/54	11/59
16	TA 5924	Leyland OPSU2/1	540554	BBA	M1240	B53F	12/54	12/54	4/69
20	TA 11180	Leyland OPSU2/1	542302	BBA	120/1	B67F	6/55	6/55	11/59
33	TA 11181	Leyland OPSU2/1	542309	BBA	120/2	B67F	6/55	6/55	11/59?
3	TA 11182	Leyland OPSU2/1	541732	Blanckenberg		B65F	6/55	6/55	1/69
4	TA 11183	Leyland OPSU2/1	540405	Blanckenberg		B65F	7/55	7/55	11/68
45	TA 11204	Leyland ECPO2/1R	545620	BBA	96/3	B46F+12	7/55	7/55	-/67
41	TA 11633	Leyland ERT2/1	551524	BBA	121/1	B67F	12/55	12/55	12/61
42	TA 11634	Leyland ERT2/1	551925	BBA	121/2	B67F	2/56	2/56	12/68
43	TA 11635	Leyland ERT2/1	551926	BBA	121/3	B67F	2/56	2/56	10/68
44	TA 11636	Leyland ERT2/1	551974	BBA	121/4	B67F	2/56	2/56	4/69
46	TA 11975	Leyland ERT2/1	552155	BBA	168/1	B67F	5/56	5/56	-/--
47	TA 11976	Leyland ERT2/1	551494	BBA	168/2	B67F	5/56	5/56	-/--
48	TA 11977	Leyland ERT2/1	560538	BBA	168/3	B67F	6/56	6/56	-/--

49	TA 11978	Leyland ERT2/1	560793	BBA	168/4	B67F	8/56	8/56	-/--
50	TA 12812	Leyland ERT2/1	571659	Blanckenberg		B62F	2/58	2/58	6/69
51	TA 12813	Leyland ERT2/1	571660	Blanckenberg		B62F	2/58	2/58	5/69
52	TA 12814	Leyland ERT1/1	572138	Blanckenberg		B62F	2/58	2/58	6/69
34	TA 8260	Leyland ERT2/1	580937	BBA	323/4	B62F	4/59	4/59	-/--
35	TA 8492	Leyland ERT2/1	580938	BBA	323/5	B62F	4/59	4/59	-/--
36	TA 13001	Leyland ERT2/1	572969	BBA	257/1	B62F	1/59	1/59	-/--
37	TA 13002	Leyland ERT2/1	572970	BBA	257/2	B62F	1/59	1/59	-/--
38	TA 13003	Leyland ERT2/1	572971	BBA	257/3	B62F	1/59	1/59	-/--
53	TA 13326	Leyland ERT2/1	572973	BBA	270/1	B62F	3/58	3/58	-/--
54	TA 13327	Leyland ERT2/1	572974	BBA	270/2	B62F	3/58	3/58	-/--
55	TA 13328	Leyland ERT2/1	573088	BBA	270/3	B62F	3/58	3/58	-/--
39	TA 8695	Leyland ERT2/1	580939	BBA	323/6	B62F	4/59	4/59	-/--
23	TA 8110	Leyland ERT2/1	580934	BBA	323/1	B62F	4/59	4/59	-/--
24	TA 8171	Leyland ERT2/1	580935	BBA	323/2	B62F	4/59	4/59	-/--
25	TA 8174	Leyland ERT2/1	580936	BBA	323/3	B62F	4/59	4/59	-/--
		Leyland ERT2/1	582460	BBA	582/1	B55F	4/61	4/61	-/--
8	TA 18121	Leyland ERT2/1	611107	Blanckenberg		B61F	6/62	6/62	-/--
2	TA 18122	Leyland ERT2/1	611108	Blanckenberg		C49F	8/62	8/62	-/--
13	TA 18123	Leyland ERT2/1	611358	Craftsman		B61F	8/62	8/62	-/--
14	TA 18124	Leyland ERT2/1	612153	Craftsman		B61F	8/62	8/62	-/--
15	TA 18125	Leyland ERT2/1	612154	Craftsman		B61F	9/62	9/62	-/--
20	TA 18126	Leyland ERT2/1	612155	Craftsman		B61F	8/62	8/62	-/--
21	TA 18130	Leyland ERT2/1	612156	Craftsman		B61F	12/62	12/62	-/--
	TA 5780	Leyland PSUC1/3	584114	BBA	291/2	B55F	10/60	-/62	-/--
6	TA 18127	AEC Regal VI	U2RA014	Craftsman		B62F	11/62	11/62	-/--
1	TA 18128	AEC Regal VI	U2RA013	Craftsman		B62F	11/62	11/62	-/--
22	TA 18129	AEC Regal VI	U2RA012	Craftsman		B62F	11/62	11/62	-/--
		AEC Kudu	2S2RA008	?		B--F	11/62	11/62	-/--
		AEC Kudu	2S2RA001	?		B--F	2/63	2/63	-/--
		AEC Kudu	2S2RA029	?		B--F	8/63	8/63	-/--
11	TA 18648	AEC Kudu	2S2RA052	Craftsman		B62F	12/64	12/64	-/--
17	TA 18649	AEC Kudu	2S2RA053	Craftsman		B62F	3/65	3/65	-/--
19	TA 18650	AEC Kudu	2S2RA054	Craftsman		B62F	12/64	12/64	-/--
26	TA 18651	AEC Kudu	2S2RA055	Craftsman		B62F	2/65	2/65	-/--
27	TA 18652	AEC Kudu	2S2RA059	Craftsman		B62F	4/65	4/65	-/--
28	TA 18653	AEC Kudu	2S2RA060	Craftsman		B62F	9/65	9/65	-/--
40	TA 20039	Guy Warrior	WUM4999	TMBB		B61F+15	1/66	1/66	-/--
41	TA 20040	Guy Warrior	WUM4995	TMBB		B61F+15	1/66	1/66	-/--
11		Ford R226	45570	BBA	2267/1	B--F	6/66	6/66	-/--
		Ford R226	45571	BBA	2267/2	B--F	6/66	6/66	-/--
		Ford R226	45315	BBA	2267/3	B--F	6/66	6/66	-/--
		Ford R226	45698	BBA	2267/4	B--F	6/66	6/66	-/--
56	TA 16774	Guy Warrior	WTB5665	BBA	2308/1	B64F	12/66	12/66	-/--
57	TA 11790	Guy Warrior	WTB5666	BBA	2308/2	B64F	12/66	12/66	-/--
58	TA 20180	Guy Warrior	WTB5667	BBA	2308/3	B64F	12/66	12/66	-/--
59	TA 13080	Guy Warrior	WTB5668	BBA	2308/4	B64F	12/66	12/66	-/--
60	TA 17675	Guy Warrior	WTB5684	BBA	2308/5	B64F	12/66	12/66	-/--
61	TA 10867	Guy Warrior	WTB5685	BBA	2308/6	B64F	12/66	12/66	-/--
62	TA 10407	Guy Warrior	WTB5686	BBA	2308/7	B64F	12/66	12/66	-/--
18	TA 25092	AEC Kudu	3S2RA596	TMBB		B61F	7/69	7/69	-/--
5	TA 25974	AEC Kudu	3S2RA595	TMBB		B61F	2/69	2/69	-/--
7	TA 25975	AEC Kudu	3S2RA597	TMBB		B61F	2/69	2/69	-/--
9	TA 25976	AEC Kudu	3S2RA600	TMBB		B61F	2/69	2/69	-/--
10	TA 25977	AEC Kudu	3S2RA598	TMBB		B61F	4/69	4/69	-/--
12	TA 25978	AEC Kudu	3S2RA599	TMBB		B61F	3/69	3/69	-/--
29	TA 25980	AEC Kudu	3S2RA601	TMBB		B61F	4/69	4/69	-/--
30	TA 25981	AEC Kudu	3S2RA602	TMBB		B61F	4/69	4/69	-/--
31	TA 25982	AEC Kudu	3S2RA603	TMBB		B61F	4/69	4/69	-/--
		Mercedes-Benz		TMBB		B--F	-/71	-/71	-/--
		Mercedes-Benz		TMBB		B--F	-/71	-/71	-/--
		Mercedes-Benz		TMBB		B--F	-/71	-/71	-/--
		Mercedes-Benz		TMBB		B--F	-/71	-/71	-/--
		Mercedes-Benz		TMBB		B--F	-/71	-/71	-/--

		Mercedes-Benz		TMBB		B--F	-/71	-/71	-/--
		Mercedes-Benz		TMBB		B--F	-/71	-/71	-/--
		Mercedes-Benz OH1417		BBA	2742/1	B--F	6/71	6/71	-/--
		687272							
42	TA 31641	Mercedes-Benz O302		Brockhouse		B--F	-/73	-/73	-/--
		Mercedes-Benz O302		Brockhouse		B--F	-/73	-/73	-/--
		Mercedes-Benz O302		Brockhouse		B--F	-/73	-/73	-/--
45	TA 31644	Mercedes-Benz O302		Brockhouse		B--F	-/73	-/73	-/--
		Mercedes-Benz O302		Brockhouse		B--F	-/73	-/73	-/--
		Mercedes-Benz O302		Brockhouse		B--F	-/73	-/73	-/--
		Mercedes-Benz OF1617		Brockhouse		B--F	-/73	-/73	-/--
		Mercedes-Benz OF1617		Brockhouse		B--F	-/73	-/73	-/--
		Mercedes-Benz OF1617		Brockhouse		B--F	-/73	-/73	-/--
		Mercedes-Benz OF1617		Brockhouse		B--F	-/73	-/73	-/--
		Mercedes-Benz OF1617		Brockhouse		B--F	-/73	-/73	-/--
		Mercedes-Benz OF1617		Brockhouse		B--F	-/73	-/73	-/--
		Mercedes-Benz OF1617		Brockhouse		B--F	-/73	-/73	-/--
		Mercedes-Benz OF1617		Brockhouse		B--F	-/73	-/73	-/--
		Mercedes-Benz OF1617		Brockhouse		B--F	-/73	-/73	-/--
		Mercedes-Benz OF1617	?	Brockhouse		B--F	-/73	-/73	-/--
	TA 8340	AEC Kudu	?	?		B--F	by-/74	by-/74	-/--
71		AEC Kudu	?	?		B--F	-/--	-/--	-/--
72	TA 34481	AEC Kudu	?	?		B--F	-/--	-/--	-/--
74	TA 34483	AEC Kudu	?	?		B--F	by11/77	by11/77	-/--
75	TA 34484	Mercedes-Benz	?	?		B--F	by11/77	by11/77	-/--
77	TA 34486	Mercedes-Benz	?	?		B--F	by11/77	by11/77	-/--
79	TA 3448x	Mercedes-Benz	?	?		B--F	by11/77	by11/77	-/--
80	TA 34489	Mercedes-Benz	?	?		B--F	by11/77	by11/77	-/--
	TA 37079	?	?	?		B--F	-/--	-/--	-/--
	TA 37080	?	?	?		B--F	-/--	-/--	-/--
		Nissan CB20	00016	BBA	3272/1	B--F	3/77	3/77	-/--
		Nissan CB20	00021	BBA	3272/2	B--F	3/77	3/77	-/--
		Hino BY340	40017 ?	BBA	3355/1	B--F	3/78	3/78	-/--
		Hino BY340	40036	BBA	3355/2	B--F	3/78	3/78	-/--
		Hino BY340	40017 ?	BBA	3355/3	B--F	3/78	3/78	-/--
		Hino BY340	40054	BBA	3355/4	B--F	3/78	3/78	-/--
		Hino BY340	40055	BBA	3355/5	B--F	3/78	3/78	-/--
		Leyland PSU3C/2R	7602152	BBA	3356/1	B--F	3/78	3/78	-/--
		Leyland PSU3C/2R	7602154	BBA	3356/2	B--F	3/78	3/78	-/--
		Leyland PSU3C/2R	7601666	BBA	3356/3	B--F	3/78	3/78	-/--
		Leyland PSU3C/2R	7601670	BBA	3356/4	B--F	3/78	3/78	-/--
		Hino BY340	40089	BBA	3461/1	B--F	1/79	1/79	-/--
		Hino BY340	40091	BBA	3461/2	B--F	1/79	1/79	-/--
		Hino BY340	40092	BBA	3461/3	B--F	1/79	1/79	-/--
		Hino BY340	40096	BBA	3461/4	B--F	1/79	1/79	-/--
		Hino BY340	40090	BBA	3462/1	B--F	1/79	1/79	-/--
		Hino BY340	40093	BBA	3462/2	B--F	1/79	1/79	-/--
		Hino BY340	40094	BBA	3462/3	B--F	1/79	1/79	-/--
		Hino BY340	40095	BBA	3462/4	B--F	1/79	1/79	-/--
		Hino BY340	40097	BBA	3462/5	B--F	1/79	1/79	-/--
		Hino BY340	40098	BBA	3462/6	B--F	1/79	1/79	-/--
		Magirus Deutz 230EV110		BBA	3637/1	B--F	4/80	4/80	-/--
		551.0151.001							
		Mercedes-Benz O305		BBA	3926/1	B54F+37	7/82	7/82	-/--
		307001 61 030764							
		Mercedes-Benz O305		BBA	3926/2	B54F+37	7/82	7/82	-/--
		307001 61 030800							
	FVZ 794T	Mercedes-Benz O305		BBA	3926/3	B54F+37	7/82	7/82	-/--
		307001 61 030838							
	FVZ 795T	Mercedes-Benz O305		BBA	3926/4	B54F+37	8/82	8/82	-/--
		307001 61 030874							
		Mercedes-Benz O305		BBA	3926/5	B54F+37	8/82	8/82	-/--
		307001 61 030875							

| 754 | FVZ 797T | Mercedes-Benz O305 307001 61 030913 | | BBA | 3926/6 | B54F+37 | 8/82 | 8/82 | 1/00 |

Notes:

Leyland RTS8 16914/5 had Park Royal body numbers B4949/50, order unknown.

19/20 (Daimler COG5) had Park Royal body numbers B5318/9, order unknown.

TA 39, 922 (34, 14) carried chassis numbers 460655/78 as initially allocated by Leyland. They were later officially changed to the numbers shown above.

It is not certain whether there were 4 or 5 Daimlers in 1947/8. TA 211 (35) has also been recorded with chassis no 13999 which may have been attributed incorrectly to Kimberley Municipality.

TA 9695 (5) is also recorded as TA 9693.

TA 9695-7, 5208 (5, 7, 32, 9) were built on Weymann frames, nos L98-100/11.

? (unknown Leyland ? / BBA, new 1952-1961 renumbered 68 and re-registered TA 8675 by 11/77.

TA 5780 (-) was a demonstrator, on hire from Leyland Albion.

TA 20039/40, 16774, 11790, 20180, 13080, 17675, 10867 (40/1, 56-61) are Guy Warrior 2 with AV470 engines.

FVZ 797T (754) re-registered CWL 946 GP c1996. This was also recorded as 745.

Disposals:

TA 814 (36): Tuckers Springs.

TA 481, 354, 211 (39, 25, 35): Greyhound, Johannesburg.

TA 922 (14): Mart Motors.

TA 442 (24): Johannesburg Metals.

TA 7076/9, 8214/7 (27, 40, 26, 31): Keysers, for scrap.

TA 8212 (2): Vaal Transport Corporation (Pty) Ltd., Vereeniging.

TA 9840/1, 5924, 11182/3, 11634-6, 12812-4 (10/2/6, 3, 4, 42-4, 50-2): scrapped.

TA 10904, 11180/1 (21/0, 33): Rand Bus Lines, Johannesburg 130-2.

TA 11204 (45): breakdown lorry.

TA 11633 (41): burnt out.

Three Leyland PSU3/2R and two Mercedes-Benz O305: Durban Municipality by -/90.

FVZ 794/5T (?, ?): Roodepoort Municipality 59, 60.

FVZ 797T (as CWL 946 GP) (754): Ekurhuleni Transport 754.

BOKSBURG MUNICIPALITY

Boksburg Municipality experimented with six Railless trolleybuses from 1914 till c1919 but may not have operated buses until 1939. In 1984 the fleet totalled 40 buses. This had risen to 51 buses in 1986. Much of fleet was destroyed in a fire in the depot c1999. The Municipality became part of the new Ekurhuleni Metropolitan City in January 2000, along with Benoni and Germiston. The Boksburg municipal bus fleet was then transferred to the new Ekurhuleni Transport.

1	Railless	?	Railless	B28R	-/14	-/14	c-/19
2	Railless	?	Railless	B28R	-/14	-/14	c-/19
3	Railless	?	Railless	B28R	-/14	-/14	c-/19
4	Railless	?	Railless	B28R	-/14	-/14	c-/19
5	Railless	?	Railless	B28R	-/14	-/14	c-/19
6	Railless	?	Railless	B28R	-/14	-/14	c-/19
	Leyland RKPZ04	200792	?	B---	-/39	-/39	-/--
	Leyland RKPZ04	200793	?	B---	-/39	-/39	-/--
	Leyland RKPZ04	201691	?	B---	-/39	-/39	-/--
	Leyland RKPZ04	201692	?	B---	-/39	-/39	-/--
	AEC Regal	O6624247		B---	10/46	10/46	-/--
	AEC Regal	O6624697	Brush	B--F	11/46	11/46	-/--
	AEC Regal	O6624248		B---	12/46	12/46	-/--
	AEC Regal	O6624700		B---	12/46	12/46	-/--
	AEC Regal	O6624698		B---	2/47	2/47	-/--
	AEC Regal	O6624702		B---	2/47	2/47	-/--
	AEC Regal	O6624699		B---	4/47	4/47	-/--
	AEC Regal	O6624703		B---	9/47	9/47	-/--
	AEC Regal	O6624706		B---	-/47	-/47	-/--

	TB 217	AEC Regal	(one of above)	Wevell	B--F	by-/47	by-/47	-/--
		AEC Regal III	O682392		B---	12/48	12/48	-/--
		AEC Regal III	O682304		B---	1/49	1/49	-/--
		AEC Regal III	O682302		B---	2/49	2/49	-/--
13	TB 644	AEC Regal III	O682303	Wevell	B--F	3/49	3/49	by-/69
14	TB 64	Leyland OPS3/1	?	Wevell	B--F	5/49	5/49	by-/69
16	TB 699	Leyland OPS3/1	482526	Wevell	B--F	-/49	-/49	-/69
17	TB 670	Leyland OPS3/1	482530	Wevell	B--F	-/49	-/49	by-/69
18	TB 674	Leyland OPS3/1	482531	Wevell	B--F	-/49	-/49	-/--
19	TB 6511	Leyland OPS3/1	482532	Wevell	B--F	-/49	-/49	-/--
20	TB 6512	Leyland OPS3/1	482534	Wevell	B--F	-/49	-/49	-/--
21	TB 6514	Leyland OPS3/1	482533	Wevell	B--F	-/49	-/49	-/--
22	TB 5584	AEC Regal III	9621A860	Craftsman	B47F	7/51	7/51	-/69
23	TB 667	AEC Regal III	9621A863	Craftsman	B47F	11/51	11/51	-/--
24	TB 6872	AEC Regal III	9621A862	Craftsman	B47F	12/51	12/51	-/--
25	TB 5040	AEC Regal III	9621A864	Craftsman	B47F	6/52	6/52	-/--
26	TB 5045	AEC Regal III	9621A865	Craftsman	B47F	7/52	7/52	-/--
27	TB 5056	AEC Regal III	9621A861	Craftsman	B47F	6/52	6/52	-/--
28	TB 4850	AEC Regal IV	9821E1708	Craftsman	B56F	8/54	8/54	-/--
29	TB 5612	AEC Regal IV	9821E1707	Craftsman	B56F	11/54	11/54	-/--
	TB 4552	Henschel HS100		Brockhouse	B42F	-/56	-/56	-/--
	TB 4568	Henschel HS100		Brockhouse	B42F	-/56	-/56	-/--
	TB 4572	Henschel HS100		Brockhouse	B42F	-/56	-/56	-/--
	TB 4580	Henschel HS100		Brockhouse	B42F	-/56	-/56	-/--
14	TB 4625	Henschel HS100	36809	Brockhouse	B46F	-/56	-/56	by-/69
40	TB 10323	AEC Regal IV	9825E2200	Blanckenberg	B67F	10/57	10/57	by-/73
41	TB 10324	AEC Regal IV	9825E2196	Blanckenberg	B67F	10/57	10/57	by-/73
40	TB 10325	AEC Regal IV	?	Brockhouse	B67F	10/57	10/57	by-/73
41	TB 10326	AEC Regal IV	?	Brockhouse	B67F	11/57	11/57	by-/73
42	TB 10327	AEC Regal IV	?	Brockhouse	B67F	11/57	11/57	by-/73
43	TB 10328	AEC Regal IV	?	Brockhouse	B67F	11/57	11/57	by-/73
6	TB 10091	AEC Regal IV	9825E2218	Craftsman	B61F	6/58	6/58	by-/78
7	TB 10093	AEC Regal IV	9825E2217	Craftsman	B61F	7/58	7/58	by-/71
8	TB 10090	AEC Regal IV	9825E2221	Craftsman	B61F	5/58	5/58	by-/81
4	TB 11129	Mercedes-Benz 319	022058	Craftsman	B11F	-/59	-/59	by-/82
5	TB 11128	Mercedes-Benz 319	021634	Craftsman	B11F	-/59	-/59	by-/84
51	TB 11303	AEC Regal IV	9826E2520	TMBB	B71F	4/61	4/61	-/--
52	TB 11304	AEC Regal IV	9826E2519	TMBB	B71F	4/61	4/61	-/--
2	TB 10049	AEC Regal VI	U2RA036	Craftsman	B61F	1/63	1/63	by-/82
3	TB 11175	AEC Regal VI	U2RA037	Craftsman	B61F	1/63	1/63	by-/82
53	TB 10146	Leyland ERT2/1	622415	TMBB	B68F	-/63	-/63	-/--
54	TB 10184	Leyland ERT2/1	622414	TMBB	B68F	-/63	-/63	-/--
55	TB 10359	Leyland ERT2/1	622161	TMBB	B68F	-/63	-/63	-/--
56	TB 10515	Leyland ERT2/1	622416	TMBB	B68F	-/63	-/63	-/--
57	TB 10617	Leyland ERT2/1	622417	TMBB	B68F	-/63	-/63	-/--
58	TB 10677	Leyland ERT2/1	622162	TMBB	B68F	-/63	-/63	-/--
59	TB 10741	Leyland ERT2/1	622784	TMBB	B68F	-/63	-/63	-/--
60		Guy Arab V 6LX	?	TMBB	FB63F	9/65	9/65	by-/71
30	TB 10508	Guy Arab V 6LX	FD76074	TMBB	FB63F	-/67	-/67	-/--
61	TB 12541	AEC Kudu	2S2RA325	TMBB	B65F	-/67	-/67	-/--
62	TB 12542	AEC Kudu	2S2RA324	TMBB	B65F	-/67	-/67	-/--
63	TB 12543	AEC Kudu	2S2RA327	TMBB	B65F	-/67	-/67	-/--
64	TB 12544	AEC Kudu	2S2RA326	TMBB	B65F	-/67	-/67	-/--
65	TB 11272	AEC Kudu	2S2RA323	TMBB	B65F	-/67	-/67	by-/87
1	TB 12456	Guy Victory 6LX	WTB5782	AB&C	B65F	-/67	-/67	by-/86
31	TB 12567	Guy Victory 6LX	WTB5893	Craftsman	B63F	-/68	-/68	-/--
9	TB 12801	Mercedes-Benz	044053	TMBB	B50F	-/68	-/68	by-/81
10	TB 12802	Mercedes-Benz	043013	TMBB	B50F	-/68	-/68	by-/82
11	TB 12803	Mercedes-Benz	044128	TMBB	B50F	-/68	-/68	by-/82
12	TB 12804	Mercedes-Benz	048014	TMBB	B50F	-/68	-/68	by-/82
		Hino	?	?	B--F	-/68	-/68	-/--
13	TB 13319	Mercedes-Benz OF1113	?	TMBB	B50F	-/69	-/69	-/--
14	TB 13320	Mercedes-Benz OF1113	?	TMBB	B50F	-/69	-/69	-/--
15	TB 13321	Mercedes-Benz OF1113	?	TMBB	B50F	-/69	-/69	-/--

16	TB 13322	Mercedes-Benz OF1113	?	TMBB		B50F	-/68	-/68	-/--
17	TB 13323	Mercedes-Benz OF1113	?	TMBB		B50F	-/68	-/68	-/--
18	TB 13324	Mercedes-Benz OF1113	?	TMBB		B50F	-/68	-/68	-/--
19	TB 13325	Mercedes-Benz OF1113	?	TMBB		B50F	-/68	-/68	-/--
20	TB 13550	Mercedes-Benz OF1113	?	TMBB		B50F	by -/71	by -/71	-/--
21	TB 13783	Mercedes-Benz OF1113	?	TMBB		B50F	by -/71	by -/71	-/--
22	TB 25163	Mercedes-Benz OF1113	?	TMBB		B50F	-/71	-/71	-/--
23	TB 25164	Mercedes-Benz OF1113	?	TMBB		B50F	-/71	-/71	-/--
24	TB 25165	Mercedes-Benz OF1113	?	TMBB		B50F	-/71	-/71	-/--
25	TB 25166	Mercedes-Benz OF1113	?	TMBB		B50F	-/71	-/71	-/--
26	TB 25167	Mercedes-Benz OF1113	?	TMBB		B50F	-/71	-/71	-/--
27	TB 25168	Mercedes-Benz OF1313	?	TMBB		B65F	-/71	-/71	-/--
32	TB 25169	Mercedes-Benz OF1313	?	TMBB		B65F	-/71	-/71	-/--
60	TB 25170	Mercedes-Benz OF1313	?	TMBB		B65F	-/71	-/71	-/--
68	TB 25171	Mercedes-Benz OF1313	?	TMBB		B65F	-/71	-/71	-/--
69	TB 25172	Mercedes-Benz OF1313	?	TMBB		B65F	-/71	-/71	-/--
70	TB 25173	Mercedes-Benz OF1313	?	TMBB		B65F	-/71	-/71	-/--
33	?	?	?	?		B--F	-/71-/72	-/71-/72	-/--
34	?	?	?	?		B--F	-/71-/72?	-/71-/72?	-/--
35	TB 11183	Mercedes-Benz OF1313	?	TMBB ?		B65F?	-/71-/72?	-/71-/72?	-/--
36	TB 11194	Mercedes-Benz OF1313	?	TMBB ?		B65F?	-/71-/72?	-/71-/72?	-/--
37	TB 11444	Mercedes-Benz OF1313	?	TMBB ?		B65F?	-/71-/72?	-/71-/72?	-/--
39	TB 11618	Seddon Pennine 4-V8	48452	TMBB		B65F	5/72	5/72	-/--
		Seddon Pennine 4	48459	BBA	2770/1	B--F	5/72	5/72	-/--
		Seddon Pennine 4	48460	BBA	2770/2	B--F	6/72	6/72	-/--
28	KLB 167T	Guy Victory 2	?	VSA		B63F	by -/86	by -/86	by1/00
29	KLB 168T	Guy Victory 2	?	VSA		B63F	by -/86	by -/86	by1/00
30	KLB 169T	Guy Victory 2	?	VSA		B63F	by -/86	by -/86	by1/00
31	LCB 940T	Guy Victory 2	?	BBL ?		B68F	by -/86	by -/86	by1/00
1	LBZ 751T	?	?	BBL ?		B--F	by -/87	by -/87	-/--
11	GLF 017T	Hino BY340	?	BBL ?		B--F	by -/87	by -/87	-/--
12	GRC 929T	?	?	BBL ?		B--F	by -/87	by -/87	-/--
43	GPJ 813T?	Nissan CB20	?	BBL ?		B--F	by -/87	by -/87	-/--
65	GPJ 813T?	Hino BY340	?	?		B--F	by -/87	by -/87	-/--
67	JHL 925T	Hino BY340	?	BBL ?		B--F	by -/87	by -/87	-/--
76	DGG 563T	Hino BY340	?	BBL ?		B--F	by -/87	by -/87	-/--
		ERF	51539	?		B--F	8/87	8/87	by 1/00
		ERF	52927	?		B--F	8/87	8/87	by 1/00
		ERF	53182	?		B--F	8/87	8/87	by 1/00
		ERF	57881	?		B--F	9/88	9/88	by 1/00
		ERF	57882	?		B--F	10/88	10/88	by 1/00
		ERF	57883	?		B--F	10/88	10/88	by 1/00
193	HZB 809GP	ERF Trailblazer 64GXB	37490	BBA	3596/11	B57F+24	2/80	by1/00	1/00

Notes:

TB 644 (13) rebodied TMBB B44F at an unknown date.
TB 699, 674, 6511 (16/8/9) rebodied Craftsman B44F at an unknown date (18/9 by -/73).
TB 670 (17) rebodied Craftsman B40F at an unknown date.
TB 6512/4 (20/1) rebodied Craftsman B47F by -/73.
TB 4552/68/72/80 had body contract no. R3300.
TB 4625 (14) chassis no also recorded as 36109.
TB 10323/4 (40/1) renumbered 66/7 at an unknown date.
TB 10325-8 (40-3) had chassis nos 9825E2197-9/201, order unknown and are also recorded with
Blanckenberg bodies.
TB 10677 (58) is recorded with chassis no 622152 but this is BMMO 5202, a PSU3/4R. The version shown
is believed to be correct.
? (33/4) one of these was registered TB 11093, renumbered 2 by -/87.
The six ERFs new in 1987/8 were Super Trailblazers.
HZB 809GP (193) ex Germiston 193.

Disposals:

HZB 809GP (193): Ekurhuleni Transport 95.

1	FWX 710GP	Nissan CB20		02503	VSA		B63F+20	-/86	-/86	1/00

2	FVM 616GP	Hino BY340	40216	BBL	?	B70F+16	-/82	-/82	1/00
3	FWX 681GP	Hino BY340	40211	BBL	655/4	B70F+27	-/82	-/82	1/00
4	FBK 945GP	Hino BY340	40209	BBL	655/2 (?)	B70F+16	-/82	-/82	1/00
5	FRK 873GP	Hino BY340	40220	BBL	753/1	B70F+27	-/84	-/84	1/00
6	TB 5091	Hino BY340	40064	De Haan		B69F+28	-/78	-/78	1/00
7	FFM 054GP	Mercedes-Benz OF1417 35209720724924		?		B57F	-/71	-/71	1/00
8	FGW 805GP	Hino BY340	40134	BBL	?	B62F+29	-/81	-/81	1/00
9	FFM 065GP	Hino BY340	40174	BBL	?	B62F+29	-/81	-/81	1/00
10	FSX 089GP	Hino BY340	40215	BBL	655/6	B70F+27	-/82	-/82	1/00
11	FNC 846GP	Hino BY340	40212	BBL	655/5	B70F+27	-/82	-/82	1/00
12	FGW 813GP	Hino BY340	?	BBL	655/2 (?)	B70F+27	-/82	-/82	1/00

Notes:

It seems likely that 1-12 above had been renumbered, possibly in the late 1990s. Some may appear earlier in this list with their former registration numbers.

TB 5091 (6) also recorded as TB 50921, re-registered FWX 702GP.

Disposals:

FWX 710GP, FVM 616GP, FWX 681GP (1/2/3): Ekurhuleni Transport 76/0/2.

FBK 945GP, FRK 873GP, FFM 054GP, FGW 805GP (4/5/7/8): Ekurhuleni Transport 54/62/55/8.

TB 5091 (as FWX 702GP) (6): Ekurhuleni Transport 74.

FFM 065GP, FSX 089GP, FNC 846GP, FGW 813GP (9-12): Ekurhuleni Transport 57/69/3/59.

BRAKPAN MUNICIPALITY

Brackpan Municipality started operating buses in the early 1930s. The fleet numbered 99 buses in 1984 and appears to have ceased soon afterwards.

		AEC Ranger	665038	?		B---	-/32	-/32	-/--
		Albion SpPW69	16409J	?		B---	10/35	10/35	-/--
		Albion SpPW69	16409K	?		B---	10/35	10/35	-/--
25		Albion SpCX13	?	?		FB--F	by-/39	by-/39	-/--
		Ford tractor unit	?	BMS		AB---	by 3/44	by 3/44	-/--
		AEC Regal	O6624251	?		B---	9/46	9/46	-/--
		AEC Regal	O6624229	?		B---	10/46	10/46	-/-
		AEC Regal	O6624246	?		B---	11/46	11/46	-/--
		Daimler CVD6	14762	?		B---	-/47	-/47	-/--
		Daimler CVD6	14763	?		B---	-/47	-/47	-/--
		AEC Regal III	O962014	BMS (?)		B--F	3/48	3/48	-/--
		AEC Regal III	O962015	BMS (?)		B--F	3/48	3/48	-/--
		AEC Regal III	O962016	BMS (?)		B--F	2/48	2/48	-/--
		AEC Regal III	O962017	BMS (?)		B--F	2/48	2/48	-/--
		AEC Regal III	O962018	BMS (?)		B--F	3/48	3/48	-/--
		AEC Regal III	O962019	BMS (?)		B--F	3/48	3/48	-/--
39	TO 817	AEC Regal III	(from above)	BMS (?)		B--F	by3/48	by3/48	-/--
41	TO 825	AEC Regal III	(from above)	BMS (?)		B--F	by3/48	by3/48	-/--
5		Guy Arab III	?	TMBB		B--F	-/--	-/--	-/68
7		Guy Arab III	?	TMBB		B--F	-/--	-/--	-/68
		Daimler CVD6	15095	?		B---	-/48	-/48	-/--
		Daimler CVG6DD	14678	?		B---	-/49	-/49	-/--
		Daimler CVG6DD	14679	?		B---	-/49	-/49	-/--
		Daimler CVG6DD	14680	?		B---	-/49	-/49	-/--
		Daimler CVG6DD	14681	?		B---	-/49	-/49	-/--
		Daimler CVG6DD	14682	?		B---	-/49	-/49	-/--
		Daimler CVG6DD	14683	?		B---	-/49	-/49	-/--
		Daimler CVG6	17922	?		B---	-/51	-/51	-/--
		Daimler CVG6	17923	?		B---	-/51	-/51	-/--
		Daimler CVG6	17924	?		B---	-/51	-/51	-/--
58	TO 13222	AEC Regal IV	?	Brockhouse		B53F	10/54	10/54	-/68

59	TO 13223	AEC Regal IV	?	Brockhouse		B53F	11/54	11/54	-/--
60	TO 13224	AEC Regal IV	?	Brockhouse		B53F	10/54	10/54	-/--
61	TO 13225	AEC Regal IV	?	Brockhouse		B53F	11/54	11/54	-/--
1		Daimler D650HS	25545	BBA	140/1	B64F	4/56	4/56	-/--
2		Daimler D650HS	25546	BBA	140/2	B64F	4/56	4/56	-/--
3	TO 8765	Daimler D650HS	25550	BBA	140/3	B64F	4/56	4/56	-/67
4		Daimler D650HS	25569	BBA	140/4	B64F	5/56	5/56	-/--
9	TO 11103	Leyland 14B/1XL	?	TMBB		B63F	-/60	-/60	-/--
10	TO 11104	Leyland 14B/1XI	?	TMBB		B63F	-/00	-/80	-/--
11	TO 11105	Leyland 14B/1XL	?	TMBB		B63F	-/60	-/60	-/--
12	TO 11106	Leyland 14B/1XL	?	TMBB		B63F	-/60	-/60	-/--
13	TO 11107	Leyland 14B/1XL	?	TMBB		B63F	-/60	-/60	-/--
14	TO 11108	Leyland 14B/1XL	?	TMBB		B63F	-/60	-/60	-/--
15	TO 11313	Leyland 14B/1XL	?	TMBB		B63F	-/60	-/60	-/--
16	TO 12511	Ford Thames Trader	?	TMBB		B45F	-/62	-/62	-/--
17	TO 12513	Ford Thames Trader	?	TMBB		B45F	-/62	-/62	-/--
18	TO 13509	Ford Thames Trader	?	TMBB		B45F	-/62	-/62	-/--
19	TO 13513	Ford Thames Trader	?	TMBB		B45F	-/62	-/62	-/--
20	TO 13517	Ford Thames Trader	?	TMBB		B45F	-/62	-/62	-/--
21	TO 12946	Ford Thames Trader	?	TMBB		B45F	-/63	-/63	-/--
22	TO 12943	Ford Thames Trader	?	TMBB		B45F	-/63	-/63	-/--
23	TO 12936	Ford Thames Trader	?	TMBB		B45F	-/63	-/63	-/--
24	TO 12940	Ford Thames Trader	?	TMBB		B45F	-/63	-/63	-/--
25	TO 12959	Ford Thames Trader	?	TMBB		B45F	-/63	-/63	-/--
26	TO 862	DAF	?	TMBB		B60F	-/63	-/63	-/--
27	TO 863	Leyland OPS4/5	?	Brockhouse		B63F	-/63	-/63	-/--
28	TO 846	Leyland OPS4/5	?	Brockhouse		B63F	-/63	-/63	-/--
29	TO 835	Leyland OPS4/5	?	Brockhouse		B63F	-/63	-/63	-/--
30	TO 9488	Leyland	?	Brockhouse		B63F	-/63	-/63	-/--
31	TO 13029	AEC Kudu	?	AB&C		B63F	-/68	-/68	-/--
32	TO 9821	Leyland	?	Brockhouse		B63F	-/63	-/63	-/--
33	TO 11157	Leyland	?	Brockhouse		B63F	-/63	-/63	-/--
34	TO 12396	Leyland	?	Brockhouse		B63F	-/64	-/64	-/--
35	TO 12663	Leyland	?	Brockhouse		B63F	-/64	-/64	-/--
36	TO 13396	Leyland	?	Brockhouse		B63F	-/64	-/64	-/--
37	TO 13493	AEC Kudu	?	AB&C		B65F	-/68	-/68	-/--
38	TO 13508	AEC Kudu	?	AB&C		B65F	-/68	-/68	-/--
40	TO 13240	AEC Kudu	?	AB&C		B65F	-/68	-/68	-/--
42	TO 2988	AEC Kudu	?	AB&C		B65F	-/68	-/68	-/--
43	TO 12169	AEC Kudu	?	AB&C		B65F	-/65	-/65	-/--
44	TO 12426	AEC Kudu	?	AB&C		B65F	-/65	-/65	-/--
45	TO 13047	Guy Warrior 6LX	WTB5243	Rhino		B68F	1/66	1/66	-/--
46	TO 13775	Guy Warrior 6LX	WTB5259	Rhino		B68F	1/66	1/66	-/--
47	TO 11183	Guy Warrior 6LX	WTB5236	Rhino		B68F	1/66	1/66	-/--
48	TO 13189	Guy Warrior 6LX	WTB5237	Rhino		B68F	1/66	1/66	-/--
49	TO 8193	Guy Warrior 6LX	WTB5244	Rhino		B68F	2/66	2/66	-/--
50	TO 13200	Guy Warrior 6LX	WTB5256	Rhino		B68F	2/66	2/66	-/--
51	TO 12202	Guy Warrior 6LX	WTB5512	Rhino		B65F	6/66	6/66	-/--
52	TO 11389	AEC Regal VI	?	Rhino		B63F	-/66	-/66	-/--
53	TO 12472	AEC Kudu	?	Rhino		B65F	-/67	-/67	-/--
54	TO 14112	AEC Kudu	?	Rhino		B65F	-/67	-/67	-/--
55	TO 12838	AEC Kudu	?	Rhino		B65F	-/67	-/67	-/--
		Guy Warrior 6LX	WTB5921	?		B--F	3/69	3/69	-/--
		Guy Warrior 6LX	WTB5988	?		B--F	3/69	3/69	-/--
3	TO 12665	AEC Ranger	?	?		B--F	-/69	-/69	-/--
6	TO 15165	AEC Ranger	?	?		B--F	-/69?	-/69	-/--
8	TO 13222	Mercedes-Benz	?	?		B--F	-/68?	-/68?	-/--
	TO 17290	Mercedes-Benz	?	?		B--F	-/70	-/70	-/--
	TO 17292	?	?	?		B--F	/70	-/70	-/--
	TO 17293	Mercedes-Benz	?	?		B--F	-/70	-/70	-/--
	TO 17294	?	?	?		B--F	-/70	-/70	-/--
	TO 17295	?	?	?		B--F	-/70	-/70	-/--
13		Mercedes-Benz	?	?		B--F	by11/77	by11/77	-/--
14	TO 18111	Leyland	?	?		B--F	by11/77	by11/77	-/--

16	TO 12511	Leyland	?	?		B--F	by11/77	by11/77	-/--
20		Mercedes-Benz	?	?		B--F	by11/77	by11/77	-/--
23	TO 11303	Mercedes-Benz	?	?		B--F	by11/77	by11/77	-/--
26		?	?	De Haan		B--F	by11/77	by11/77	-/--
28	TO 18113	Leyland	?	?		B--F	by11/77	by11/77	-/--
29	TO 18114	Leyland	?	?		B--F	by11/77	by11/77	-/--
	TO 18116	Leyland	?	?		B--F	by11/77	by11/77	-/--
32	TO 12946	Mercedes-Benz	?	?		B--F	by11/77	by11/77	-/--
39	TO 13418	Mercedes-Benz	?	?		B--F	by11/77	by11/77	-/--
48	TO 13189	Mercedes-Benz	?	?		B--F	by11/77	by11/77	-/--
60	TO 16695	Guy Victory	?	?		B--F	by11/77	by11/77	-/--
61	TO 16697	Mercedes-Benz	?	?		B--F	by11/77	by11/77	-/--
66		Mercedes-Benz	?	?		B--F	by11/77	by11/77	-/--
67		Mercedes-Benz	?	?		B--F	by11/77	by11/77	-/--
80	TO 13029	International	?	?		B--F	by11/77	by11/77	-/--
85	TO 16970	International	?	?		B--F	by11/77	by11/77	-/--
		Toyota Dyna	036932	BBA	3697/1	M--	8/80	8/80	-/--

Notes:

AEC Regal O6624229 was diverted from Nigel Municipality.
AEC Regal III O962014-9 are also recorded with AB&C B39F bodies. 39 & 41 were rebodied AB&C B39F
   so perhaps all were similarly rebodied.
TO 13222-5 (58-61) have chassis nos 9822E1701-4, order unknown.
TO 11103-8 (9-15) were Leyland VoortrekkeR model, a special PSV design for South Africa.
TO 12169/426 (43/4) also reported with TMBB bodies.

Disposal:

TO 8765 (3): Nigel Municipality (for spares).

EKURHULENI TRANSPORT

Ekurhuleni Transport was formed in January 2000 for the new Metropolitan Municipality. This was achieved by
merging the fleets of Germiston, Benoni & Boksburg Municipalities. Also Alberton, Brakpan, Kempton Park, Nigel
& Springs, all of whom were former bus operators and Edenvale which never ran buses.
Vehicles from Germiston are numbered in a 23xxx series on paper but the "23" is an asset register prefix and is not
displayed on the vehicles. Boksburg has a similar "30" prefix.
See publication WWK3 for full details of the Germiston Municipality fleet.

1	HWJ 543GP	Ld ERT1/1		572129	BBL	916/1	B52+17F	12/57	1/00	7/06
3	JMN 937GP	Ld ERT1/1		572132	BBL	?	B53F+17	12/57	1/00	7/05
4	JWF 941GP	MB L613D			BBL	1018/1	B27F+3	3/88	1/00	1/05
			31040426004235							
5	HPH 474GP	MB L613D			BBL	1018/2	B27F+6	3/88	1/00	1/05
			31040426004234							
6	HWK 864GP	MB L613D			BBL	1018/4	B28F+3	3/88	1/00	1/05
			31040426005041							
7	JMN 940GP	MB L613D			BBL	1018/6	B27F+3	3/88	1/00	
			31040426005518							
8	JPM 237GP	MB L613D			BBL	1018/3	B28F+3	3/88	1/00	1/05
			31040426005040							
9	KCH 347GP	MB L613D			BBL	1018/5	B28F+3	3/88	1/00	
			31040426005349							
10	KCH 346GP	MB L613D			BBL	1018/7	B28F+3	3/88	1/00	
			31040426005350							
11	KCH 345GP	ERF Super Trailblazer	60377	BBL		1319/1	B65F+23	3/90	1/00	
12	HTJ 831GP	ERF Super Trailblazer	60376	BBL		1319/2	B66F+23	3/90	1/00	
13	HZB 810GP	ERF Super Trailblazer	67307	BBL		1382/1	B66F+12	4/91	1/00	
14	JWF 939GP	ERF Super Trailblazer	67308	BBL		1382/2	B66F+12	4/91	1/00	
15	KCH 349GP	ERF Super Trailblazer	69757	BBL		1514/1	B60F+25	-/92	1/00	
16	KCH 352GP	ERF Super Trailblazer	70357	BBL		1514/2	B60F+25	-/92	1/00	7/00

No	Reg	Make/Model	Chassis	Body	Fleet No	Config	In	Out	Notes
17	HWK 870GP	ERF Super Trailblazer	72371	Santini		B61F+22	-/93	1/00	
18	HZB 811GP	ERF Super Trailblazer	72370	Santini		B61F+22	-/93	1/00	
21	JMN 938GP	Leyland ERT1/1	572134	BBL	?	B53F+17	1/58	1/00	by5/05
24	JMN 613GP	Leyland ERT1/1	572135	BBL	887/4	B63F+17	1/58	1/00	7/05
25	HZB 820GP	Leyland ERT1/1	572131	BBL	917/1	B53F+17	1/58	1/00	7/05
28	JMN 935GP	Leyland ERT1/1	581628	BBL	916/4	B53F+17	858	1/00	7/05
33	JYR 279GP	MB O305 30700161040836		BBL	848/1	B55F+16	9/84	1/00	
34	HWK 866GP	MB O305 30700161041077		DDL	048/2	B54F+16	9/84	1/00	7/06
35	HWJ 539GP	Leyland ERT2/1	572889	BBL	916/3	B52F+17	2/58	1/00	7/05
36	JWF 943GP	MB O305 30700161041078		BBL	848/3	B54F+16	9/84	1/00	
37	HTJ 846GP	MB O305 30700161041093		BBL	848/4	B54F+16	9/84	1/00	
38	JWF 938GP	MB O305 30700161041094		BBA	4174/1	H55/39F+6	3/85	1/00	
39	JYR 281GP	MB O305 30700161041110		BBA	4174/2	H55/39F+6	3/85	1/00	
40	HZB 799GP	Saurer	2617	Springfield		H55/38F	-/79	1/00	by5/05
45	HZB 813GP	Leyland Victory 2	8401039	BBL	919/3	B62F+20	6/86	1/00	7/06
46	HZB 815GP	Leyland Victory 2	8401037	BBL	919/1 (?)	B62F+25	6/86	1/00	7/06
47	HPH 466GP	Leyland Victory 2	8401038	BBL	919/2	B63F+25	6/86	1/00	
48	HZB 806GP	Leyland Victory 2	8401042	BBL	919/5	B66F+25	6/86	1/00	7/06
49	HZB 802GP	Leyland Victory 2	8401013	BBL	919/4	B64F+25	6/86	1/00	7/06
50	JWF 940GP	Leyland Victory 2	8401040	BBL	919/6	B66F+25	6/86	1/00	
51	JGC 246GP	Leyland Victory 2	8401041	BBL	919/7 (?)	B--F	6/86	1/00	8/03
54	FBK 945GP	Hino BY340	40209	BBL	655/2 (?)	B70F+16	-/82	1/00	
55	FFM 054GP	MB OF1417 35209720724924		?		B57F	-/71	1/00	
57	FFM 065GP	Hino BY340	40174	BBL	?	B62F+29	-/81	1/00	
58	FGW 805GP	Hino BY340	40134	BBL	?	B62F+29	-/81	1/00	
59	FGW 813GP	Hino BY340	?	BBL	655/2 (?)	B70F+27	-/82	1/00	
62	FRK 873GP	Hino BY340	40220	BBL	753/1	B70F+27	-/84	1/00	
63	FNC 846GP	Hino BY340	40212	BBL	655/5	B70F+27	-/82	1/00	
68	JMN 932GP	Leyland ERT2/1	561558	BBL	917/2	B52F+17	2/57	1/00	
69	FSX 089GP	Hino BY340	40215	BBL	655/6	B70F+27	-/82	1/00	
70	FVM 616GP	Hino BY340	40216	BBL	?	B70F+16	-/82	1/00	
72	FWX 681GP	Hino BY340	40211	BBL	655/4	B70F+27	-/82	1/00	
74	FWX 702GP	Hino BY340	40064	De Haan		B69F+28	-/78	1/00	
75	HZB 797GP	Leyland ERT1/1	581627	BBL	917/4	B52F+17	9/58	1/00	7/05
76	JPM 236GP	Leyland ERT1/1	573105	BBL	917/3	B52F+17	9/58	1/00	by8/05
76	FWX 710GP	Nissan CB20	02503	VSA		B63F+20	-/86	1/00	
103	JMN 931GP	Leyland ERT2/1	801477	BBL	1206/1	B66F+20	12/69	1/00	by5/05
104	HWJ 542GP	Leyland ERT2/1	801476	BBL	1206/2	B--F	1/70	1/00	by5/05
105	JMN 932GP	Leyland ERT2/1	800533	BBL	1206/3	B65F+15	1/70	1/00	by5/05
19	LFW 020GP	MAN 18.232 AAMA630571PX05730		BBL	?	B61F+22	6/00	6/00	
134	RVC 274GP	MB O500M1725L 9BM3821884B368131		Marcopolo	01171?	B61F+12	12/02	12/02	
135	RVC 281GP	MB O500M1725L 9BM3821884B368121		Marcopolo	01168	B61F+12	12/02	12/02	
136	RVC 283GP	MB O500M1725L 9BM3821884B368125		Marcopolo	01170	B61F+12	12/02	12/02	
137	RVC 265GP	MB O500M1725L 9BM3821884B372090		Marcopolo	01163?	B61F+12	12/02	12/02	
138	RVC 259GP	MB O500M1725L 9BM3821884B370814		Marcopolo	01160	B61F+12	12/02	12/02	
139	RVC 254GP	MB O500M1725L 9BM3821884B371537		Marcopolo	01162	B61F+12	12/02	12/02	
140	RTY 049GP	MB O500M1725L 9BM3821884B370394		Marcopolo	01159	B61F+12	10/02	10/02	
141	RVC 251GP	MB O500M1725L 9BM3821884B372613		Marcopolo	01165	B61F+12	12/02	12/02	

142	RTY 055GP	MB O500M1725L		Marcopolo	01169?	B60F+12	10/02	10/02	
		9BM3821884B368127							
143	RVC 284GP	MB O500M1725L		Marcopolo	01171?	B60F+12	12/02	12/02	
		9BM3821884B368306							
144	RVC 276GP	MB O500M1725L		Marcopolo	01164	B60F+12	12/02	12/02	
		9BM3821884B372095							
145	RVC 285GP	MB O500M1725L		Marcopolo	01161	B60F+12	12/02	12/02	
		9BM3821884B371213							
146	?	MB O500M1725L		Marcopolo	?	B60F+12	12/02	12/02	by-/08
		?							
147	RVC 287GP	MB O500M1725L		Marcopolo	01157	B60F+12	12/02	12/02	
		9BM3821884B368403							
148	RVC 290GP	MB O500M1725L		Marcopolo	01166	B60F+12	12/02	12/02	
		9BM3821884B372615							
149	RVC 045GP	MB O500M1725L		Marcopolo	01158	B60F+12	12/02	12/02	
		9BM3821884B370084							
150	RVC 270GP	MB O500M1725L		Marcopolo	01156	B60F+12	12/02	12/02	
		9BM3821884B368395							
151	RVC 267GP	MB O500M1725L		Marcopolo	01155	B60F+12	12/02	12/02	
		9BM3821884B368310							
152	RVC 278GP	MB O500M1725L		Marcopolo	01167	B60F+12	12/02	12/02	
		9BM3821884B372619							
25	CWL 946GP	MB O305		BBA	3926/6	B54F+37	8/82	by5/05	
		307001 61 030913							
153	SJG 646GP	MB O500M1725L		Marcopolo	501221	B61F+12	6/05	6/05	
		9BM3821884B405488							
154	SJG 642GP	MB O500M1725L		Marcopolo	501222	B61F+12	6/05	6/05	
		9BM3821884B405698							
155	SJG 630GP	MB O500M1725L		Marcopolo	501244	B61F+12	6/05	6/05	
		9BM3821884B407145							
156	SJG 637GP	MB O500M1725L		Marcopolo	501223	B61F+12	6/05	6/05	
		9BM3821884B406597							
189	KCG 387GP	ERF Trailblazer 64GXB	38003	BBA	3596/7	B65F+15	2/80	1/00	7/06
193	HZB 809GP	ERF Trailblazer 64GXB	37490	BBA	3596/11	B57F+24	2/80	1/00	
226	JGC 249GP	Guy Victory 2	800044	De Haan		B65F+30	6/83	1/00	7/06
235	JMN 941GP	ERF Trailblazer	47330	De Haan		B66F+14	-/83	1/00	7/06
237	JGV 638GP	ERF Trailblazer	48470	De Haan		B71F+26	5/84	1/00	
238	JWF 942GP	ERF Trailblazer	47295	De Haan		B66F+26	5/84	1/00	
239	HZB 792GP	ERF Trailblazer	48471	De Haan		B71F+34	6/84	1/00	7/06

Notes:

HWJ 543GP, JMN 937/8/613GP (1, 3, 21/4) ex Germiston 1, 3, 21/4. Rebodied by BBL -/85.
JWF 941GP, HPH 474GP, HWK 864GP (4-6) ex Germiston 4-6.
JMN 940GP, KCH 346GP (7, 10) ex Germiston 7, 10. Transferred to Boksburg by 5/06.
JPM 237GP, KCH 352GP, HWK 866GP, HZB 799GP (8, 16, 34, 40) ex Germiston 8, 16, 34, 40.
KCH 347/5GP, HTJ 831GP (9, 11/2) ex Germiston 9, 11/2. Renumbered 130/28, 82 by 5/06.
HZB 810GP, JWF 939GP, KCH 349GP (13-5) ex Germiston 13-5. Renumbered 96, 117/31 by 5/06.
HWK 870GP, HZB 811GP, KGT 975 T (17/8, 33) ex Germiston 17/8, 33. Renumbered 89, 97, 123 by 5/06.
HZB 820GP, JMN 935GP, HWJ 539GP (25/8, 35) ex Germiston 25/8, 35. Rebodied by BBL -/85.
JWF 943GP, HTJ 846GP, JWF 938GP (36-8) ex Germiston 36-8. Renumbered 121, 83, 116 by 5/06.
JYR 281GP (39) ex Germiston 39. Renumbered 124 by 5/06.
HZB 813/5/06/2GP, JGC 246GP, FBK 945GP (45/6/8/9, 51/4) ex Germiston 45/6/8/9, 51, 4.
HPH 466GP, JWF 940GP (47, 50) ex Germiston 47, 50. Transferred to Boksburg by 5/06.
FFM 054/65GP, FGW 805/13GP, FRK 873GP, FNC 846GP (55/7-9, 62/3) ex Boksburg 7, 9, 8, 12, 5, 11.
JMN 932GP (68) ex Germiston 68. Rebodied by BBL -/85. Noted as 58 5/05.
FSX 089GP, FVM 616GP, FWX 681/702/10GP (69, 70/2/4/6) ex Boksburg 10, 2, 3, 6, 1.
HZB 797GP, JPM 236GP (75/6) ex Germiston 75/6. Rebodied by BBL -/85.
JMN 931GP, HWJ 542GP, JMN 932GP (103-5) ex Germiston 103-5. Rebodied BBL -/90.
LFW 020GP (19) ordered by Germiston. Renumbered 132 by 8/05. Also noted as RTY 049GP.
134-56 have Marcopolo Torino bodies, body numbers prefixed BUSUCFBSN365, suffixed POLO.
CWL 946GP (25) ex Benoni 754 (or 745).
KCG 387GP, JGC 249GP, JMN 941GP (189, 226/35) ex Germiston 189, 226/35.
HZB 809GP (193) ex Boksburg 193, new as Germiston 193.
JGV 638GP (237/8) ex Germiston 237/8. Renumbered 103/20 by 5/06

Known previous registrations:
HWJ 543GP, JMN 937/8/613GP, HZB 820GP (1, 3, 21/4/5) ex LZG 716-8/20/1T, TG 18415/7/9/21/2.
JWF 941GP, HPH 474GP, HWK 864GP, JMN 940GP, JPM 237GP (4-8) ex MMR 721/2T, MPB 461/2/4T.
KCH 347/6/5GP, HTJ 831GP, HZB 810GP, (9-13) ex MPB 463/5T. NXH 965/6T, PPW 253T.
JWF 939GP, KCH 349GP, KCH 352GP, HWK 870GP (14-7) ex PPW 254T, RJF 243/8T, RVL 314T.
HZB 811GP, JYR 279GP, HWK 866GP, JWF 943GP (18, 33/4/6) ex RWD 005T, KGT 975/7T.
JMN 935GP, HWJ 539GP, JMN 932GP (28, 35, 68) ex LZG 722/5/6T, new as TG 18445/23, 15197.
JWF 943GP, HTJ 846GP, JWF 938GP, JYR 281GP, HZB 799GP (30-40) ex KGT 9/8/4/6/3T, CDN 881T.
HZB 013/5GP, HPH 466GP, HZB 806/2GP (45-9) ex KYF 186/7T, KZC 558/9T, KZT 182T.
JWF 940GP, JGC 246GP (50-1) ex KZT 177T, KZZ 526T.
HZB 797GP, JPM 236GP (75/6) ex LZG 728T, MBX 186T, new as TG 18447/8.
JMN 931GP, HWJ 542GP (103-5) ex LZG 736-8T, new as TG 40818-20.
KCG 387GP (189) ex DDT 928T, new as CZG 659T
HZB 809GP, JGC 249GP, JMN 941GP (193, 226/35) ex CZG 664T, HWM 712T, JBR 520T.
JGV 638GP, JWF 942GP, HZB 792GP (237-9) ex JBJ 335/4T, JTY 326T.

Disposals:
HWJ 543GP, JMN 937GP, JWF 941GP, HPH 474GP, HWK 864GP, JPM 237GP (1, 3-6, 8): scrapped.
KCH 352GP, JMN 613GP, HZB 820GP, JMN 935GP, HWK 866GP (16, 24/5/8, 34): scrapped.
HWJ 539GP, HZB 799/813/5/06/2/797GP, JPM 236GP (35, 40/5/6/8/9, 75/6): scrapped.
JMN 931GP, HWJ 542GP, JMN 932GP, KCG 387GP (103-5/89): scrapped.
JGC 249GP, JMN 941GP, HZB 792GP (226/35/9): scrapped.

HERCULES MUNICIPALITY

The boundaries of Pretoria were extended in 1949 to include Hercules. At that point Hercules Municipality and its buses became part of Pretoria Municipality.

	Reo	?	Wayne	-/--	-/--	-/49
TP 48050	Reo	?	Wayne	-/--	-/--	-/49
	Leyland OPS1	?	Brush	-/49	-/49	-/49
	Leyland OPS1	?	Brush	-/49	-/49	-/49
	Leyland OPS1	?	BMS (ex trailer)	-/49	-/49	-/49
	Leyland OPS1	?	BMS (ex trailer)	-/49	-/49	-/49
	Leyland OPS1	?	BMS (ex trailer)	-/49	-/49	-/49
	Leyland OPS1	?	BMS (ex trailer)	-/49	-/49	-/49
	Leyland OPS1	?	BMS (ex trailer)	-/49	-/49	-/49
	Leyland OPS1	?	BMS (ex trailer)	-/49	-/49	-/49
	Leyland OPS1	?	BMS (ex trailer)	-/49	-/49	-/49
	Leyland OPS1	?	Brush	-/49	-/49	-/49
	Leyland OPS1	?	Brush	-/49	-/49	-/49

Disposals:
? (Reo), TP 48050: Pretoria Municipality 229/30.
? (Leyland OPS1): Pretoria Municipality 281-92.

JOHANNESBURG MUNICIPAL TRANSPORT
JOHANNESBURG METROPOLITAN BUS SERVICE

The City and Suburban Tramway Co started operating horse trams in Johannesburg in 1891. This company was acquired by Johannesburg City Council in 1904 and soon after started operating electric trams. These continued till 1961, with over 200 in use. Trolleybuses were introduced in 1936 and ran till June 1984 although a few prototypes were operated after this. However, they were not deemed sufficiently successful so the system closed completely in 1986. Motor buses were used briefly from 1913 to 1915 and were then fully used from 1927.

The bus fleet total has been around 500 buses in recent years. Internally, the organisation has been known as Johannesburg Transportation Department or Directorate. In July 2001 this changed to Johannesburg Metropolitan Bus Service, trading as Metrobus, a stand-alone company wholly owned by the City of Johannesburg.
The municipality of Roodepoort was incorporated into the city of Johannesburg in 2003 and the Roodepoort municipal bus fleet was absorbed into Metrobus.

		TSM petrol-electric	?	?	B--	3/13	3/13	6/15
		Thornycroft	?	?	B--	3/13	3/13	6/15
	TJ 1481	TSM	?	?	B--	10/13	10/13	6/15
		TSM	?	?	B--	10/13	10/13	6/15
		TSM	?	?	B--	10/13	10/13	6/15
		TSM	?	?	B--	10/13	10/13	6/15
1		Dennis E	?	?	B31	4/27	4/27	by-/36
2		Dennis E	?	?	B31	4/27	4/27	by-/36
3		Dennis E	?	?	B31	4/27	4/27	by-/36
4	TJ 11789	Dennis E	17085	?	B31	4/27	4/27	-/--
5		Dennis E	?	?	B31	4/27	4/27	by-/36
6	TJ 11783	Leyland LSC1	45377	?	B30D	4/27	4/27	by-/45
7	TJ 11787	Leyland LSC1	45383	?	B30D	4/27	4/27	by-/45
8	TJ 11782	Leyland LSC1	45375	?	B30D	4/27	4/27	by-/45
9	TJ 11781	Leyland LSC1	45374	?	B30D	4/27	4/27	-/36
10	TJ 11790	Leyland LSC1	45381	?	B29D	4/27	4/27	by-/45
11	TJ 11791	Leyland LSC1	45436	Leyland	B30D	4/27	4/27	by-/45
12	TJ 11792	Leyland LSC1	45382	?	B30D	4/27	4/27	by-/45
13	TJ 11793	Leyland LSC1	45380	?	B29D	4/27	4/27	by-/45
14	TJ 11794	Leyland LSC1	45379	?	B29D	4/27	4/27	by-/45
15	TJ 11795	Leyland LSC1	45378	?	B29D	4/27	4/27	by-/45
16	TJ 11796	TSM B9A	4947	?	B32D	4/27	4/27	by-/39
17	TJ 11797	TSM B9A	4951	?	B32D	4/27	4/27	by-/39
18	TJ 11798	TSM B9A	4948	?	B32D	4/27	4/27	by-/39
19	TJ 11799	TSM B9A	4949	?	B32D	4/27	4/27	by-/39
20	TJ 11800	TSM B9A	4950	?	B32D	4/27	4/27	by-/39
21	TJ 16307	Leyland LSC3	46972	Vickers (SA)	B35D	4/28	4/28	by-/45
22	TJ 16308	Leyland LSC3	46971	Vickers (SA)	B35D	4/28	4/28	by-/45
23	TJ 16309	Leyland LSC3	47380	Vickers (SA)	B35D	7/28	7/28	by-/45
24	TJ 16310	Leyland LSC3	47375	Vickers (SA)	B35D	7/28	7/28	by-/45
25	TJ 16311	Leyland LSC3	47389	Vickers (SA)	B35D	7/28	7/28	by-/45
26	TJ 16312	Leyland LSC3	47388	Vickers (SA)	B35D	7/28	7/28	by-/45
27	TJ 16313	Leyland LSC3	47378	Vickers (SA)	B35D	7/28	7/28	by-/45
28	TJ 16314	Leyland LSC3	47387	Vickers (SA)	B35D	7/28	7/28	by-/45
29	TJ 16315	Leyland LSC3	47376	Vickers (SA)	B35D	7/28	7/28	by-/45
30	TJ 16316	Leyland LSC3	47381	Vickers (SA)	B35D	7/28	7/28	by-/45
31	TJ 16317	Leyland LSC3	47386	Vickers (SA)	B35D	7/28	7/28	by-/45
32	TJ 16318	Leyland LSC3	47379	Vickers (SA)	B35D	7/28	7/28	by-/45
33	TJ 16319	Leyland LSC3	47377	Vickers (SA)	B35D	7/28	7/28	by-/45
34	TJ 16320	Leyland LSC3	46970	Vickers (SA)	B35D	4/28	4/28	by-/45
35	TJ 16321	Leyland LSC3	46285	Vickers (SA)	B35D	12/27	12/27	by-/45
41	TJ 19913	Leyland TA4	65541	Millhouse	B24F	4/30	4/30	by-/40
42	TJ 19914	Leyland TA4	65567	Millhouse	B24F	4/30	4/30	by-/40
43	TJ 19915	Leyland TA4	65564	Millhouse	B24F	4/30	4/30	by-/40
44	TJ 23748	AEC Ranger	665027	Griffin	B36F	-/31	-/31	by-/47
45	TJ 23749	AEC Ranger	665024	Griffin	B36F	-/31	-/31	by-/47
46	TJ 23750	AEC Ranger	665029	Griffin	B36F	-/31	-/31	by-/47
47	TJ 23751	AEC Ranger	665028	Griffin	B36F	-/31	-/31	by-/47
48	TJ 23752	AEC Ranger	665025	Griffin	B36F	-/31	-/31	by-/47
49	TJ 23753	AEC Ranger	665030	Griffin	B36F	-/31	-/31	by-/47
50	TJ 23754	AEC Ranger	665031	Griffin	B36F	-/31	-/31	by-/47
51	TJ 23755	AEC Ranger	665026	Griffin	B36F	-/31	-/31	by-/47
52	TJ 23756	Guy C28	C23718	Cooper	B28	-/31	-/31	-/--
53	TJ 23757	Guy C28	C23716	Cooper	B28	-/31	-/31	-/--
54	TJ 23758	Guy C28	C23717	Cooper	B28	-/31	-/31	-/--
55	TJ 23759	Guy FC48	FC23334	Vickers (SA)	H25/26R	10/31	10/31	-/--
56	TJ 23760	Guy FC48	FC23336	Vickers (SA)	H25/26R	10/31	10/31	-/--
57	TJ 12844	Karrier Monitor 6LW	48004	Vickers (SA)	H30/26R	-/33	-/33	-/48

58	TJ 12845	Karrier Monitor 6LW	48005	Vickers (SA)	H30/26R	-/33	-/33	by -/48
59	TJ 12846	Karrier Monitor	48008	Vickers (SA)	H30/26R	-/33	-/33	by -/48
60	TJ 12847	Karrier Monitor	48011	Vickers (SA)	H30/26R	-/33	-/33	-/48
61	TJ 12848	Karrier Monitor	48013	Vickers (SA)	H30/26R	-/33	-/33	by -/48
62	TJ 12849	Karrier Monitor	48009	Vickers (SA)	H30/26R	-/33	-/33	by -/48
63	TJ 12850	Karrier Monitor	48012	Vickers (SA)	H30/26R	-/33	-/33	by -/48
64	TJ 12851	Karrier Monitor	48010	Vickers (SA)	H30/26R	-/33	-/33	-/48
65	TJ 12852	Karrier Monitor 6LW	48006	Vickers (SA)	H30/26R	-/33	-/33	-/48
66	TJ 12853	Karrier Monitor 6LW	48007	Vickers (SA)	H30/26R	-/33	-/33	-/48
67	TJ 39986	AEC Regent	O6612951	MCCW	H30/26R	10/34	10/34	-/48--/52
68	TJ 39987	AEC Regent	O6612949	MCCW	H30/26R	10/34	10/34	-/48--/52
69	TJ 39988	AEC Regent	O6612956	MCCW	H30/26R	10/34	10/34	-/48--/52
70	TJ 39989	AEC Regent	O6612944	MCCW	H30/26R	10/34	10/34	-/48--/52
71	TJ 39990	AEC Regent	O6612952	MCCW	H30/26R	10/34	10/34	-/48--/52
72	TJ 39991	AEC Regent	O6612953	MCCW	H30/26R	10/34	10/34	-/48--/52
73	TJ 39992	AEC Regent	O6612945	MCCW	H30/26R	10/34	10/34	-/48--/52
74	TJ 39993	AEC Regent	O6612946	MCCW	H30/26R	10/34	10/34	-/48--/52
75	TJ 39994	AEC Regent	O6612955	MCCW	H30/26R	10/34	10/34	-/48--/52
76	TJ 39995	AEC Regent	O6612948	MCCW	H30/26R	10/34	10/34	-/48--/52
77	TJ 39996	AEC Regent	O6612957	MCCW	H30/26R	10/34	10/34	-/48--/52
78	TJ 39997	AEC Regent	O6612943	MCCW	H30/26R	10/34	10/34	-/48--/52
79	TJ 39998	AEC Regent	O6613199	MCCW	H30/26R	10/34	10/34	-/48--/52
80	TJ 39999	AEC Regent	O6612950	MCCW	H30/26R	10/34	10/34	-/48--/52
81	TJ 40001	AEC Regent	O6612954	MCCW	H30/26R	10/34	10/34	-/48--/52
82	TJ 40002	AEC Regent	O6612947	MCCW	H30/26R	10/34	10/34	-/48--/52
83	TJ 40003	Leyland TD4c	5635	MCCW	H30/26R+8	12/35	12/35	-/48--/52
84	TJ 40004	Leyland TD4c	5633	MCCW	H30/26R	12/35	12/35	-/48--/52
85	TJ 40005	Leyland TD4c	5631	MCCW	H30/26R	12/35	12/35	-/48--/52
86	TJ 40006	Leyland TD4c	5643	MCCW	H30/26R	12/35	12/35	-/48--/52
87	TJ 40007	Leyland TD4c	5642	MCCW	H30/26R	12/35	12/35	-/48--/52
88	TJ 40008	Leyland TD4c	5636	MCCW	H30/26R	12/35	12/35	-/48--/52
89	TJ 40009	Leyland TD4c	5637	MCCW	H30/26R	12/35	12/35	-/48--/52
90	TJ 40010	Leyland TD4c	5640	MCCW	H30/26R	12/35	12/35	-/48--/52
91	TJ 40011	Leyland TD4c	5638	MCCW	H30/26R	12/35	12/35	-/48--/52
92	TJ 40012	Leyland TD4c	5632	MCCW	H30/26R	12/35	12/35	-/48--/52
93	TJ 40013	Leyland TD4c	5639	MCCW	H30/26R	12/35	12/35	-/48--/52
94	TJ 40014	Leyland TD4c	5644	MCCW	H30/26R	12/35	12/35	-/48--/52
95	TJ 40015	Leyland TD4c	5641	MCCW	H30/26R	12/35	12/35	-/48--/52
96	TJ 40016	Leyland TD4c	5634	MCCW	H30/26R	12/35	12/35	-/48--/52
97	TJ 40017	Leyland TD4c	5645	MCCW	H30/26R	12/35	12/35	-/48--/52
98	TJ 40018	Leyland TD4c	5647	MCCW	H30/26R	12/35	12/35	-/48--/52
99	TJ 40019	Leyland TD4c	5646	MCCW	H30/26R	12/35	12/35	-/48--/52

Notes:

It has also been reported that two further Thornycrofts were purchased in 3/13.

With the exception of 11, 1-20 are thought to have been bodied locally by Wevell. The bodies were of generally British appearance except for having windows of full drop type. They all had pneumatic tyres, including the Leyland LSC1.

TJ 11789/92/4/5/8 (4, 12/45/8) were renumbered N4, N12 (?), N14 (?), N15 (?), N18 (?). Vehicles prefixed N were allocated to "Native Services".

5 vehicles were reported acquired from I. Lopis in 4/28 and 8 vehicles from Rapid Motor Transport(s) in 5/28. Five of these vehicles may have become 36-40.

TJ 16307 21 (21-35) had bodies built in South Africa by the Vickers and Metropolitan Carriage Co (SA) Ltd, an organisation associated with the British Vickers company (which later became the MCCW bus building company). These buses were fitted with pneumatic tyres when new.

TJ 16308-14/7-9, 19913 (22-8, 31-3, 41) renumbered N12/7-22, 2/3, 23, 41, all subject to confirmation.

TJ 16317 (31) has also been reported with chassis no. 46284 but this is a City Tramways vehicle.

TJ 23750 (46) renumbered 440 in 1948, believed as an ancillary vehicle.

TJ 19913-5 (41-43) also reported as TJ 19913/2/4 and were paid for by the Johannesburg Consolidated Investment Co Ltd to operate a service to a housing development in Lower Houghton. 42/3 are also recorded with chassis nos. in reverse order.

TJ 23748-55 (44-51) were originally fitted with petrol engines but 44 was converted to diesel power after a short time, an early experiment with this type of engine.

TJ 23756-60 (52-6) were fitted with Guy petrol engines.

TJ 23759/60 (55/6) had upstairs seating arranged as 7 rows of 3 with gangways on both sides, plus 4 at the back.

TJ 12844/5/52/3 (57/8, 65/6) were fitted with Gardner 6LW engines from new. The experience so gained was to influence JMT's future engine policy.

TJ 12846-51 (59-64) were fitted with Karrier petrol engines.

TJ 12844-53 (57-66) have also been reported as having bodies built by Seale & Frank.

TJ 39986-99, 40001/2 (67-82) were renumbered 340-55 in 1948.

TJ 40003-19 (83-99) were renumbered 302-18 in 1948.

Disposals:

? (?): (two of the 1913 vehicles): converted into tower wagons for the tramways service.

TJ 11781 (9): chassis reused for a lorry.

TJ 23748-55 (44-51): several of these vehicles became tow-cars with the rear part of the body cut away.

TJ 23759/60 (55/6): one became a tramway overhead wire greasing wagon.

100	TJ 24742	White 61R	M4092	?		B24-	by -/35	-/35	-/37
101	TJ 5030	Bedford WLG	115715	?		B24-	by -/35	-/35	-/37
102	TJ 27859	Bedford	?	?		B24-	by -/35	-/35	-/37
103	TJ 1123	Dennis A	11080	?		B32-	by -/35	-/35	-/--
104	TJ 3218	Dennis Lancet	170087	?		B35-	-/32	-/35	by-/40
105	TJ 4441	Reo	?	?		B---	by -/35	-/35	-/35
106	TJ 1174	Reo	?	?		B34-	by -/35	-/35	by-/40
107	TJ 275	White 65AR	871135	?		B32-	by -/35	-/35	-/--
108	TJ 11946	Diamond T	52553	?		B24-	by -/35	-/35	by-/40
109	TJ 26083	Bussing NAG	37159	?		B---	by -/35	-/35	-/37
110	TJ 25526	Reo Gold Crown	1743GB	?		B27-	by -/35	-/35	by-/40
111	TJ 23664	Chevrolet	?	?		B---	by -/35	-/35	-/35
112	TJ 839	White 61R	174707	?		B28-	by -/35	-/35	-/37
113	TJ 115	Reo	?	?		B36-	by -/35	-/35	by-/40
114	TJ 11496	Reo ?	3K30	?		B28-	by -/35	-/35	by-/40
115	TJ 5582	Reo	?	?		B34-	by -/35	-/35	-/37
116	TJ 1799	Reo Gold Crown	?	?		B34-	by -/35	-/35	by-/40
117	TJ 11280	Reo Gold Crown	?	?		B---	by -/35	-/35	-/36
118	TJ 19652	Reo Gold Crown	?	?		B34-	by -/35	-/35	by-/40
119	TJ 5090	Reo Gold Crown	?	?		B---	by -/35	-/35	-/36
120	TJ 9555	Reo Gold Crown	?	?		B28-	by -/35	-/35	by-/40
121	TJ 6828	Reo Gold Crown	2D385	?		B24-	by -/35	-/35	-/37
122	TJ 6710	Chevrolet	?	?		B---	by -/35	-/35	-/35

Notes:

A total of 43 vehicles is recorded as purchased in 6/33 with 2 more in 10/36 and a further two in 10/37. It is presumed that 100-122 above were the only ones which were deemed fit for further service although it is not clear why these are shown as acquired in 1935.

The 6/33 vendors are listed as Blake (6 vehicles), Smuts (4), Frank (3), Enwright (3), van den Berg (5+1), Levine (3), Lamb & Pienaar (3), Van Graevenitz (4), Smith (1), Williams (1), Templeton (1) and van Deventer (8).

The 12/36 vehicles were bought from Williams (2).

The 10/37 vehicles were bought from Pretorius (2).

It is not known which vehicles emanated from which vendor.

122	TJ 40020	Leyland TD4c	7343	MCCW	H30/26R	-/36	-/36	-/48--/52
123	TJ 40021	Leyland TD4c	7341	MCCW	H30/26R	-/36	-/36	-/48--/52
124	TJ 40022	Leyland TD4c	7344	MCCW	H30/26R	-/36	-/36	-/48--/52
125	TJ 40023	Leyland TD4c	7342	MCCW	H30/26R	-/36	-/36	-/48--/52
126	TJ 40024	Leyland TD4c	7345	MCCW	H30/26R	-/36	-/36	-/48--/52
127	TJ 40027	Leyland TD4c	7348	MCCW	H30/26R	-/36	-/36	-/48--/52
128	TJ 40028	Leyland TD4c	7346	MCCW	H30/26R	-/36	-/36	-/48--/52
129	TJ 40029	Leyland TD4c	7347	MCCW	H30/26R	-/36	-/36	-/48--/52
1	TJ 40025	AEC Renown	O664253	MCCW	H34/30R	-/35	-/35	-/48--/52
2	TJ 40026	Leyland TT4c	5880	MCCW	H34/30R	-/35	-/35	-/54
3	TJ 59132	AEC Regent	O6615024	MCCW	H32/26R+8	2/37	2/37	-/--
4	TJ 59133	AEC Regent	O6615028	MCCW	H32/26R	2/37	2/37	-/--
5	TJ 59134	AEC Regent	?	MCCW	H32/26R	2/37	2/37	-/--
9	TJ 59135	AEC Regent	O6615022	MCCW	H32/26R	2/37	2/37	-/--

16	TJ 59136	AEC Regent	O6615025	MCCW		H32/26R	2/37	2/37	-/--
19	TJ 59137	AEC Regent	O6615021	MCCW		H32/26R	2/37	2/37	-/--
20	TJ 59138	AEC Regent	O6615023	MCCW		H32/26R	2/37	2/37	-/--
36	TJ 59139	AEC Regent	O6615027	MCCW		H32/26R	2/37	2/37	-/--
37	TJ 50140	AEC Regent	O6615031	MCCW		H32/26R	2/37	2/37	-/--
38	TJ 59141	AEC Regent	O6615033	MCCW		H32/26R	2/37	2/37	-/--
39	TJ 59142	AEC Regent	O6615026	MCCW		H32/26R	2/37	2/37	-/--
40	TJ 59143	AEC Regent	?	MCCW		H32/26R	2/37	2/37	-/--
102	TJ 59144	AEC Regent	O6615029	MCCW		H32/26R	2/37	2/37	-/--
105	TJ 59145	AEC Regent	O6615034	MCCW		H32/26R	2/37	2/37	-/--
111	TJ 59146	AEC Regent	O6615035	MCCW		H32/26R	2/37	2/37	-/--
6	TJ 63674	Daimler COG6	10148	MCCW		H32/26R+8	-/37	-/37	-/--
12	TJ 63675	Daimler COG6	10150	MCCW		H32/26R	-/37	-/37	-/--
14	TJ 63676	Daimler COG6	10149	MCCW		H32/26R	-/37	-/37	-/--
15	TJ 63677	Daimler COG6	10152	MCCW		H32/26R	-/37	-/37	-/--
17	TJ 63678	Daimler COG6	10158	MCCW		H32/26R	-/37	-/37	-/--
18	TJ 63679	Daimler COG6	10156	MCCW		H32/26R	-/37	-/37	-/--
31	TJ 63680	Daimler COG6	10154	MCCW		H32/26R	-/37	-/37	-/--
41	TJ 63681	Daimler COG6	10157	MCCW		H32/26R	-/37	-/37	-/--
100	TJ 63682	Daimler COG6	10153	MCCW		H32/26R	-/37	-/37	-/--
101	TJ 63683	Daimler COG6	10155	MCCW		H32/26R	-/37	-/37	-/--
109	TJ 63684	Daimler COG6	10151	MCCW		H32/26R	-/37	-/37	-/--
112	TJ 63685	Daimler COG6	10159	MCCW		H32/26R	-/37	-/37	-/--
115	TJ 63686	Daimler COG6	10160	MCCW		H32/26R	-/37	-/37	-/--
117	TJ 63687	Daimler COG6	10161	MCCW		H32/26R	-/37	-/37	-/--
119	TJ 63688	Daimler COG6	10163	MCCW		H32/26R	-/37	-/37	-/--
121	TJ 63689	Daimler COG6	10162	MCCW		H32/26R	-/37	-/37	-/--
130	TJ 63690	Daimler COG6	10164	MCCW		H32/26R	-/37	-/37	-/--
131	TJ 63691	Daimler COG6	10281	MCCW		H32/26R	-/37	-/37	-/--
132	TJ 63692	Daimler COG6	10165	MCCW		H32/26R	-/37	-/37	-/--
133	TJ 63693	Daimler COG6	10284	MCCW		H32/26R	-/37	-/37	-/--
134	TJ 63694	Daimler COG6	10288	MCCW		H32/26R	-/37	-/37	-/--
135	TJ 63695	Daimler COG6	10286	MCCW		H32/26R	-/37	-/37	-/--
136	TJ 63696	Daimler COG6	10166	MCCW		H32/26R	-/37	-/37	-/--
137	TJ 63697	Daimler COG6	10282	MCCW		H32/26R	-/37	-/37	-/--
138	TJ 63698	Daimler COG6	10285	MCCW		H32/26R	-/37	-/37	-/--
139	TJ 63699	Daimler COG6	10283	MCCW		H32/26R	-/37	-/37	-/--
140	TJ 63700	Daimler COG6	10287	MCCW		H32/26R	-/37	-/37	-/--
141	TJ 63701	Daimler COG6	10289	MCCW		H32/26R	-/37	-/37	-/--
142	TJ 63702	Daimler COG6	10290	MCCW		H32/26R	-/37	-/37	-/--
143	TJ 63703	Daimler COG6	10291	MCCW		H32/26R	-/37	-/37	-/--
144	TJ 63704	Daimler COG6	10292	MCCW		H32/26R	-/37	-/37	-/--
145	TJ 63705	Daimler COG6	10294	MCCW		H32/26R	-/37	-/37	-/--
146	TJ 63706	Daimler COG6	10293	MCCW		H32/26R	-/37	-/37	-/--
147	TJ 63707	Daimler COG6	10295	MCCW		H32/26R	-/37	-/37	-/--
148	TJ 63708	Daimler COG6	10167	MCCW		H32/26R	-/37	-/37	-/--
32	TJ 48610	Bedford ?	?	?		B25-	-/37	-/37	-/--
42	TJ 36198	Leyland KPZ4	202101	Duple	7257/2	C24F	3/40	3/40	-/--

Notes:

TJ 40020-4/7-9/5/6 (122-9, 2) renumbered 319-327/01 in 1948.
TJ 59134/43 (5, 40) had chassis numbers O6615030/2, order unknown.
TJ 59146 (111) also recorded by JMT as fleet no 10.
TJ 59132-46 (3-5, 9, 16/9, 20, 36-40, 102/5/11) renumbered 328-39, 356-8 in 1948.
TJ 63674-708 (6, 12/4/5/7/8, 31, 41, 100/1/9/12/5.7.9.21/30-48) entered service between 10/37 and 4/38.
They were renumbered 359-393 in 1948.

Five Daimler / MCCW were ordered in 1939. They were diverted by the U.K. Ministry of Supply to Birmingham City
Transport and West Monmouth Omnibus Board and were new in 1940 as follows:

FVP 921	Daimler COG6	11151	MCCW	H32/26R	Birmingham CT 1321
EAX 729	Daimler COG6	11152	MCCW	H32/26R	West Monmouth OB 20
FVP 920	Daimler COG6	11153	MCCW	H32/26R	Birmingham CT 1320
FVP 922	Daimler COG6	11154	MCCW	H32/26R	Birmingham CT 1322
FVP 923	Daimler COG6	11155	MCCW	H32/26R	Birmingham CT 1323

51	TJ 41351	Mack EE1SH	3609	BMS		B35F	10/43	10/43	by2/56
52	TJ 41352	Mack EE1SH	3624	BMS		B35F	1/44	1/44	by2/56
53	TJ 41383	Mack EE1SH	3625	BMS		B35F	11/43	11/43	by2/56
54	TJ 41386	Mack EE1SH	3621	BMS		B35F	9/43	9/43	by2/56
55	TJ 41409	Mach EE1SH	3623	BMS		B35F	12/43	12/43	by2/56
56	TJ 41422	Mack EE1SH	3615	BMS		B35F	11/43	11/43	by2/56
57	TJ 41430	Mack EE1SH	3616	BMS		B35F	10/43	10/43	by2/56
58	TJ 41437	Mack EE1SH	3614	BMS		B35F	9/43	9/43	by2/56
59	TJ 41451	Mack EE1SH	3617	BMS		B35F	12/43	12/43	by2/56
60	TJ 41459	Mack EE1SH	3620	BMS		B35F	10/43	10/43	by2/56
61	TJ 43864	Mack EE1SH	3622	BMS		B35F	10/43	10/43	by2/56
62	TJ 43888	Mack EE1SH	3607	BMS		B35F	10/43	10/43	by2/56
63	TJ 43904	Mack EE1SH	3608	BMS		B35F	11/43	11/43	by2/56
64	?	Mack EE1SH	3618	BMS		B35F	9/43	9/43	by2/56
65	TJ 44315	Mack EE1SH	3610	BMS		B35F	8/43	8/43	by2/56
66	TJ 44338	Mack EE1SH	3619	BMS		B35F	-/43	-/43	by2/56
151	TJ 69947	Daimler CVG6	13062	BMS		H32/26R+12	-/47	-/47	by-/60
152	TJ 60919	Daimler CVG6	12659	BMS		H32/26R+12	-/47	-/47	by-/66
153	TJ 61190	Daimler CVG6	13287	BMS		H32/26R+12	-/47	-/47	by-/66
154	TJ 61227	Daimler CVG6	13288	BMS		H32/26R+12	-/47	-/47	by-/66
155	TJ 61238	Daimler CVG6	12660	BMS		H32/26R+12	-/47	-/47	by-/62
156	TJ 61240	Daimler CVG6	12620	BMS		H32/26R+12	-/47	-/47	by-/62
157	TJ 61619	Daimler CVG6	13060	BMS		H32/26R+12	-/47	-/47	by-/66
158	TJ 61713	Daimler CVG6	12639	BMS		H32/26R+12	-/47	-/47	by-/66
159	TJ 61749	Daimler CVG6	13063	BMS		H32/26R+12	-/47	-/47	-/--
160	TJ 61750	Daimler CVG6	12640	BMS		H32/26R+12	-/47	-/47	-/--
161	TJ 61779	Daimler CVG6	13289	BMS		H32/26R+12	-/47	-/47	-/--
162	TJ 61818	Daimler CVG6	13542	BMS		H32/26R+12	-/47	-/47	by-/66
163	TJ 61888	Daimler CVG6	13551	BMS		H32/26R+12	-/47	-/47	by-/66
164	TJ 61917	Daimler CVG6	13543	BMS		H32/26R+12	-/47	-/47	-/--
165	TJ 61968	Daimler CVG6	13545	BMS		H32/26R+12	-/47	-/47	-/--
166	TJ 61969	Daimler CVG6	13546	BMS		H32/26R+12	-/47	-/47	by-/66
167	TJ 61986	Daimler CVG6	13556	BMS		H32/26R+12	-/47	-/47	by-/62
168	TJ 62104	Daimler CVG6	13554	BMS		H32/26R+12	-/47	-/47	by-/66
169	TJ 62113	Daimler CVG6	13547	BMS		H32/26R+12	-/47	-/47	by-/66
170	TJ 62160	Daimler CVG6	13553	BMS		H32/26R+12	-/47	-/47	by-/66
171	TJ 74692	Daimler CVG6	12534	MCCW		H32/26R+12	-/48	-/48	by-/62
172	TJ 74693	Daimler CVG6	12515	MCCW		H32/26R+12	-/48	-/48	by-/66
173	TJ 74694	Daimler CVG6	12514	MCCW		H32/26R+12	-/48	-/48	by-/62
174	TJ 74695	Daimler CVG6	12554	MCCW		H32/26R+12	-/48	-/48	-/--
175	TJ 74696	Daimler CVG6	12535	MCCW		H32/26R+12	-/48	-/48	by-/66
419	TJ 94698	Daimler CD650DD	17339	Brockhouse		H32/26R+12	-/50	-/50	-/--
420	TJ 94699	Daimler CD650DD	17340	Brockhouse		H32/26R+12	-/50	-/50	-/--
421	TJ 94700	Daimler CD650DD	17341	Brockhouse		H32/26R+12	-/50	-/50	by-/70
422	TJ 94701	Daimler CD650DD	17342	Brockhouse		H32/26R+12	-/50	-/50	-/--
423	TJ 94702	Daimler CD650DD	17343	Brockhouse		H32/26R+12	-/50	-/50	-/--
424	TJ 94703	AEC Regent III	9612E4683	BMS		H32/26R+12	3/50	3/50	-/--
425	TJ 94704	AEC Regent III	9612E4684	BMS		H32/26R+12	4/50	4/50	-/--
426	TJ 94705	AEC Regent III	9612E4685	BMS		H32/26R+12	3/50	3/50	-/--
427	TJ 94706	AEC Regent III	9612E4686	BMS		H32/26R+12	3/50	3/50	-/--
428	TJ 94707	AEC Regent III	9612E4687	BMS		H32/26R+12	3/50	3/50	-/--
429	TJ 94708	AEC Regent III	9612E4688	BMS		H32/26R+12	3/50	3/50	-/--
430	TJ 94709	AEC Regent III	9612E4689	BMS		H32/26R+12	3/50	3/50	-/--
431	TJ 94710	AEC Regent III	9612E4690	BMS		H32/26R+12	4/50	4/50	-/--
432	TJ 94711	AEC Regent III	9612E4691	BMS		H32/26R+12	4/50	4/50	-/--
433	TJ 94712	AEC Regent III	9612E4692	BMS		H32/26R+12	5/50	5/50	-/--
434	TJ 94713	AEC Regent III	9612E4693	BMS		H32/26R+12	5/50	5/50	-/--
435	TJ 94714	AEC Regent III	9612E4694	BMS		H32/26R+12	5/50	5/50	-/--
436	TJ 94715	AEC Regent III	9612E4695	BMS		H32/26R+12	5/50	5/50	-/--
437	TJ 94716	AEC Regent III	9612E4696	BMS		H32/26R+12	4/50	4/50	-/--
438	TJ 94717	AEC Regent III	9612E4697	BMS		H32/26R+12	4/50	4/50	-/--
439	TJ 116.046	AEC Regent III	9613E7175	BBA	M838	H32/26R+12	12/52	12/52	-/--
440	TJ 116.047	AEC Regent III	9613E7176	BBA	M845	H32/26R+12	2/53	2/53	-/--

441	TJ 116.048	AEC Regent III	9613E7177	BBA	M839	H32/26R+12	12/52	12/52	-/--
442	TJ 116.049	AEC Regent III	9613E7178	BBA	M846	H32/26R+12	2/53	2/53	-/--
443	TJ 116.050	AEC Regent III	9613E7179	BBA	M841	H32/26R+12	12/52	12/52	-/--
444	TJ 116.051	AEC Regent III	9613E7180	BBA	M836	H32/26R+12	12/52	12/52	-/--
445	TJ 116.052	AEC Regent III	9613E7181	BBA	M842	H32/26R+12	12/52	12/52	-/--
446	TJ 116.053	AEC Regent III	9613E7182	BBA	M847	H32/26R+12	2/53	2/53	-/--
447	TJ 116.054	AEC Regent III	9613E7183	BBA	M843	H32/26R+12	2/53	2/53	-/--
448	TJ 116.055	AEC Regent III	9613E7184	BBA	M837	H32/26R+12	12/52	12/52	-/--
449	TJ 116.056	AEC Regent III	9613E7185	DDA	M044	H32/26R+12	2/53	2/53	-/--
450	TJ 116.057	AEC Regent III	9613E7186	BBA	M849	H32/26R+12	2/53	2/53	-/--
451	TJ 116.058	AEC Regent III	9613E7187	BBA	M848	H32/26R+12	2/53	2/53	-/--
452	TJ 116.059	AEC Regent III	9613E7188	BBA	M840	H32/26R+12	12/52	12/52	-/72
301	TJ 50978	Daimler G6HS	25347	BBA	M1035	B36F+15	6/54	6/54	-/--
302	TJ 51101	Daimler G6HS	25348	BBA	M1033	B36F+15	5/54	5/54	-/--
303	TJ 51208	Daimler G6HS	25349	BBA	M1032	B36F+15	5/54	5/54	-/--
304	TJ 51258	Daimler G6HS	25350	BBA	M1034	B36F+15	5/54	5/54	-/--
305	TJ 51269	Daimler G6HS	25328	BBA	M1036	B44F+24	6/54	6/54	by-/68
306	TJ 51487	Daimler G6HS	25329	BBA	M1037	B44F+24	6/54	6/54	by-/68
307	TJ 51529	Daimler G6HS	25330	BBA	M1038	B44F+24	6/54	6/54	by-/68
308	TJ 51582	Daimler G6HS	25331	BBA	M1039	B44F+24	6/54	6/54	by-/68
309	TJ 54297	Daimler G6HS	25335	BBA	M1040	B44F+24	8/54	8/54	by-/68
310	TJ 54319	Daimler G6HS	25336	BBA	M1041	B44F+24	8/54	8/54	by-/68
311	TJ 54327	Daimler G6HS	25341	BBA	M1042	B44F+24	8/54	8/54	by-/68
312	TJ 54334	Daimler G6HS	25342	BBA	M1043	B44F+24	8/54	8/54	by-/68
313	TJ 54339	Daimler G6HS	25343	BBA	M1044	B44F+24	8/54	8/54	by-/68
314	TJ 54389	Daimler G6HS	25344	BBA	M1045	B44F+24	8/54	8/54	by-/68
315	TJ 54391	Daimler G6HS	25332	Brockhouse		B53F+19	-/54	-/54	by-/68
316	TJ 54521	Daimler G6HS	25333	Brockhouse		B53F+19	-/54	-/54	by-/68
317	TJ 54588	Daimler G6HS	25334	Brockhouse		B53F+19	-/54	-/54	by-/68
318	TJ 54764	Daimler G6HS	25337	Brockhouse		B53F+19	-/54	-/54	by-/68
319	TJ 54798	Daimler G6HS	25338	Brockhouse		B53F+19	-/54	-/54	by-/68
320	TJ 54851	Daimler G6HS	25339	Brockhouse		B53F+19	-/54	-/54	by-/68
321	TJ 55299	Daimler G6HS	25340	Brockhouse		B53F+19	-/54	-/54	by-/68
322	TJ 55334	Daimler G6HS	25345	Brockhouse		B53F+19	-/54	-/54	-/67
323	TJ 55369	Daimler G6HS	25346	Brockhouse		B53F+19	-/54	-/54	-/67
324	TJ 79483	Leyland ER44	?	BBA	?	B44F+24	-/54	-/54	by-/76

Notes:

TJ 41351/2/83/6/409/22/30/7/51/9, 43864/88/904, ?, 44315/38 (51-66) were austerity normal control single-deckers with right hand drive (looking very like Bedford OWB heavy duty chassis) and fitted with Mack 77 bhp petrol engines. They were renumbered as follows:

	In 1948	In 1950
TJ 41351 (51)	429	484
TJ 41352 (52)	430	
TJ 41383 (53)	431	486
TJ 41386 (54)	443	494
TJ 41409 (55)	444	
TJ 41422 (56)	432	487
TJ 41430 (57)	445	496
TJ 41437 (58)	433	488
TJ 41451 (59)	446	
TJ 41459 (60)	434	489
TJ 43864 (61)	435	490
TJ 4388 (62)	447	
TJ 43904 (63)	448	498
? (64)	436	491

TJ 69947, 60919, 61190/227/38/40/619/713/49/50/79/818/88/917/68/9/86, 62104/13/60, 74692-6 (151-75) were renumbered 394-418 in 1948.

TJ 74692-6 (171-5) are also reported as having been H30/26R when new.

TJ 61238/40/968/86, 62014 (398/9, 408, 410/1 later became driver training vehicles F8-12.

TJ 61749/50/79/917/68, 74695 (402/3/4/7/8/17) were reported extant in 1970.

TJ 50978/1101/208/58 (301-4) renumbered 501-4 by 9/68.

TJ 79483 (324) has not been traced in BBA records. It may, however, have been Leyland 522591 (BBA M1029) which is recorded by BBA for Bloemfontein. Note that 488 was later transferred to Bloemfontein - perhaps in exchange for 324 ? 324 was renumbered 484 by 12/62.
Daimler CVG6 chassis numbered 13558/9 have been attributed to JMT but not traced. It has been suggested that they may have been diverted to Roodepoort Municipality.

Disposal:

TJ 116.059 (452): smallholding, Johannesburg; Suncrush Drinks, re-registered NU 111.184 and converted to a mobile bar for use on staff outings, starting in 4/87. Donated to the Durban Historical Transport Society and kept at the Natal Parks Board's open-air museum at Midmar. Assegaai Tours, Assegaaibosch Country Lodge, Kareeedouw, Eastern Cape by 5/09.

453	TJ 34408	Guy Arab III 5LW	?	?		B---	7/46	2/56	-/58
454	TJ 30505	Guy Arab III 5LW	?	?		B---	10/46	2/56	-/57
455	TJ 14362	Guy Arab III 5LW	?	?		B---	1/47	2/56	-/57
456	TJ 6267	Guy Arab III 5LW	?	?		B---	1/47	2/56	-/58
457	TJ 8846	Guy Arab III 5LW	?	?		B---	3/47	2/56	-/58
458	TJ ??381	Guy Arab III 5LW	?	?		B---	3/47	2/56	-/--
459	TJ 13908	Guy Arab III 5LW	?	Northern BS		B---	5/47	2/56	-/--
460	TJ 13867	Guy Arab III 5LW	?	?		B---	6/47	2/56	-/57
461	TJ 10026	Guy Arab III 5LW	?	?		B---	7/47	2/56	-/57
462	TJ 11554	Guy Arab III 5LW	?	?		B---	4/47	2/56	-/61
463	TJ 18913	Guy Arab III 5LW	?	Northern BS		B---	10/47	2/56	-/57
464	TJ 64358	Guy Arab III 5LW	?	?		B---	9/47	2/56	-/58
465	TJ 9278	Guy Arab III 5LW	?	?		B---	2/48	2/56	-/58
466	TJ 82525	Guy Arab III 5LW	?	AB&C (new 1954)		B---	10/48	2/56	-/57
467	TJ 65892	Guy Arab III 5LW	?	?		B---	8/49	2/56	-/58
468	TJ 35604	Guy Arab III 5LW	?	?		B---	10/49	2/56	-/58
469	TJ 93405	Guy Arab III 5LW	?	?		B---	1/50	2/56	-/58
470	TJ 90179	Guy Arab III 5LW	?	?		B---	2/50	2/56	-/58
471	TJ 33586	Daimler COG6	?	Weymann		B---	-/--	2/56	-/--
472	TJ 97903	Daimler COG6	?	Weymann		B---	-/--	2/56	-/--
473	TJ 97904	Daimler COG6	?	Weymann		B---	-/--	2/56	-/--
474	TJ 97905	Daimler COG6	?	Weymann		B---	-/--	2/56	-/--
475	TJ 110.012	Daimler COG6	?	Weymann		B---	-/--	2/56	-/--
476	TJ 110.013	Daimler COG6	?	Weymann		B---	-/--	2/56	-/--
477	TJ 110.014	Daimler COG6	?	Weymann		B---	-/--	2/56	-/--
478	TJ 110.015	Daimler COG6	?	Weymann		B---	-/--	2/56	-/--
479	TJ 14666	Daimler COG6	?	Weymann		B---	-/--	2/56	-/--
480	TJ 58156	Daimler G6HS	25050	Swiss Aluminium Co		B64F+16	-/54	2/56	-/--
481	TJ 111.759	Daimler G6HS	25377	Gove		B54F+13	10/54	2/56	-/--
482	TJ 125.931	Daimler D650HS	25396	Swiss Aluminium Co		B51F+24	-/55	2/56	-/--
483	TJ 121.484	Bussing Tu11	?	Bussing		B---	7/54	2/56	-/--
484	TJ 121.341	Bussing 4500T	?	Bussing		B35D	7/54	2/56	-/--
485	TJ 83413	Leyland ER44	522598	BBA	M673	B51F+20	8/54	2/56	-/--
486	TJ 125.932	Leyland ER44	521951	BBA	M687	B51F+20	3/55	2/56	-/--
487	TJ 125.933	Leyland ER44	521952	BBA	M859	B51F+20	4/55	2/56	-/--
488	TJ 49022	Leyland ER44	521958	BBA	M865	B51F+20	4/55	2/56	-/56
489	TJ 123.598	Leyland HR44	521588	BBA	M709	B45F+16	12/54	2/56	by-/76
490	TJ 123.599	Leyland HR44	521589	BBA	M710	B45F+16	12/54	2/56	by-/76
491	TJ 70949	Leyland ER44 (SA2)	560219	BBA	171/1	B64F+16	6/56	6/56	by-/75
492	TJ 70971	Leyland ER44 (SA2)	560220	BBA	171/2	B64F+16	6/56	6/56	by-/76
493	TJ 71029	Leyland ER44 (SA2)	560224	BBA	171/3	B64F+16	9/56	9/56	by-/76
494	TJ 71067	Leyland ER44 (SA2)	560225	BBA	171/4	B64F+16	9/56	9/56	by-/76
495	TJ 41430	Leyland ER44 (SA2)	560226	BBA	171/5	B64F+16	10/56	10/56	by-/75
251	TJ 137.500	AEC Regent V	D2RA110	BBA	137/1	H39/30R+16	11/56	11/56	-/--
252	TJ 137.501	AEC Regent V	D2RA111	BBA	137/2	H39/30R	11/56	11/56	by-/73
253	TJ 137.502	AEC Regent V	D2RA112	BBA	137/3	H39/30R	11/56	11/56	by-/73
254	TJ 137.503	AEC Regent V	D2RA113	BBA	137/4	H39/30R	11/56	11/56	-/--
255	TJ 137.504	AEC Regent V	D2RA114	BBA	137/5	H39/30R	12/56	12/56	-/--
256	TJ 137.505	AEC Regent V	D2RA115	BBA	137/6	H39/30R	12/56	12/56	-/--
257	TJ 137.506	AEC Regent V	D2RA116	BBA	137/7	H39/30R	12/56	12/56	-/--
258	TJ 137.507	AEC Regent V	D2RA117	BBA	137/8	H39/30R	12/56	12/56	-/--

259	TJ 137.508	AEC Regent V	D2RA118	BBA	137/9	H39/30R	12/56	12/56	-/--
260	TJ 137.509	AEC Regent V	D2RA119	BBA	137/10	H39/30R	12/56	12/56	by-/73
261	TJ 137.510	AEC Regent V	D2RA120	BBA	137/11	H39/30R	12/56	12/56	-/--
262	TJ 137.511	AEC Regent V	D2RA121	BBA	137/12	H39/30R	12/56	12/56	-/--
263	TJ 137.512	AEC Regent V	D2RA122	BBA	137/13	H39/30R	2/57	2/57	by-/73
264	TJ 137.513	AEC Regent V	D2RA123	BBA	137/14	H39/30R	2/57	2/57	by-/73
265	TJ 137.414	AEC Regent V	D2RA124	BBA	137/15	H39/30R	2/57	2/57	by-/73
266	TJ 137.515	AEC Regent V	D2RA125	BBA	137/16	H39/30R	2/57	2/57	by-/73
267	T.I 137.516	AEC Regent V	D2RA126	DDA	137/17	H39/30R	2/57	2/57	by-/73
268	TJ 137.517	AEC Regent V	D2RA127	BBA	137/18	H39/30R	2/57	2/57	by-/73
269	TJ 137.518	AEC Regent V	D2RA128	BBA	137/19	H39/30R	2/57	2/57	by-/73
270	TJ 137.519	AEC Regent V	D2RA129	BBA	137/20	H39/30R	2/57	2/57	by-/73
271	TJ 137.520	AEC Regent V	D2RA130	BBA	137/21	H39/30R	2/57	2/57	by-/73
272	TJ 137.521	AEC Regent V	D2RA131	BBA	137/22	H39/30R	2/57	2/57	by-/73
273	TJ 137.522	AEC Regent V	D2RA132	BBA	137/23	H39/30R	2/57	2/57	by-/73
274	TJ 137.523	AEC Regent V	D2RA133	BBA	137/24	H39/30R	3/57	3/57	by-/73
275	TJ 137.524	AEC Regent V	D2RA134	BBA	137/25	H39/30R	3/57	3/57	by-/73
276	TJ 137.525	AEC Regent V	D2RA135	BBA	137/26	H39/30R	3/57	3/57	by-/73
277	TJ 137.526	AEC Regent V	D2RA136	BBA	137/27	H39/30R	3/57	3/57	by-/73
278	TJ 137.527	AEC Regent V	D2RA137	BBA	137/28	H39/30R	3/57	3/57	by-/73
279	TJ 137.528	AEC Regent V	D2RA138	BBA	137/29	H39/30R	3/57	3/57	by-/73
280	TJ 137.529	AEC Regent V	D2RA139	BBA	137/30	H39/30R	3/57	3/57	by-/73
281	TJ 137.530	AEC Regent V	D2RA327	BBA	137/31	H39/30R	3/57	3/57	by-/73
282	TJ 137.531	AEC Regent V	D2RA328	BBA	137/32	H39/30R	4/57	4/57	by-/73
283	TJ 137.531	AEC Regent V	D2RA329	BBA	137/33	H39/30R	4/57	4/57	by-/73
284	TJ 137.533	AEC Regent V	D2RA330	BBA	137/34	H39/30R	4/57	4/57	by-/73
285	TJ 137.534	AEC Regent V	D2RA331	BBA	137/35	H39/30R	5/57	5/57	by-/73
286	TJ 137.535	AEC Regent V	D2RA332	BBA	137/36	H39/30R+16	5/57	5/57	by-/73
287	TJ 137.536	AEC Regent V	D2RA333	BBA	137/37	H39/30R+16	5/57	5/57	by-/73
288	TJ 137.537	AEC Regent V	D2RA334	BBA	137/38	H39/30R+16	5/57	5/57	by-/73
289	TJ 137.538	AEC Regent V	D2RA335	BBA	137/39	H39/30R+16	5/57	5/57	by-/73
290	TJ 137.539	AEC Regent V	D2RA336	BBA	137/40	H39/30R+16	4/57	4/57	by-/73
291	TJ 137.540	AEC Regent V	D2RA337	BBA	137/41	H39/30R+16	4/57	4/57	by-/73
292	TJ 137.541	AEC Regent V	D2RA338	BBA	137/42	H39/30R+16	5/57	5/57	by-/73
293	TJ 137.542	AEC Regent V	D2RA339	BBA	137/43	H39/30R+16	5/57	5/57	by-/73
294	TJ 137.543	AEC Regent V	D2RA340	BBA	137/44	H39/30R+16	4/57	4/57	by-/73
295	TJ 137.544	AEC Regent V	D2RA341	BBA	137/45	H39/30R+16	5/57	5/57	by-/73
296	TJ 137.545	AEC Regent V	D2RA342	BBA	137/46	H39/30R+16	4/57	4/57	by-/73
297	TJ 137.546	AEC Regent V	D2RA343	BBA	137/47	H39/30R+16	4/57	4/57	by-/73
298	TJ 137.547	AEC Regent V	D2RA344	BBA	137/48	H39/30R+16	4/57	4/57	by-/73
299	TJ 137.548	AEC Regent V	D2RA345	BBA	137/49	H39/30R+16	5/57	5/57	by-/73
300	TJ 137.549	AEC Regent V	D2RA346	BBA	137/50	H39/30R+16	5/57	5/57	by-/73
470	TJ 24274	AEC Regal IV	9825E2182	BBA	246/1	B64F+5	12/57	12/57	by3/76
471	TJ 35392	AEC Regal IV	9825E2184	BBA	246/3	B64F+5	12/57	12/57	by -/73
472	TJ 35408	AEC Regal IV	9825E2185	BBA	246/4	B64F+5	12/57	12/57	by -/73
473	TJ 35461	AEC Regal IV	9825E2186	BBA	246/5	B64F+5	12/57	12/57	-/--
474	TJ 35514	AEC Regal IV	9825E2189	BBA	246/8	B64F+5	1/58	1/58	-/--
475	TJ 35561	AEC Regal IV	9825E2188	BBA	246/7	B64F+5	1/58	1/58	-/--
476	TJ 35695	AEC Regal IV	9825E2187	BBA	246/6	B64F+5	1/58	1/58	-/--
477	TJ 35812	AEC Regal IV	9825E2183	BBA	246/2	B64F+5	1/58	1/58	by3/76
478	TJ 35813	AEC Regal IV	9825E2190	BBA	246/9	B64F+5	1/58	1/58	by -/73
479	TJ 35857	AEC Regal IV	9825E2191	BBA	246/10	B64F+5	1/58	1/58	by -/74
453	TJ 161.240	Guy Arab IV RR	FDR73970	BBA	175/1	H51/34D+21	9/58	9/58	-/--
454	TJ 161.241	Guy Arab IV RR	FDR73971	BBA	175/2	H51/34D+21	9/58	9/58	-/--
455	TJ 161.242	Guy Arab IV RR	FDR73972	BBA	175/3	H51/34D+21	9/58	9/58	-/--
456	TJ 161.243	Guy Arab IV RR	FDR73973	BBA	175/4	H51/34D+21	9/58	9/58	-/--
457	TJ 161.244	Guy Arab IV RR	FDR73974	BBA	175/5	H51/34D+21	9/58	9/58	-/--
458	TJ 161.245	Guy Arab IV RR	FDR73975	BBA	175/6	H51/34D+21	9/58	9/58	-/--
459	TJ 161.246	Guy Arab IV RR	FDR73976	BBA	175/7	H51/34D+21	9/58	9/58	-/--
460	TJ 161.247	Guy Arab IV RR	FDR73978	BBA	175/8	H51/34D+21	9/58	9/58	-/--
461	TJ 161.248	Guy Arab IV RR	FDR73979	BBA	175/9	H51/34D+21	9/58	9/58	-/--
462	TJ 161.249	Guy Arab IV RR	FDR73977	BBA	175/10	H51/34D+21	9/58	9/58	-/--
500	TJ 52219	Leyland ERT	?	Wevell		B46F+30	-/53	-/--	-/--
171	TJ 171.560	AEC Regal IV	9825E2359	Brockhouse		B65F+16	6/59	6/59	-/--

172	TJ 171.561	AEC Regal IV	9825E2360	Brockhouse		B65F+16	6/59	6/59	-/--
173	TJ 171.562	AEC Regal IV	9825E2361	Brockhouse		B65F+16	6/59	6/59	-/--
174	TJ 171.563	AEC Regal IV	9825E2362	Brockhouse		B65F+16	4/59	4/59	-/--
175	TJ 171.564	AEC Regal IV	9825E2363	Brockhouse		B65F+16	7/59	7/59	-/--
176	TJ 171.565	AEC Regal IV	9825E2364	Brockhouse		B65F+16	4/59	4/59	-/--
177	TJ 171.566	AEC Regal IV	9825E2365	Brockhouse		B65F+16	6/59	6/59	-/--
178	TJ 171.567	AEC Regal IV	9825E2366	Brockhouse		B65F+16	5/59	5/59	-/--
179	TJ 161.568	AEC Regal IV	9825E2367	Brockhouse		B65F+16	6/59	6/59	-/--
180	TJ 161.569	AEC Regal IV	9825E2368	Brockhouse		B65F+16	4/59	4/59	-/--
181	TJ 161.570	AEC Regal IV	9825E2369	Brockhouse		B65F+16	6/59	6/59	-/--
182	TJ 161.571	AEC Regal IV	9825E2370	Brockhouse		B65F+16	3/59	3/59	-/--
183	TJ 171.572	AEC Regal IV	9825E2371	Brockhouse		B65F+16	4/59	4/59	-/--
184	TJ 171.573	AEC Regal IV	9825E2372	Brockhouse		B65F+16	5/59	5/59	by3/76
185	TJ 171.574	AEC Regal IV	9825E2373	Brockhouse		B65F+16	5/59	5/59	by3/76
186	TJ 171.575	AEC Regal IV	9825E2374	Brockhouse		B65F+16	6/59	6/59	-/--
187	TJ 171.576	AEC Regal IV	9825E2375	Brockhouse		B65F+16	-/59	-/59	-/--
188	TJ 171.577	AEC Regal IV	9825E2376	Brockhouse		B65F+16	4/59	4/59	-/--
189	TJ 171.578	AEC Regal IV	9825E2377	Brockhouse		B65F+16	-/59	-/59	-/--
190	TJ 171.579	AEC Regal IV	9825E2378	Brockhouse		B65F+16	5/59	5/59	-/--
191	TJ 171.500	AEC Regent V	D2RA599	BBA	295/1	H39/30R	3/59	3/59	-/--
192	TJ 171.501	AEC Regent V	D2RA600	BBA	295/2	H39/30R	3/59	3/59	by -/98
193	TJ 171.502	AEC Regent V	D2RA601	BBA	295/3	H39/30R	3/59	3/59	-/--
194	TJ 171.503	AEC Regent V	D2RA602	BBA	295/4	H39/30R	3/59	3/59	-/--
195	TJ 171.504	AEC Regent V	D2RA603	BBA	295/5	H39/30R	3/59	3/59	-/--
196	TJ 171.505	AEC Regent V	D2RA604	BBA	295/6	H39/30R	3/59	3/59	-/--
197	TJ 171.506	AEC Regent V	D2RA605	BBA	295/7	H39/30R	3/59	3/59	-/--
198	TJ 171.507	AEC Regent V	D2RA606	BBA	295/8	H39/30R	3/59	3/59	-/--
199	TJ 171.508	AEC Regent V	D2RA607	BBA	295/9	H39/30R	3/59	3/59	-/--
200	TJ 171.509	AEC Regent V	D2RA608	BBA	295/10	H39/30R	3/59	3/59	-/--
201	TJ 171.510	AEC Regent V	D2RA609	BBA	295/11	H39/30R	4/59	4/59	-/--
202	TJ 171.511	AEC Regent V	D2RA610	BBA	295/12	H39/30R	4/59	4/59	-/--
203	TJ 171.512	AEC Regent V	D2RA611	BBA	295/13	H39/30R	5/59	5/59	-/--
204	TJ 171.513	AEC Regent V	D2RA612	BBA	295/14	H39/30R	5/59	5/59	-/--
205	TJ 171.514	AEC Regent V	D2RA613	BBA	295/15	H39/30R	5/59	5/59	-/--
206	TJ 171.515	AEC Regent V	D2RA614	BBA	295/16	H39/30R	5/59	5/59	-/--
207	TJ 171.516	AEC Regent V	D2RA615	BBA	295/17	H39/30R	5/59	5/59	-/--
208	TJ 171.517	AEC Regent V	D2RA616	BBA	295/18	H39/30R	4/59	4/59	-/--
209	TJ 171.518	AEC Regent V	D2RA617	BBA	295/19	H39/30R	5/59	5/59	-/--
210	TJ 171.519	AEC Regent V	D2RA618	BBA	295/20	H39/30R	5/59	5/59	-/--
211	TJ 171.520	AEC Regent V	D2RA619	BBA	295/21	H39/30R	4/59	4/59	-/--
212	TJ 171.521	AEC Regent V	D2RA620	BBA	295/22	H39/30R	5/59	5/59	-/--
213	TJ 171.522	AEC Regent V	D2RA621	BBA	295/23	H39/30R	5/59	5/59	-/--
214	TJ 171.523	AEC Regent V	D2RA622	BBA	295/24	H39/30R	5/59	5/59	-/--
215	TJ 171.524	AEC Regent V	D2RA623	BBA	295/25	H39/30R	5/59	5/59	-/--
216	TJ 171.525	AEC Regent V	D2RA624	BBA	295/26	H39/30R	6/59	6/59	-/--
217	TJ 171.526	AEC Regent V	D2RA625	BBA	295/27	H39/30R	6/59	6/59	-/--
218	TJ 171.527	AEC Regent V	D2RA626	BBA	295/28	H39/30R	6/59	6/59	-/--
219	TJ 171.528	AEC Regent V	D2RA627	BBA	295/29	H39/30R	6/59	6/59	-/--
220	TJ 171.529	AEC Regent V	D2RA628	BBA	295/30	H39/30R	6/59	6/59	-/--
221	TJ 171.530	AEC Regent V	D2RA629	BBA	295/31	H39/30R	6/69	6/59	-/--
222	TJ 171.531	AEC Regent V	D2RA630	BBA	295/32	H39/30R	6/59	6/59	-/--
223	TJ 171.532	AEC Regent V	D2RA631	BBA	295/33	H39/30R	6/59	6/59	by-/98
224	TJ 171.533	AEC Regent V	D2RA632	BBA	295/34	H39/30R	6/59	6/59	-/--
225	TJ 171.534	AEC Regent V	D2RA633	BBA	295/35	H39/30R	6/59	6/59	-/--
226	TJ 171.535	AEC Regent V	D2RA634	BBA	295/36	H39/30R	6/59	6/59	-/--
227	TJ 171.536	AEC Regent V	D2RA635	BBA	295/37	H39/30R	6/59	6/59	-/--
228	TJ 171.537	AEC Regent V	D2RA636	BBA	295/38	H39/30R	7/59	7/59	-/--
229	TJ 171.538	AEC Regent V	D2RA637	BBA	295/39	H39/30R	7/59	7/59	-/--
230	TJ 171.539	AEC Regent V	D2RA638	BBA	295/40	H39/30R	7/59	7/59	-/--
231	TJ 171.540	AEC Regent V	D2RA639	BBA	295/41	H39/30R	7/59	7/59	-/--
232	TJ 171.541	AEC Regent V	D2RA640	BBA	295/42	H39/30R	7/59	7/59	-/--
233	TJ 171.542	AEC Regent V	D2RA641	BBA	295/43	H39/30R	7/59	7/59	-/--
234	TJ 171.543	AEC Regent V	D2RA642	BBA	295/44	H39/30R	7/59	7/59	-/--
235	TJ 171.544	AEC Regent V	D2RA643	BBA	295/45	H39/30R	7/59	7/59	-/--

236	TJ 171.545	AEC Regent V	D2RA644	BBA	295/46	H39/30R	7/59	7/59	-/--
237	TJ 171.546	AEC Regent V	D2RA645	BBA	295/47	H39/30R	8/59	8/59	-/--
238	TJ 171.547	AEC Regent V	D2RA646	BBA	295/48	H39/30R	8/59	8/59	-/--
239	TJ 171.548	AEC Regent V	D2RA647	BBA	295/49	H39/30R	8/59	8/59	-/--
240	TJ 171.549	AEC Regent V	D2RA648	BBA	295/50	H39/30R	8/59	8/59	-/--
241	TJ 171.550	AEC Regent V	D2RA649	BBA	295/51	H39/30R	8/59	8/59	-/--
242	TJ 171.551	AEC Regent V	D2RA650	BBA	295/52	H39/30R	8/59	8/59	-/--
243	TJ 171.552	AEC Regent V	D2RA651	BBA	295/53	H39/30R	9/59	9/59	-/--
244	TJ 171.553	AEC Regent V	D2RA652	BBA	295/54	H39/30R	9/59	9/59	-/--
245	TJ 171.554	AEC Regent V	D2RA653	BBA	295/55	H39/30R	9/59	9/59	-/--
246	TJ 171.555	AEC Regent V	D2RA654	BBA	295/56	H39/30R	9/59	9/59	-/--
247	TJ 171.556	AEC Regent V	D2RA655	BBA	295/57	H39/30R	9/59	9/59	-/--
248	TJ 171.557	AEC Regent V	D2RA656	BBA	295/58	H39/30R	9/59	9/59	-/--
249	TJ 171.558	AEC Regent V	D2RA657	BBA	295/59	H39/30R	9/59	9/59	-/--
250	TJ 171.559	AEC Regent V	D2RA658	BBA	295/60	H39/30R	9/59	9/59	-/--
151	TJ 130.752	Guy Arab IV RR	FDR74651	BBA	179/1	H51/34D+21	11/60	11/60	-/--
152	TJ 130.841	Guy Arab IV RR	FDR74652	BBA	179/2	H51/34D+21	11/60	11/60	-/--
153	TJ 130.877	Guy Arab IV RR	FDR74663	BBA	179/3	H51/34D+21	11/60	11/60	-/--
154	TJ 130.934	Guy Arab IV RR	FDR74664	BBA	179/4	H51/34D+21	11/60	11/60	-/--
155	TJ 130.944	Guy Arab IV RR	FDR74665	BBA	179/5	H51/34D+21	11/60	11/60	-/--
156	TJ 130.989	Guy Arab IV RR	FDR74666	BBA	179/6	H51/34D+21	11/60	11/60	-/--
157	TJ 131.008	Guy Arab IV RR	FDR74667	BBA	179/7	H51/34D+21	11/60	11/60	-/--
158	TJ 131.120	Guy Arab IV RR	FDR74668	BBA	179/8	H51/34D+21	11/60	11/60	-/--
159	TJ 131.193	Guy Arab IV RR	FDR74669	BBA	179/9	H51/34D+21	11/60	11/60	-/--
160	TJ 131.224	Guy Arab IV RR	FDR74670	BBA	179/10	H51/34D+21	12/60	12/60	-/--
161	TJ 131.467	Guy Arab IV RR	FDR74671	BBA	179/11	H51/34D+21	12/60	12/60	-/--
162	TJ 131.511	Guy Arab IV RR	FDR74672	BBA	179/12	H51/34D+21	12/60	12/60	-/--
163	TJ 131.575	Guy Arab IV RR	FDR74673	BBA	179/13	H51/34D+21	12/60	12/60	-/--
164	TJ 131.577	Guy Arab IV RR	FDR74674	BBA	179/14	H51/34D+21	12/60	12/60	-/--
165	TJ 131.674	Guy Arab IV RR	FDR74675	BBA	179/15	H51/34D+21	1/61	1/61	-/--
166	TJ 131.784	Guy Arab IV RR	FDR74676	BBA	179/16	H51/34D+21	1/61	1/61	-/--
167	TJ 131.838	Guy Arab IV RR	FDR74677	BBA	179/17	H51/34D+21	2/61	2/61	-/--
168	TJ 131.920	Guy Arab IV RR	FDR74678	BBA	179/18	H51/34D+21	2/61	2/61	-/--
169	TJ 131.952	Guy Arab IV RR	FDR74650	BBA	179/19	H51/34D+21	2/61	2/61	-/--
170	TJ 131.976	Guy Arab IV RR	FDR74679	BBA	179/20	H51/34D+21	2/61	2/61	-/--

Notes:

TJ 34408 (453) ex Northern BS, Johannesburg 2.

TJ 30505 (454) ex Northern BS, Johannesburg 3. Also recorded as TJ 306?5.

TJ 14362 (455) ex Northern BS, Johannesburg 5. Also recorded as TJ 15362.

TJ 6267 (456) ex Northern BS, Johannesburg 6.

TJ 8846 (457) ex Northern BS, Johannesburg 8. Also recorded as TJ 6846, it had a body rebuilt by Northern BS.

TJ ??381, 13908 (458/9) ex Northern BS, Johannesburg 10/2.

TJ 13867 (460) ex Northern BS, Johannesburg 13. It had a body rebuilt by Northern BS.

TJ 10026 (461) ex Northern BS, Johannesburg 15.

TJ 11554 (462) ex Northern BS, Johannesburg 11. It was renumbered 500 in 1960.

TJ 18913 (463) ex Northern BS, Johannesburg 17.

TJ 64358 (464) ex Northern BS, Johannesburg 18. Also recorded as TJ 64258, it had a body rebuilt by Northern BS.

TJ 9278, 82525, 65892, 35604, 93405, 90179 (465-70) ex Northern BS, Johannesburg 20-5.

TJ 18913, 64358, 9278, 82525, 65892, 35604, 93405, 90179 (463-70) are also recorded with 6LW engines.

TJ 33586, 97903 -5, 110.012 -5, 14666 (471-9) ex Northern BS 30-8, originally Durban, passing to Northern in 1951/2. They are also recorded with MCCW B--- bodies. They were presumably from the 1939/40 batch originally registered ND 23357-70 with H32/26R bodies. 479 was acquired via Volksrust.

TJ 58156, 111.759, 125.931 (480-2) ex Northern BS, Johannesburg 50-2; renumbered 324/5/6 by 12/62.

TJ 58156 (480) also reported with a Gove B51F body.

TJ 121.484/341, 83413, 125.932/3, 49022 (483-8) ex Northern BS, Johannesburg 41-6.

TJ 125.598/9 (489/90) ex Northern BS, Johannesburg 60/1. Also reported with identities reversed.

Guy Arabs shown as RR had Rolls Royce engines.

Leyland vehicles listed as ER44 were found not to be sufficiently rugged for South African conditions. The chassis components for later vehicles reconfigured by BBA both as to strength and dimensions and were termed "SA2".

TJ 161.240-9 (453-62) renumbered 771-80, probably after rebuilding in 1972 to H49/35F+23.

TJ 24274, 35392/408/61/514/61/695/812/3/57 (470-9) originally recorded as B64F+5 but a JMT report of 3/76 quotes them as B63F+16. Renumbered 921-30 in 1959.

TJ 52219 (500) is a mystery, possibly an acquired vehicle.

TJ 137.500-49 (251-300) renumbered 851-900, date unknown.

TJ 171.560-79 (171-90) renumbered 901-920, date unknown.

TJ 171.500-59 (191-250) renumbered 791-850, date unknown.

TJ 171.501 (192) rebodied BBA FH73F+21 (3270/1) and renumbered 999 7/77; re-registered LVJ 697T -/79 and converted to O73F by-/93.

TJ 130.752/841/77/934/44/89, 131.008/120/93/224/467/511/75/7/674/784/838/920/52/76 (151-70) renumbered 751-70, probably after rebuilding to H49/35F+23 in 1971/2. The above version is from BBA records but 169/70 have also been reported with chassis numbers reversed.

Disposals:

TJ 49022 (488): Bloemfontein 74 (OB 9051), possibly in exchange for TJ 79483 (324).

TJ 130.934/44 (154/5 as 754/5): Namibia Breweries, Windhoek by -/93.

TJ 171.501 (192) as LVJ 697T (999): Algoa Bus 100 (BJJ 177EC).

TJ 171.532 (223) preserved by B. Suddaby, Durban, as 823 (ND 194.372).

TJ 171 548 (239 later 839) at the James Hall Museum of Transport, La Rochelle, Johannesburg.

One of TJ161 240-9 (now fitted with an AEC AV760 engine) later to Durban Historical Transport Society, and kept at the Natal Parks Board's open-air museum at Midmar, painted in Durban's blue/white livery. Later to James Hall Museum of Transport, La Rochelle, Johannesburg.

1	TJ 202.051	AEC Regal VI	3U2RA258	Craftsman	B64F+16	9/64	9/64	-/--
2	TJ 202.052	AEC Regal VI	3U2RA259	Craftsman	B64F+16	9/64	9/64	-/--
3	TJ 202.053	AEC Regal VI	3U2RA260	Craftsman	B64F+16	6/64	6/64	-/--
4	TJ 202.054	AEC Regal VI	3U2RA261	Craftsman	B64F+16	6/64	6/64	-/--
5	TJ 202.055	AEC Regal VI	3U2RA262	Craftsman	B64F+16	9/64	9/64	-/--
6	TJ 202.056	AEC Regal VI	3U2RA263	Craftsman	B64F+16	10/64	10/64	-/--
7	TJ 202.057	AEC Regal VI	3U2RA264	Craftsman	B64F+16	10/64	10/64	-/--
8	TJ 202.058	AEC Regal VI	3U2RA265	Craftsman	B64F+16	9/64	9/64	-/--
9	TJ 202.059	AEC Regal VI	3U2RA266	Craftsman	B64F+16	11/64	11/64	-/--
10	TJ 202.060	AEC Regal VI	3U2RA267	Craftsman	B64F+16	5/65	5/65	-/--
11	TJ 202.061	AEC Regal VI	3U2RA268	Craftsman	B64F+16	8/64	8/64	-/--
12	TJ 202.062	AEC Regal VI	3U2RA269	Craftsman	B64F+16	4/65	4/65	-/--
13	TJ 202.063	AEC Regal VI	3U2RA270	Craftsman	B64F+16	4/65	4/65	-/--
14	TJ 202.064	AEC Regal VI	3U2RA271	Craftsman	B64F+16	12/64	12/64	-/--
15	TJ 202.065	AEC Regal VI	3U2RA272	Craftsman	B64F+16	11/64	11/64	-/--
16	TJ 202.066	AEC Regal VI	3U2RA358	Craftsman	B64F+16	5/65	5/65	-/--
17	TJ 202.067	AEC Regal VI	3U2RA359	Craftsman	B64F+16	5/65	5/65	-/--
18	TJ 202.068	AEC Regal VI	3U2RA360	Craftsman	B64F+16	6/65	6/65	-/--
19	TJ 202.069	AEC Regal VI	3U2RA361	Craftsman	B64F+16	5/65	5/65	-/--
20	TJ 202.070	AEC Regal VI	3U2RA362	Craftsman	B64F+16	6/65	6/65	-/--
21	TJ 243.227	AEC Regal VI	3U2RA501	Craftsman	B65F+19	-/66	-/66	-/--
22	TJ 243.228	AEC Regal VI	3U2RA502	Craftsman	B65F+19	-/66	-/66	-/--
23	TJ 243.229	AEC Regal VI	3U2RA503	Craftsman	B65F+19	-/66	-/66	-/--
24	TJ 243.230	AEC Regal VI	3U2RA504	Craftsman	B65F+19	-/66	-/66	-/--
25	TJ 243.231	AEC Regal VI	3U2RA505	Craftsman	B65F+19	-/66	-/66	-/--
26	TJ 234.232	AEC Regal VI	3U2RA506	Craftsman	B65F+19	-/66	-/66	-/--
27	TJ 243.233	AEC Regal VI	3U2RA507	Craftsman	B65F+19	-/66	-/66	-/--
28	TJ 243.234	AEC Regal VI	3U2RA508	Craftsman	B65F+19	-/66	-/66	-/--
29	TJ 243.235	AEC Regal VI	3U2RA509	Craftsman	B65F+19	-/66	-/66	-/--
30	TJ 243.236	AEC Regal VI	3U2RA510	Craftsman	B65F+19	-/66	-/66	-/--
31	TJ 243.237	AEC Regal VI	3U2RA511	Craftsman	B65F+19	-/66	-/66	-/--
32	TJ 243.238	AEC Regal VI	3U2RA512	Craftsman	B65F+19	-/66	-/66	-/--
33	TJ 243.329	AEC Regal VI	3U2RA513	Craftsman	B65F+19	-/66	-/66	-/--
34	TJ 243.240	AEC Regal VI	3U2RA514	Craftsman	B65F+19	-/66	-/66	-/--
35	TJ 243.241	AEC Regal VI	3U2RA515	Craftsman	B65F+19	-/66	-/66	-/--
36	TJ 243.242	AEC Regal VI	3U2RA516	Craftsman	B65F+19	-/66	-/66	-/--
37	TJ 243.244	AEC Regal VI	3U2RA517	Craftsman	B65F+19	-/66	-/66	-/--
38	TJ 243.245	AEC Regal VI	3U2RA518	Craftsman	B65F+19	-/66	-/66	-/--
39	TJ 243.246	AEC Regal VI	3U2RA519	Craftsman	B65F+19	-/66	-/66	-/--
40	TJ 243.247	AEC Regal VI	3U2RA520	Craftsman	B65F+19	-/66	-/66	-/--
41	TJ 243.248	AEC Regal VI	3U2RA521	Craftsman	B65F+19	-/66	-/66	-/--

42	TJ 243.249	AEC Regal VI	3U2RA522	Craftsman		B65F+19	-/66	-/66	-/--
43	TJ 243.250	AEC Regal VI	3U2RA523	Craftsman		B65F+19	-/66	-/66	-/--
44	TJ 243.251	AEC Regal VI	3U2RA524	Craftsman		B65F+19	-/66	-/66	-/--
45	TJ 243.252	AEC Regal VI	3U2RA525	Craftsman		B65F+19	-/66	-/66	-/--
301	TJ 279.801	Daimler CRG6-36	62651	BBA	2374/1	H48/37D+15	12/68	12/68	-/--
302	TJ 279.802	Daimler CRG6-36	62652	BBA	2374/2	H48/37D+15	12/68	12/68	-/--
303	TJ 279.803	Daimler CRG6-36	62653	BBA	2374/3	H48/37D+15	1/69	1/69	-/--
304	TJ 279.804	Daimler CRG6-36	62654	BBA	2374/4	H48/37D+15	1/69	1/69	-/--
305	TJ 279.805	Daimler CRG6-36	62655	BBA	2374/5	H48/37D+15	12/68	12/68	-/--
306	TJ 279.806	Daimler CRG6-36	62856	BBA	2374/6	H48/37D+15	1/69	1/69	-/--
307	TJ 279.807	Daimler CRG6-36	62657	BBA	2374/7	H48/37D+15	1/69	1/69	-/--
308	TJ 279.808	Daimler CRG6-36	62658	BBA	2374/8	H48/37D+15	1/69	1/69	-/--
309	TJ 279.809	Daimler CRG6-36	62659	BBA	2374/9	H48/37D+15	2/69	2/69	-/--
310	TJ 279.810	Daimler CRG6-36	62660	BBA	2374/10	H48/37D+15	2/69	2/69	-/--
311	TJ 279.811	Daimler CRG6-36	62661	BBA	2374/11	H48/37D+15	2/69	2/69	-/--
312	TJ 279.812	Daimler CRG6-36	62662	BBA	2374/12	H48/37D+15	2/69	2/69	-/--
313	TJ 279.813	Daimler CRG6-36	62663	BBA	2374/13	H48/37D+15	2/69	2/69	-/--
314	TJ 279.814	Daimler CRG6-36	62690	BBA	2374/14	H48/37D+15	2/69	2/69	-/--
315	TJ 279.815	Daimler CRG6-36	62891	BBA	2374/15	H48/37D+15	3/69	3/69	-/--
316	TJ 279.816	Daimler CRG6-36	62892	BBA	2374/16	H48/37D+15	3/69	3/69	-/--
317	TJ 279.817	Bristol VRL-LH6L	101	BBA	2373/1	H50/35D+22	8/68	8/68	-/--
318	TJ 279.818	Bristol VRL-LH6L	103	BBA	2373/2	H50/35D+22	9/68	9/68	-/--
319	TJ 279.819	Bristol VRL-LH6L	104	BBA	2373/3	H50/35D+22	9/68	9/68	-/--
320	TJ 279.820	Bristol VRL-LH6L	105	BBA	2373/4	H50/35D+22	9/68	9/68	-/--
321	TJ 279.821	Bristol VRL-LH6L	106	BBA	2373/5	H50/35D+22	9/68	9/68	-/--
322	TJ 279.822	Bristol VRL-LH6L	107	BBA	2373/6	H50/35D+22	9/68	9/68	-/--
323	TJ 279.823	Bristol VRL-LH6L	108	BBA	2373/7	H50/35D+22	1/69	1/69	-/--
324	TJ 279.824	Bristol VRL-LH6L	109	BBA	2373/8	H50/35D+22	9/68	9/68	-/--
325	TJ 279.825	Bristol VRL-LH6L	110	BBA	2373/9	H50/35D+22	9/68	9/68	-/--
326	TJ 279.826	Bristol VRL-LH6L	111	BBA	2373/10	H50/35D+22	10/68	10/68	-/--
327	TJ 279.827	Bristol VRL-LH6L	112	BBA	2373/11	H50/35D+22	10/68	10/68	-/--
328	TJ 279.828	Bristol VRL-LH6L	113	BBA	2373/12	H50/35D+22	10/68	10/68	-/--
329	TJ 279.829	Bristol VRL-LH6L	114	BBA	2373/13	H50/35D+22	10/68	10/68	-/--
330	TJ 279.830	Bristol VRL-LH6L	115	BBA	2373/14	H50/35D+22	10/68	10/68	-/--
46	TJ 301.117	Daimler SRC6	36305	Craftsman	CC-07-01	B61F+20	-/69	-/69	-/--
47	TJ 301.118	Daimler SRC6	36306	Craftsman	CC-07-08	B61F+20	-/69	-/69	-/--
48	TJ 301.119	Daimler SRC6	36307	Craftsman	CC-07-10	B61F+20	-/69	-/69	-/--
49	TJ 301.120	Daimler SRC6	36308	Craftsman	CC-07-05	B61F+20	-/69	-/69	-/--
50	TJ 301.121	Daimler SRC6	36309	Craftsman	CC-07-03	B61F+20	-/69	-/69	-/--
51	TJ 301.122	Daimler SRC6	36310	Craftsman	CC-07-02	B61F+20	-/69	-/69	-/--
52	TJ 301.123	Daimler SRC6	36311	Craftsman	CC-07-09	B61F+20	-/69	-/69	-/--
53	TJ 301.124	Daimler SRC6	36312	Craftsman	CC-07-04	B61F+20	-/69	-/69	-/--
54	TJ 301.125	Daimler SRC6	36313	Craftsman	CC-07-06	B61F+20	-/69	-/69	-/--
55	TJ 301.126	Daimler SRC6	36314	Craftsman	CC-07-07	B61F+20	-/69	-/69	-/--
56	TJ 329.052	AEC Kudu	3S2RA796	Craftsman		B62F+18	-/70	-/70	-/--
57	TJ 329.053	AEC Kudu	3S2RA797	Craftsman		B62F+18	-/70	-/70	-/--
58	TJ 329.054	AEC Kudu	3S2RA798	Craftsman		B62F+18	-/70	-/70	-/--
59	TJ 329.055	AEC Kudu	3S2RA799	Craftsman		B62F+18	-/70	-/70	-/--
60	TJ 329.056	AEC Kudu	3S2RA800	Craftsman		B62F+18	12/70	12/70	-/--
61	TJ 329.057	AEC Kudu	3S2RA801	Craftsman		B62F+18	-/71	-/71	-/--
62	TJ 329.058	AEC Kudu	3S2RA802	Craftsman		B62F+18	-/71	-/71	-/--
63	TJ 329.059	AEC Kudu	3S2RA803	Craftsman		B62F+18	-/71	-/71	-/--
64	TJ 329.060	AEC Kudu	3S2RA804	Craftsman		B62F+18	-/71	-/71	-/--
65	TJ 329.061	AEC Kudu	3S2RA805	Craftsman		B62F+18	-/71	-/71	-/--
66	TJ 345.501	Mercedes-Benz O305 305220 20 001109		Craftsman		B60F+20	7/71	7/71	by5/95
67	TJ 345.502	Mercedes-Benz O305 305220 20 001319		Craftsman		B60F+20	-/71	-/71	by5/95
68	TJ 345.504	Mercedes-Benz O305 305220 20 001304		Craftsman		B60F+20	-/71	-/71	by5/95
69	TJ 345.505	Mercedes-Benz O305 305220 20 001276		Craftsman		B60F+20	-/71	-/71	by5/95
70	TJ 345.503	Mercedes-Benz O305 305220 20 001313		Craftsman		B60F+20	-/71	-/71	by5/95

71	TJ 345.506	Mercedes-Benz O305 305220 20 001288	Craftsman	B60F+20	-/71	-/71	by5/95
72	TJ 345.507	Mercedes-Benz O305 305220 20 001294	Craftsman	B60F+20	-/71	-/71	by5/95
73	TJ 345.508	Mercedes-Benz O305 305220 20 001299	Craftsman	B60F+20	-/71	-/71	by5/95
74	TJ 345.509	Mercedes-Benz O305 305220 20 001309	Craftsman	B60F+20	-/71	-/71	by5/95
75	TJ 345.510	Mercedes-Benz O305 305220 20 001332	Craftsman	B60F+20	-/71	-/71	by5/95
76	TJ 345.511	Mercedes-Benz O305 305220 20 001381	Craftsman	B60F+20	-/71	-/71	by5/95
77	TJ 345.512	Mercedes-Benz O305 305220 20 001419	Craftsman	B60F+20	-/71	-/71	by5/95
78	TJ 345.513	Mercedes-Benz O305 305220 20 001412	Craftsman	B60F+20	-/71	-/71	by5/95
79	TJ 345.514	Mercedes-Benz O305 305220 20 001408	Craftsman	B60F+20	-/71	-/71	by5/95
80	TJ 345.515	Mercedes-Benz O305 305220 20 001416	Craftsman	B60F+20	-/71	-/71	by5/95
81	TJ 345.516	Mercedes-Benz O305 305220 20 001422	Craftsman	B60F+20	-/71	-/71	by5/95
82	TJ 345.517	Mercedes-Benz O305 305220 20 001466	Craftsman	B60F+20	-/71	-/71	by5/95
83	TJ 345.518	Mercedes-Benz O305 305220 20 001282	Craftsman	B60F+20	-/72	-/72	by5/95
84	TJ 345.519	Mercedes-Benz O305 305220 20 001458	Craftsman	B60F+20	-/72	-/72	by5/95
85	TJ 345.520	Mercedes-Benz O305 305220 20 001461	Craftsman	B60F+20	-/72	-/72	by5/95
86	TJ 345.521	Mercedes-Benz O305 305220 20 001337	Craftsman	B60F+20	-/72	-/72	by5/95
87	TJ 345.522	Mercedes-Benz O305 305220 20 001327	Craftsman	B60F+20	-/72	-/72	by5/95
88	TJ 345.523	Mercedes-Benz O305 305220 20 001335	Craftsman	B60F+20	2/72	2/72	-/--
89	TJ 345.524	Mercedes-Benz O305 305220 20 001340	Craftsman	B60F+20	-/72	-/72	by5/95
90	TJ 345.525	Mercedes-Benz O305 305220 20 001342	Craftsman	B60F+20	-/72	-/72	by5/95
91	TJ 345.526	Mercedes-Benz O305 305220 20 001346	Craftsman	B60F+20	-/72	-/72	by5/95
92	TJ 345.527	Mercedes-Benz O305 305220 20 001402	Craftsman	B60F+20	-/72	-/72	by5/95
93	TJ 345.528	Mercedes-Benz O305 305220 20 001405	Craftsman	B60F+20	-/72	-/72	by5/95
94	TJ 345.529	Mercedes-Benz O305 305220 20 001470	Craftsman	B60F+20	-/72	-/72	by5/95
95	TJ 345.530	Mercedes-Benz O305 305220 20 001474	Craftsman	B60F+20	-/72	-/72	by5/95
96	TJ 345.531	Mercedes-Benz O305 305220 20 001478	Craftsman	B60F+20	-/72	-/72	by5/95
97	TJ 345.532	Mercedes-Benz O305 305220 20 001482	Craftsman	B60F+20	-/72	-/72	by5/95
98	TJ 345.533	Mercedes-Benz O305 305220 20 001490	Craftsman	B60F+20	-/72	-/72	by5/95
99	TJ 345.534	Mercedes-Benz O305 305220 20 001497	Craftsman	B60F+20	-/72	-/72	by5/95
100	TJ 345.535	Mercedes-Benz O305 305220 20 001508	Craftsman	B60F+20	-/72	-/72	by5/95
101	TJ 345.536	Mercedes-Benz O305 305220 20 001515	Craftsman	B60F+20	-/72	-/72	by5/95
08/42	LVH 342T	Mercedes-Benz O302 241/20/009659	?	B24	-/70	-/--	-/--

102	TJ 345.537	Mercedes-Benz O305 305220 20 001519	Craftsman	B60F+20	12/71	12/71	by5/95
103	TJ 345.538	Mercedes-Benz O305 305220 20 001564	Craftsman	B60F+20	6/72	6/72	12/90
104	TJ 345.539	Mercedes-Benz O305 305220 20 001571	Craftsman	B60F+20	-/72	-/72	by5/95
105	TJ 345.540	Mercedes-Benz O305 305220 20 001640	Craftsman	B60F+20	-/71	-/71	by5/95
106	TJ 345.541	Mercedes-Benz O305 305220 20 001651	Craftsman	B60F+20	-/71	-/71	by5/95
107	TJ 345.542	Mercedes-Benz O305 305220 20 001662	Craftsman	B60F+20	-/71	-/71	4/91
108	TJ 345.543	Mercedes-Benz O305 305220 20 001673	Craftsman	B60F+20	-/71	-/71	5/91
109	TJ 345.544	Mercedes-Benz O305 305220 20 001674	Craftsman	B60F+20	-/71	-/71	by5/95
110	TJ 345.545	Mercedes-Benz O305 305220 20 001685	Craftsman	B34D+64	-/72	-/72	by5/95
111	TJ 345.546	Mercedes-Benz O305 305220 20 002211	Craftsman	B34D+64	-/72	-/72	by5/95
112	TJ 345.547	Mercedes-Benz O305 305220 20 002215	Craftsman	B34D+64	-/72	-/72	by5/95
113	TJ 345.548	Mercedes-Benz O305 305220 20 002222	Craftsman	B34D+64	-/72	-/72	by5/95
114	TJ 345.549	Mercedes-Benz O305 305220 20 002226	Craftsman	B34D+64	-/72	-/72	by5/95
115	TJ 345.550	Mercedes-Benz O305 305220 20 002230	Craftsman	B34D+64	-/72	-/72	by5/95
116	TJ 345.551	Mercedes-Benz O305 305220 20 002234	Craftsman	B34D+64	-/72	-/72	by5/95
117	TJ 345.552	Mercedes-Benz O305 305220 20 002241	Craftsman	B34D+64	-/72	-/72	by5/95
118	TJ 345.553	Mercedes-Benz O305 305220 20 002245	Craftsman	B34D+64	-/72	-/72	by5/95
119	TJ 345.554	Mercedes-Benz O305 305220 20 002249	Craftsman	B34D+64	-/72	-/72	by5/95
120	TJ 345.555	Mercedes-Benz O305 305220 20 002042	Craftsman	B60F+20	-/72	-/72	by5/95
121	TJ 345.556	Mercedes-Benz O305 305220 20 002047	Craftsman	B60F+20	7/72	7/72	by5/95
122	TJ 345.557	Mercedes-Benz O305 305220 20 002052	Craftsman	B60F+20	8/72	8/72	by5/95
123	TJ 345.558	Mercedes-Benz O305 305220 20 002062	Craftsman	B60F+20	8/72	8/72	by5/95
124	TJ 345.559	Mercedes-Benz O305 305220 20 002068	Craftsman	B60F+20	8/72	8/72	by5/95
125	TJ 345.560	Mercedes-Benz O305 305220 20 002073	Craftsman	B60F+20	7/72	7/72	5/98
126	TJ 345.561	Mercedes-Benz O305 305220 20 002078	Craftsman	B60F+20	8/72	8/72	by5/95
127	TJ 345.562	Mercedes-Benz O305 305220 20 002088	Craftsman	B60F+20	8/72	8/72	by5/95
128	TJ 345.563	Mercedes-Benz O305 305220 20 002098	Craftsman	B60F+20	12/72	12/72	5/98
129	TJ 345.564	Mercedes-Benz O305 305220 20 002112	Craftsman	B60F+20	1/73	1/73	by5/95
130	TJ 345.565	Mercedes-Benz O305 305220 20 002115	Craftsman	B60F+20	9/72	9/72	-/--
131	TJ 345.566	Mercedes-Benz O305 305220 20 002119	Craftsman	B60F+20	9/72	9/72	by5/95
132	TJ 345.567	Mercedes-Benz O305 305220 20 002125	Craftsman	B60F+20	12/72	12/72	5/98
133	TJ 345.568	Mercedes-Benz O305 305220 20 002126	Craftsman	B60F+20	12/72	12/72	by5/95

134	TJ 345.569	Mercedes-Benz O305 305220 20 002132	Craftsman	B60F+20	1/73	1/73	-/--
135	TJ 345.570	Mercedes-Benz O305 305220 20 002135	Craftsman	B60F+20	10/72	10/72	by5/95
136	TJ 345.571	Mercedes-Benz O305 305220 20 002139	Craftsman	B60F+20	8/72	8/72	by5/95
137	TJ 345.572	Mercedes-Benz O305 305220 20 002145	Craftsman	B60F+20	-/72	-/72	by5/95
138	TJ 345.573	Mercedes-Benz O305 305220 20 002148	Craftsman	B60F+20	10/72	10/72	by5/95
139	TJ 345.574	Mercedes-Benz O305 305220 20 002152	Craftsman	B52F+32	10/72	10/72	5/98
140	TJ 345.575	Mercedes-Benz O305 305220 20 002155	Craftsman	B60F+20	9/72	9/72	by5/95
141	TJ 345.576	Mercedes-Benz O305 305220 20 002164	Craftsman	B60F+20	1/73	1/73	5/98
142	TJ 345.577	Mercedes-Benz O305 305220 20 022167	Craftsman	B52F+32	10/72	10/72	by5/95
143	TJ 345.578	Mercedes-Benz O305 305220 20 002171	Craftsman	B60F+20	10/72	10/72	by5/95
144	TJ 345.579	Mercedes-Benz O305 305220 20 002174	Craftsman	B52F+32	11/72	11/72	by5/95
145	TJ 345.580	Mercedes-Benz O305 305220 20 002181	Craftsman	B52F+32	11/72	11/72	by5/95
146	TJ 345.581	Mercedes-Benz O305 305220 20 002188	Craftsman	B52F+32	10/72	10/72	by5/95
147	TJ 345.582	Mercedes-Benz O305 305220 20 002192	Craftsman	B60F+20	2/73	2/73	by5/95
148	TJ 345.583	Mercedes-Benz O305 305220 20 002196	Craftsman	B60F+20	1/73	1/73	5/98
149	TJ 345.584	Mercedes-Benz O305 305220 20 002203	Craftsman	B60F+20	1/73	1/73	4/95
150	TJ 345.585	Mercedes-Benz O305 305220 20 002207	Craftsman	B60F+20	2/73	2/73	5/98
151	TJ 421.501	Mercedes-Benz O305 305220 20 002631	Craftsman	B58F+29	6/73	6/73	5/98
152	TJ 421.502	Mercedes-Benz O305 305220 20 002658	Craftsman	B58F+29	6/73	6/73	5/98
153	TJ 421.503	Mercedes-Benz O305 305220 20 002659	Craftsman	B58F+29	6/73	6/73	by5/95
154	TJ 421.504	Mercedes-Benz O305 305220 20 002680	Craftsman	B58F+29	5/73	5/73	5/98
155	TJ 421.505	Mercedes-Benz O305 305220 20 002692	Craftsman	B58F+29	6/73	6/73	5/98
156	TJ 421.506	Mercedes-Benz O305 305220 20 002693	Craftsman	B58F+29	2/74	2/74	by5/95
157	TJ 421.507	Mercedes-Benz O305 305220 20 002710	Craftsman	B58F+29	3/74	3/74	by5/95
158	TJ 421.508	Mercedes-Benz O305 305220 20 002729	Craftsman	B58F+29	3/74	3/74	4/95
159	TJ 421.509	Mercedes-Benz O305 305220 20 002742	Craftsman	B58F+29	4/74	4/74	4/95
160	TJ 421.510	Mercedes-Benz O305 305220 20 002746	Craftsman	B58F+29	3/74	3/74	4/95
161	TJ 421.511	Mercedes-Benz O305 305220 20 002747	Craftsman	B58F+29	6/73	6/73	5/98
162	TJ 421.512	Mercedes-Benz O305 305220 20 002751	Craftsman	B58F+29	5/73	5/73	4/95
163	TJ 421.513	Mercedes-Benz O305 305220 20 002752	Craftsman	B58F+29	6/73	6/73	5/98
164	TJ 421.514	Mercedes-Benz O305 305220 20 002756	Craftsman	B58F+29	11/73	11/73	-/--
165	TJ 421.515	Mercedes-Benz O305 305220 20 002757	Craftsman	B58F+29	6/73	6/73	4/95

166	TJ 421.516	Mercedes-Benz O305 305220 20 002761	Craftsman	B58F+29	6/73	6/73	5/98
167	TJ 421.517	Mercedes-Benz O305 305220 20 002766	Craftsman	B58F+29	6/74	6/74	5/98
168	TJ 421.518	Mercedes-Benz O305 305220 20 002767	Craftsman	B58F+29	3/74	3/74	by5/95
169	TJ 421.519	Mercedes-Benz O305 305220 20 002771	Craftsman	B58F+29	8/73	8/73	by5/95
170	TJ 421.520	Mercedes-Benz O305 305220 20 002772	Craftsman	B58F+29	8/73	8/73	by5/95
171	TJ 421.521	Mercedes-Benz O305 305220 20 002787	Craftsman	B58F+29	9/73	9/73	4/95
172	TJ 421.522	Mercedes-Benz O305 305220 20 002789	Craftsman	B58F+29	10/73	10/73	-/--
173	TJ 421.523	Mercedes-Benz O305 305220 20 002791	Craftsman	B58F+29	4/73	4/73	by5/95
174	TJ 421.524	Mercedes-Benz O305 305220 20 002795	Craftsman	B58F+29	10/73	10/73	4/95
175	TJ 421.525	Mercedes-Benz O305 305220 20 002796	Craftsman	B58F+29	9/73	9/73	by5/95
176	TJ 421.526	Mercedes-Benz O305 305220 20 002800	Craftsman	B58F+29	3/74	3/74	5/98
177	TJ 421.527	Mercedes-Benz O305 305220 20 002801	Craftsman	B58F+29	11/73	11/73	5/98
178	TJ 421.528	Mercedes-Benz O305 305220 20 002805	Craftsman	B58F+29	3/74	3/74	by5/95
179	TJ 421.529	Mercedes-Benz O305 305220 20 002806	Craftsman	B58F+29	1/74	1/74	4/95
180	TJ 421.530	Mercedes-Benz O305 305220 20 002807	Craftsman	B58F+29	4/74	4/74	by5/95
181	TJ 421.531	Mercedes-Benz O305 305220 20 002636	Brockhouse	B58F+29	6/73	6/73	5/98
182	TJ 421.532	Mercedes-Benz O305 305220 20 002675	Brockhouse	B58F+29	7/73	7/73	5/98
183	TJ 421.533	Mercedes-Benz O305 305220 20 002723	Brockhouse	B58F+29	7/73	7/73	5/98
184	TJ 421.534	Mercedes-Benz O305 305220 20 002762	Brockhouse	B58F+29	7/73	7/73	5/98
185	TJ 421.535	Mercedes-Benz O305 305220 20 002776	Brockhouse	B58F+29	6/73	6/73	5/98
186	TJ 421.536	Mercedes-Benz O305 305220 20 002777	Brockhouse	B58F+29	6/73	6/73	by5/95
187	TJ 421.537	Mercedes-Benz O305 305220 20 002781	Brockhouse	B58F+29	7/73	7/73	5/98
188	TJ 421.538	Mercedes-Benz O305 305220 20 002782	Brockhouse	B58F+29	6/73	6/73	5/98
189	TJ 421.539	Mercedes-Benz O305 305220 20 002786	Brockhouse	B58F+29	8/73	8/73	-/--
190	TJ 421.540	Mercedes-Benz O305 305220 20 002790	Brockhouse	B58F+29	8/73	8/73	5/98
191	TJ 421.541	Mercedes-Benz O305 307001 21 000062	Craftsman	B60F+20	-/73	-/73	7/84
192	TJ 421.542	Mercedes-Benz O305 307001 21 000074	Craftsman	B60F+20	-/73	-/73	7/84
193	TJ 421.543	Mercedes-Benz O305 307001 21 000086	Craftsman	B60F+20	-/73	-/73	5/84
194	TJ 421.544	Mercedes-Benz O305 307001 21 000092	Craftsman	B60F+20	-/73	-/73	7/84
195	TJ 421.545	Mercedes-Benz O305 307001 21 000096	Craftsman	B60F+20	-/73	-/73	5/84
196	TJ 421.546	Mercedes-Benz O305 307001 21 000102	Craftsman	B60F+20	-/73	-/73	7/84
197	TJ 421.547	Mercedes-Benz O305 307001 21 000107	Craftsman	B60F+20	-/73	-/73	7/84

198	TJ 421.548	Mercedes-Benz O305 307001 21 000111	Craftsman	B60F+20	-/73	-/73	5/84
199	TJ 421.549	Mercedes-Benz O305 307001 21 000118	Craftsman	B60F+20	-/73	-/73	7/84
200	TJ 421.550	Mercedes-Benz O305 307001 21 000124	Craftsman	B60F+20	-/73	-/73	7/84
201	TJ 421.551	Mercedes-Benz O305 307001 21 000128	Craftsman	B60F+20	-/73	-/73	6/84
202	TJ 421.552	Mercedes-Benz O305 307001 21 000135	Craftsman	B60F+20	-/73	-/73	7/84
203	TJ 421.553	Mercedes-Benz O305 307001 21 000146	Craftsman	B60F+20	-/73	-/73	7/84
204	TJ 421.554	Mercedes-Benz O305 07001 21 000163	Craftsman	B60F+20	-/73	-/73	7/84
205	TJ 421.555	Mercedes-Benz O305 307001 21 000170	Craftsman	B60F+20	-/73	-/73	7/84
206	TJ 421.556	Mercedes-Benz O305 307001 21 00017	Craftsman	B60F+20	-/73	-/73	4/84
207	TJ 421.557	Mercedes-Benz O305 307001 21 000180	Craftsman	B60F+20	-/73	-/73	6/84
208	TJ 421.558	Mercedes-Benz O305 307001 21 000187	Craftsman	B60F+20	-/73	-/73	7/84
209	TJ 421.559	Mercedes-Benz O305 307001 21 000194	Craftsman	B60F+20	-/73	-/73	6/84
210	TJ 421.560	Mercedes-Benz O305 307001 21 000201	Craftsman	B60F+20	-/73	-/73	6/84
211	TJ 425.731	Mercedes-Benz O305 307001 21 000972	Craftsman	B60F+20	-/74	-/74	6/84
212	TJ 425.732	Mercedes-Benz O305 307001 21 000979	Craftsman	B60F+20	-/74	-/74	7/84
213	TJ 425.733	Mercedes-Benz O305 307001 21 000986	Craftsman	B60F+20	-/74	-/74	5/84
214	TJ 425.734	Mercedes-Benz O305 307001 21 000993	Craftsman	B60F+20	-/74	-/74	6/84
215	TJ 435.501	Mercedes-Benz O305 307001 21 002321	Craftsman	B58F+32	-/74--/75	-/74--/75	6/84
216	TJ 435.502	Mercedes-Benz O305 307001 21 002328	Craftsman	B58F+32	-/74--/75	-/74--/75	7/84
217	TJ 435.503	Mercedes-Benz O305 307001 21 002538	Craftsman	B58F+32	-/74--/75	-/74--/75	4/84
218	TJ 435.504	Mercedes-Benz O305 307001 21 002341	Craftsman	B58F+32	-/74--/75	-/74--/75	6/84
219	TJ 435.505	Mercedes-Benz O305 307001 21 002348	Craftsman	B58F+32	-/74--/75	-/74--/75	6/84
220	TJ 435.506	Mercedes-Benz O305 307001 21 002352	Craftsman	B58F+32	-/74--/75	-/74--/75	5/84
221	TJ 435.507	Mercedes-Benz O305 307001 21 002358	Craftsman	B58F+32	-/74--/75	-/74--/75	5/84
222	TJ 435.508	Mercedes-Benz O305 307001 21 002365	Craftsman	B58F+32	-/74--/75	-/74--/75	5/84
223	TJ 435.509	Mercedes-Benz O305 307001 21 002416	Craftsman	B58F+32	-/74--/75	-/74--/75	5/84
224	TJ 435.510	Mercedes-Benz O305 307001 21 002417	Craftsman	B58F+32	-/74--/75	-/74--/75	3/84
225	TJ 435.511	Mercedes-Benz O305 307001 21 002418	Craftsman	B58F+32	-/74--/75	-/74--/75	4/84
226	TJ 435.512	Mercedes-Benz O305 307001 21 002424	Craftsman	B58F+32	-/74--/75	-/74--/75	3/84
227	TJ 435.513	Mercedes-Benz O305 307001 21 002432	Craftsman	B58F+32	-/74--/75	-/74--/75	3/84
228	TJ 435.514	Mercedes-Benz O305 307001 21 002433	Craftsman	B58F+32	-/74--/75	-/74--/75	4/84
229	TJ 435.515	Mercedes-Benz O305 307001 21 002444	Craftsman	B58F+32	-/74--/75	-/74--/75	3/84

230	TJ 435.516	Mercedes-Benz O305 307001 21 002449	Craftsman	B58F+32	-/74--/75 -/74--/75	4/84
231	TJ 435.517	Mercedes-Benz O305 307001 21 002454	Craftsman	B58F+32	-/74--/75 -/74--/75	3/84
232	TJ 435.518	Mercedes-Benz O305 307001 21 002477	Craftsman	B58F+32	-/74--/75 -/74--/75	4/84
233	TJ 435.519	Mercedes-Benz O305 307001 21 002482	Craftsman	B58F+32	-/74--/75 -/74--/75	6/84
234	TJ 435.520	Mercedes-Benz O305 307001 21 002487	Craftsman	B58F+32	-/74--/75 -/74--/75	3/84
235	TJ 435.521	Mercedes-Benz O305 307001 21 002493	Craftsman	B58F+32	-/74--/75 -/74--/75	5/84
236	TJ 435.522	Mercedes-Benz O305 307001 21 002498	Craftsman	B58F+32	-/74--/75 -/74--/75	4/84
237	TJ 435.523	Mercedes-Benz O305 307001 21 002503	Craftsman	B58F+32	-/74--/75 -/74--/75	5/84
238	TJ 435.524	Mercedes-Benz O305 307001 21 002508	Craftsman	B58F+32	-/74--/75 -/74--/75	5/84
239	TJ 435.525	Mercedes-Benz O305 307001 21 002513	Craftsman	B58F+32	-/74--/75 -/74--/75	4/84
240	TJ 435.526	Mercedes-Benz O305 307001 21 002522	Craftsman	B58F+32	-/74--/75 -/74--/75	3/84
241	TJ 435.527	Mercedes-Benz O305 307001 21 002531	Craftsman	B58F+32	-/74--/75 -/74--/75	4/84
242	TJ 435.528	Mercedes-Benz O305 307001 21 002334	Craftsman	B58F+32	-/74--/75 -/74--/75	5/84
243	TJ 435.529	Mercedes-Benz O305 307001 21 002547	Craftsman	B58F+32	-/74--/75 -/74--/75	3/84
244	TJ 435.530	Mercedes-Benz O305 307001 21 002556	Craftsman	B58F+32	-/74--/75 -/74--/75	4/84
245	TJ 435.531	Mercedes-Benz O305 307001 21 002578	Craftsman	B58F+32	-/74--/75 -/74--/75	4/84

Re-registered:
TJ 345.523 (88) to LSN 526T c1979.
TJ 345.537/8/42/3 (102/3/7/8) to LSH 931/21T, LSM 022T, LST 200T c1979.
TJ 345.556-63 (121-8) to LSJ 387T, LSH 481T, LST 120T, LSH 496/88/0T, LSJ 567T, LSN 856T c1979.
TJ 345.562 (127) later to FTZ 125GP c1996.
TJ 345.564-71 (129-36) to LSJ 487/75/20T, LSM 041/28/15T, LST 190, 217T c1979.
TJ 345.569 (134) later to HKZ 410GP c1996.
TJ 345.573-85 (138-50) to LST 194T, LSJ 402/22T, LSN 323/256/74/91/85/346/56/68/76T, LST 187T c1979.
TJ 421.501-12 (151-62) to LSP 097T, LSJ 435/59, 520/01, 493/86/70, 533, 419/2/09T c1979.
TJ 421.513-24 (163-74) to LST 406/2, 345/52/82/6/92/0T, LSJ 580T, LST 400/7T, LSH 503T c1979.
TJ 421.514/22 (164/72) later to FGG 436GP, FRK 558GP c1996.
TJ 421.525-33 (175-83) to LST 327/17/093/102/6T, LSJ 469T, LSN 261T, LSM 383T, LSJ 381T c1979.
TJ 421.534-41 (184-91) to LSK 932T, LSJ 360/448T, LST 410/338T, LSP 193/49T, LSJ 371T.

Notes:
TJ 279.801-11 (301-11) fitted with GM engines by 3/76.
TJ 279.801-5 (301-5) rebuilt to H46/34F+15 by 3/76.
TJ 279.806/7 (306-7) rebuilt to H46/34F+15 after 3/76.
TJ 279.806/14 (306/14) also recorded with chassis & body number combinations reversed.
TJ 279.812-6 (312-6) fitted with Cummins V6 engines by 3/76.
TJ 279.817-30 (317-30) A JMT record of 3/76 lists these as H40/33D+22.
TJ 301.117-26 (46-55) The original Daimler engines from these vehicles were replaced by Cummins V6 engines. They had been reseated to B56F+20 by 3/76.
TJ 345.501/2/4/5/3/6-22 (66-87) rebuilt to B52F+41 by 1982.
TJ 345.523-36 (88-101) rebuilt to B58F+22 by 1982.
LVH 342T (08/42) reported extant 5/95. No further details known and it may not have been a JMT vehicle.
TJ 345.537 (102) later reported as B52F+48.
TJ 345.538 (103) rebodied and renumbered 193 in 12/90 – see later.
TJ 345.542/3 (107/8) rebodied and renumbered 192/4 in 4/91 and 5/91 – see later.
TJ 421.531 (181-90) were recorded by JMT in 3/76 as having Craftsman bodies.

TJ 421.541-60 (191-210) rebodied & renumbered 471-7, 975, 479-85, 990, 487-90 – see later.
TJ 425.731-4 (211-4) rebodied and renumbered 491/2, 991, 494 – see later.
TJ 435.501-26 (215-40) rebodied and renumbered 495/6, 995, 498-500, 974, 478, 976-89, 486/93, 992/3 –
see later.
TJ 435.527-31 (241-5) rebodied and renumbered 994, 497, 996-8 – see later.

331	TJ 321.640	Daimler CRG6LX	63325	Park Royal B56822	H47/33D+13	1/70	1/70	by5/95
332	TJ 344.851	Daimler CRG6LX	64544	BBA	2641/9	H51/36F+6	6/71	6/71	by5/95
333	TJ 344.852	Daimler CRG6LX	64545	BBA	2641/1	H51/38F+6	6/71	6/71	by5/95
334	TJ 344.853	Daimler CRG6LX	64546	BBA	2641/2	H51/38F+6	6/71	6/71	by5/95
335	TJ 344.854	Daimler CRG6LX	64547	BBA	2641/3	H51/38F+6	6/71	6/71	by5/95
336	TJ 344.855	Daimler CRG6LX	64548	BBA	2641/4	H51/38F+6	6/71	6/71	by5/95
337	TJ 344.856	Daimler CRG6LX	64549	BBA	2641/5	H51/38F+6	6/71	6/71	by5/95
338	TJ 344.857	Daimler CRG6LX	64550	BBA	2641/6	H51/38F+6	6/71	6/71	by5/95
339	TJ 344.858	Daimler CRG6LX	64551	BBA	2641/7	H51/38F+6	6/71	6/71	by5/95
340	TJ 344.859	Daimler CRG6LX	64552	BBA	2641/8	H51/38F+6	7/71	7/71	by5/95
341	TJ 344.860	Daimler CRG6LX	64553	BBA	2641/10	H51/38F+6	7/71	7/71	by5/95
342	TJ 344.861	Daimler CRG6LX	64554	BBA	2641/11	H51/38F+6	7/71	7/71	by5/95
343	TJ 344.862	Daimler CRG6LX	64555	BBA	2641/12	H51/38F+6	7/71	7/71	by5/95
344	TJ 344.863	Daimler CRG6LX	64556	BBA	2641/13	H51/38F+6	7/71	7/71	by5/95
345	TJ 344.864	Daimler CRG6LX	64557	BBA	2641/14	H51/38F+6	7/71	7/71	by5/95
346	TJ 344.865	Daimler CRG6LX	64558	BBA	2641/15	H51/38F+6	7/71	7/71	by5/95
347	TJ 344.866	Daimler CRG6LX	64559	BBA	2641/16	H51/38F+6	8/71	8/71	by5/95
348	TJ 344.867	Daimler CRG6LX	64561	BBA	2642/1	H51/38F+6	2/72	2/72	by5/95
349	TJ 344.868	Daimler CRG6LX	64562	BBA	2642/2	H51/38F+6	2/72	2/72	by5/95
350	TJ 344.869	Daimler CRG6LX	64563	BBA	2642/3	H51/38F+6	2/72	2/72	by5/95
351	TJ 344.870	Daimler CRG6LX	64564	BBA	2642/4	H51/38F+6	2/72	2/72	by5/95
352	TJ 344.871	Daimler CRG6LX	64565	BBA	2642/5	H51/38F+6	2/72	2/72	by5/95
353	TJ 344.872	Daimler CRG6LX	64566	BBA	2642/6	H51/38F+6	2/72	2/72	by5/95
354	TJ 344.873	Daimler CRG6LX	64567	BBA	2642/7	H51/38F+6	2/72	2/72	by5/95
355	TJ 344.874	Daimler CRG6LX	64568	BBA	2642/9	H51/38F+6	3/72	3/72	by5/95
356	TJ 344.875	Daimler CRG6LX	64569	BBA	2642/10	H51/38F+6	3/72	3/72	by5/95
357	TJ 344.876	Daimler CRG6LX	64570	BBA	2642/11	H51/38F+6	3/72	3/72	by5/95
358	TJ 344.877	Daimler CRG6LX	64571	BBA	2642/12	H51/38F+6	3/72	3/72	by5/95
359	TJ 344.878	Daimler CRG6LX	64572	BBA	2642/13	H51/38F+6	3/72	3/72	by5/95
360	TJ 344.879	Daimler CRG6LX	64573	BBA	2642/14	H51/38F+6	3/72	3/72	by5/95
361	TJ 344.880	Daimler CRG6LX	64574	BBA	2642/15	H51/38F+6	3/72	3/72	by5/95
362	TJ 344.881	Daimler CRG6LX	64575	BBA	2642/16	H51/38F+6	3/72	3/72	by5/95
363	TJ 344.882	Daimler CRG6LX	64560	BBA	2642/8	H51/38F+6	4/72	4/72	by5/95
364	TJ 344.883	Daimler CRG6LX	64576	BBA	2642/17	H51/38F+6	4/72	4/72	by5/95
365	TJ 344.884	Daimler CRG6LX	64577	BBA	2642/18	H51/38F+6	4/72	4/72	by5/95
366	TJ 344.885	Daimler CRG6LX	64578	BBA	2642/19	H51/38F+6	4/72	4/72	by5/95
367	TJ 344.886	Daimler CRG6LX	64579	BBA	2642/20	H51/38F+6	4/72	4/72	by5/95
368	TJ 344.887	Daimler CRG6LX	64580	BBA	2642/21	H51/38F+6	4/72	4/72	by5/95
369	TJ 344.888	Daimler CRG6LX	64581	BBA	2642/22	H51/38F+6	5/72	5/72	by5/95
370	TJ 344.889	Daimler CRG6LX	64582	BBA	2642/23	H51/38F+6	5/72	5/72	-/86
371	TJ 344.890	Daimler CRG6LX	64583	BBA	2642/24	H51/38F+6	5/72	5/72	-/86
372	TJ 344.891	Daimler CRG6LX	64584	BBA	2642/25	H51/38F+6	5/72	5/72	-/86
373	TJ 344.892	Daimler CRG6LX	64585	BBA	2642/26	H51/38F+6	5/72	5/72	-/86
374	TJ 344.893	Daimler CRG6LX	64586	BBA	2642/27	H51/38F+6	5/72	5/72	-/86
375	TJ 344.894	Daimler CRG6LX	64587	BBA	2642/28	H51/38F+6	5/72	5/72	-/86
376	TJ 344.895	Daimler CRG6LX	64588	BBA	2642/29	H51/38F+6.	6/72	6/72	-/86
377	TJ 344.896	Daimler CRG6LX	64589	BBA	2642/30	H51/38F+6	6/72	6/72	by5/95
378	TJ 344.897	Daimler CRG6LX	64590	BBA	2642/31	H51/38F+6	6/72	6/72	by5/95
379	TJ 344.898	Daimler CRG6LX	64591	BBA	2642/32	H51/38F+6	6/72	6/72	by5/95
380	TJ 344.899	Daimler CRG6LX	64592	BBA	2642/33	H51/38F+6	6/72	6/72	by5/95
381	TJ 344.900	Daimler CRG6LX	64593	BBA	2642/34	H51/38F+6	6/72	6/72	by5/95
382	TJ 344.901	Daimler CRG6LX	64594	BBA	2642/35	H51/38F+6	6/72	6/72	by5/95
383	TJ 344.902	Daimler CRG6LX	64595	BBA	2642/36	H51/38F+6	6/72	6/72	by5/95
384	TJ 344.903	Daimler CRG6LX	64596	BBA	2642/37	H51/38F+6	6/72	6/72	by5/95
385	TJ 344.904	Daimler CRG6LX	64597	BBA	2642/38	H51/38F+6	7/72	7/72	by5/95
386	TJ 344.905	Daimler CRG6LX	64543	BBA	2642/39	H51/38F+6	6/72	6/72	4/95
387	TJ 425.701	Daimler CRG6LX	67744	BBA	2873/1	H51/38F+6	6/74	6/74	by5/95
388	TJ 425.702	Daimler CRG6LX	67745	BBA	2873/2	H51/38F+6	6/74	6/74	by5/95

389	TJ 425.703	Daimler CRG6LX	67746	BBA	2873/3	H51/38F+6	6/74	6/74	by5/95
390	TJ 425.704	Daimler CRG6LX	67747	BBA	2873/4	H51/38F+6	6/74	6/74	by5/95
391	TJ 425.705	Daimler CRG6LX	67748	BBA	2873/5	H51/38F+6	7/74	7/74	10/96
392	TJ 425.706	Daimler CRG6LX	67749	BBA	2873/6	H51/38F+6	6/74	6/74	10/96
393	TJ 425.707	Daimler CRG6LX	67750	BBA	2873/7	H51/38F+6	6/74	6/74	by5/95
394	TJ 425.708	Daimler CRG6LX	67751	BBA	2873/8	H51/38F+6	8/74	8/74	10/96
395	TJ 425.709	Daimler CRG6LX	67752	BBA	2873/9	H51/38F+6	6/74	6/74	by5/95
396	TJ 425.710	Daimler CRG0LX	67763	BBA	2873/10	H51/38F+6	6/74	6/74	by5/95
397	TJ 425.711	Daimler CRG6LX	67754	BBA	2873/11	H51/38F+6	6/74	6/74	by5/95
398	TJ 425.712	Daimler CRG6LX	67755	BBA	2873/12	H51/38F+6	6/74	6/74	by5/95
399	TJ 425.713	Daimler CRG6LX	67756	BBA	2873/13	H51/38F+6	6/74	6/74	by5/95
400	TJ 425.714	Daimler CRG6LX	67757	BBA	2873/14	H51/38F+6	6/74	6/74	by5/95
401	TJ 425.715	Daimler CRG6LX	67758	BBA	2873/15	H51/35F+6	6/74	6/74	by5/95
402	TJ 425.716	Daimler CRG6LX	67759	BBA	2873/16	H51/35F+6	7/74	7/74	by5/95
403	TJ 425.717	Daimler CRG6LX	67760	BBA	2873/17	H51/35F+6	7/74	7/74	by5/95
404	TJ 425.718	Daimler CRG6LX	67761	BBA	2873/18	H51/35F+6	7/74	7/74	by5/95
405	TJ 425.719	Daimler CRG6LX	67762	BBA	2873/19	H51/35F+6	7/74	7/74	4/95
406	TJ 425.720	Daimler CRG6LX	67763	BBA	2873/20	H51/35F+6	8/74	8/74	by5/95
407	TJ 425.721	Daimler CRG6LX	67764	BBA	2873/21	H51/35F+6	8/74	8/74	by5/95
408	TJ 425.722	Daimler CRG6LX	67765	BBA	2873/22	H51/35F+6	8/74	8/74	by5/95
409	TJ 425.723	Daimler CRG6LX	67766	BBA	2873/23	H51/35F+6	9/74	9/74	by5/95
410	TJ 425.724	Daimler CRG6LX	67767	BBA	2873/24	H51/35F+6	8/74	8/74	-/--
411	TJ 425.725	Daimler CRG6LX	67768	BBA	2873/25	H51/35F+6	8/74	8/74	by5/95
412	TJ 425.726	Daimler CRG6LX	67769	BBA	2873/26	H51/35F+6	7/74	7/74	by5/95
413	TJ 425.727	Daimler CRG6LX	67770	BBA	2873/27	H51/35F+6	7/74	7/74	by5/95
414	TJ 425.728	Daimler CRG6LX	67771	BBA	2873/28	H51/35F+6	7/74	7/74	by5/95
415	TJ 425.729	Daimler CRG6LX	67772	BBA	2873/29	H51/35F+6	7/74	7/74	by5/95
416	TJ 425.730	Daimler CRG6LX	67773	BBA	2873/30	H51/35F+6	8/74	8/74	by5/95
417	TJ 435.555	Leyland FE30AGR	7505932	BBA	3077/1	H47/34F+13	10/76	10/76	by5/95
418	TJ 435.556	Leyland FE30AGR	7505933	BBA	3077/2	H47/34F+13	10/76	10/76	by5/95
419	TJ 435.557	Leyland FE30AGR	7505934	BBA	3077/3	H47/34F+13	11/76	11/76	by5/95
420	TJ 435.558	Leyland FE30AGR	7505935	BBA	3077/4	H47/34F+13	11/76	11/76	by5/95
421	TJ 435.559	Leyland FE30AGR	7600107	BBA	3077/5	H47/34F+13	10/76	10/76	by5/95
422	TJ 435.560	Leyland FE30AGR	7600108	BBA	3077/6	H47/34F+13	11/76	11/76	by5/95
423	TJ 435.561	Leyland FE30AGR	7600109	BBA	3077/7	H47/34F+13	10/76	10/76	by5/95
424	TJ 435.562	Leyland FE30AGR	7600110	BBA	3077/8	H47/34F+13	12/76	12/76	by5/95
425	TJ 435.563	Leyland FE30AGR	7600231	BBA	3077/9	H47/34F+13	11/76	11/76	by5/95
426	TJ 435.564	Leyland FE30AGR	7600232	BBA	3077/10	H47/34F+13	11/76	11/76	by5/95
427	TJ 435.565	Leyland FE30AGR	7600233	BBA	3077/11	H47/34F+13	10/76	10/76	by5/95
428	TJ 435.566	Leyland FE30AGR	7600234	BBA	3077/12	H47/34F+13	11/76	11/76	by5/95
429	TJ 435.567	Leyland FE30AGR	7600455	BBA	3077/13	H47/34F+13	11/76	11/76	by5/95
430	TJ 435.568	Leyland FE30AGR	7600456	BBA	3077/14	H47/34F+13	11/76	11/76	by5/95
431	TJ 435.569	Leyland FE30AGR	7600457	BBA	3077/15	H47/34F+13	10/76	10/76	by5/95
432	TJ 435.570	Leyland FE30AGR	7600458	BBA	3077/16	H47/34F+13	10/76	10/76	by5/95
433	TJ 435.571	Leyland FE30AGR	7600563	BBA	3077/17	H47/34F+13	11/76	11/76	4/95
434	TJ 435.572	Leyland FE30AGR	7600564	BBA	3077/18	H47/34F+13	11/76	11/76	by5/95
435	TJ 435.573	Leyland FE30AGR	7600565	BBA	3077/19	H47/34F+13	11/76	11/76	by5/95
436	TJ 435.574	Leyland FE30AGR	7600566	BBA	3077/20	H47/34F+13	11/76	11/76	by5/95
437	TJ 435.575	Leyland FE30AGR	7600634	BBA	3077/21	H47/34F+13	10/76	10/76	10/96
438	TJ 435.576	Leyland FE30AGR	7600635	BBA	3077/22	H47/34F+13	10/76	10/76	by5/95
439	TJ 435.577	Leyland FE30AGR	7600636	BBA	3077/23	H47/34F+13	12/76	12/76	by5/95
440	TJ 435.578	Leyland FE30AGR	7600637	BBA	3077/24	H47/34F+13	11/76	11/76	by5/95
441	TJ 435.579	Leyland FE30AGR	7600969	BBA	3077/25	H47/34F+13	11/76	11/76	by5/95
442	TJ 435.580	Leyland FE30AGR	7600970	BBA	3077/26	H47/34F+13	9/76	9/76	by5/95
443	TJ 435.581	Leyland FE30AGR	7600971	BBA	3077/27	H47/34F+13	10/76	10/76	by5/95
444	TJ 435.582	Leyland FE30AGR	7600972	BBA	3077/28	H47/34F+13	10/76	10/76	by5/95
445	TJ 435.583	Leyland FE30AGR	7601127	BBA	3077/29	H47/34F+13	10/76	10/76	by5/95
446	TJ 435.584	Leyland FE30AGR	7601128	BBA	3077/30	H47/34F+13	10/76	10/76	by5/95
447	TJ 435.585	Leyland FE30AGR	7601129	BBA	3078/1	H47/34F+13	10/76	10/76	4/95
448	TJ 435.586	Leyland FE30AGR	7601130	BBA	3078/2	H47/34F+13	10/76	10/76	-/--
449	TJ 435.587	Leyland FE30AGR	7601239	BBA	3078/3	H47/34F+13	10/76	10/76	by5/95
450	TJ 435.588	Leyland FE30AGR	7601240	BBA	3078/4	H47/34F+13	9/76	9/76	by5/95
451	TJ 435.589	Leyland FE30AGR	7601241	BBA	3078/5	H47/34F+13	11/76	11/76	by5/95
452	TJ 435.590	Leyland FE30AGR	7601242	BBA	3078/6	H47/34F+13	9/76	9/76	4/95

453	TJ 435.591	Leyland FE30AGR	7601243	BBA	3078/7	H47/34F+13	9/76	9/76	by5/95
454	TJ 435.592	Leyland FE30AGR	7601244	BBA	3078/8	H47/34F+13	12/76	12/76	by5/95
455	TJ 435.593	Leyland FE30AGR	7601245	BBA	3078/9	H47/34F+13	10/76	10/76	5/98
456	TJ 435.594	Leyland FE30AGR	7601246	BBA	3078/10	H47/34F+13	10/76	10/76	4/95
457	TJ 435.595	Leyland FE30AGR	7601369	BBA	3078/11	H47/34F+13	11/76	11/76	4/95
458	TJ 435.596	Leyland FE30AGR	7601370	BBA	3078/12	H47/34F+13	10/76	10/76	by5/95
459	TJ 435.597	Leyland FE30AGR	7601371	BBA	3078/13	H47/34F+13	11/76	11/76	4/95
460	TJ 435.598	Leyland FE30AGR	7601372	BBA	3078/14	H47/34F+13	11/76	11/76	by5/95
461	TJ 435.599	Leyland FE30AGR	7601550	BBA	3078/15	H47/34F+13	11/76	11/76	4/95
462	TJ 435.600	Leyland FE30AGR	7601551	BBA	3078/16	H47/34F+13	10/76	10/76	4/95
463	TJ 435.601	Leyland FE30AGR	7601552	BBA	3078/17	H47/34F+13	10/76	10/76	5/98
464	TJ 435.602	Leyland FE30AGR	7601553	BBA	3078/18	H47/34F+13	11/76	11/76	by5/95
465	TJ 435.603	Leyland FE30AGR	7601705	BBA	3078/19	H47/34F+13	10/76	10/76	4/95
466	TJ 435.604	Leyland FE30AGR	7601706	BBA	3078/20	H47/34F+13	10/76	10/76	4/95
467	TJ 435.605	Leyland FE30AGR	7601707	BBA	3078/21	H47/34F+13	10/76	10/76	4/95
468	TJ 435.606	Leyland FE30AGR	7601708	BBA	3078/22	H47/34F+13	10/76	10/76	10/96
469	TJ 435.607	Leyland FE30AGR	7601709	BBA	3078/23	H47/34F+13	11/76	11/76	by5/95
470	TJ 435.608	Leyland FE30AGR	7601710	BBA	3078/24	H47/34F+13	10/76	10/76	4/95
471	LSL 051T	Mercedes-Benz O305 307001 21 000062		BBA	4087/7	H57/41F+12	-/73	7/84	-/--
472	LSL 056T	Mercedes-Benz O305 307001 21 000074		BBA	4087/15	H57/41F+12	-/73	7/84	-/--
473	LSL 023T	Mercedes-Benz O305 307001 21 000086		BBA	4086/2	H57/41F+12	-/73	5/84	-/--
474	LSL 024T	Mercedes-Benz O305 307001 21 000092		BBA	4087/10	H57/41F+12	-/73	7/84	-/--
475	LSJ 587T	Mercedes-Benz O305 307001 21 000096		BBA	4086/5	H57/41F+12	-/73	5/84	-/--
476	LSN 254T	Mercedes-Benz O305 307001 21 000102		BBA	4087/8	H57/41F+12	-/73	7/84	-/--
477	LSN 243T	Mercedes-Benz O305 307001 21 000107		BBA	4087/4	H57/41F+12	-/73	7/84	-/--
478	LSN 160T	Mercedes-Benz O305 307001 21 002365		BBA	4086/7	H57/41F+12	-/74--/75	5/84	-/--
479	LSN 133T	Mercedes-Benz O305 307001 21 000118		BBA	4087/12	H57/41F+12	-/73	7/84	-/--
480	LSN 073T	Mercedes-Benz O305 307001 21 000124		BBA	4087/9	H57/41F+12	-/73	7/84	-/--
481	LSN 661T	Mercedes-Benz O305 307001 21 000128		BBA	4086/11	H57/41F+12	-/73	6/84	-/--
482	LSN 653T	Mercedes-Benz O305 307001 21 000135		BBA	4087/3	H57/41F+12	-/73	7/84	-/--
483	LSN 332T	Mercedes-Benz O305 307001 21 000146		BBA	4087/2	H57/41F+12	-/73	7/84	-/--
484	LSN 316T	Mercedes-Benz O305 307001 21 000163		BBA	4087/13	H57/41F+12	-/73	7/84	-/--
485	LSN 308T	Mercedes-Benz O305 307001 21 000170		BBA	4087/5	H57/41F+12	-/73	7/84	-/--
486	LSH 497T	Mercedes-Benz O305 307001 21 002503		BBA	4086/1	H57/41F+12	-/74--/75	5/84	-/--
487	LSH 489T	Mercedes-Benz O305 307001 21 000180		BBA	4086/12	H57/41F+12	-/73	6/84	-/--
488	LSS 227T	Mercedes-Benz O305 307001 21 000187		BBA	4087/11	H57/41F+12	-/73	7/84	-/--
489	?	Mercedes-Benz O305 307001 21 000194		BBA	4087/6	H57/41F+12	-/73	6/84	by3/90
490	LST 126T	Mercedes-Benz O305 307001 21 000201		BBA	4086/8	H57/41F+12	-/73	6/84	-/--
491	LSS 207T	Mercedes-Benz O305 307001 21 000972		BBA	4086/14	H57/41F+12	-/74	6/84	-/--
492	LSS 200T	Mercedes-Benz O305 307001 21 000979		BBA	4087/14	H57/41F+12	-/74	7/84	-/--
493	LSS 187T	Mercedes-Benz O305 307001 21 002508		BBA	4086/6	H57/41F+12	-/74--/75	5/84	-/--

494	LSN 710T	Mercedes-Benz O305 307001 21 000993	BBA	4086/10	H57/41+12F	-/74	6/84	-/--
495	LSN 721T	Mercedes-Benz O305 307001 21 002321	BBA	4087/1	H57/41+12F	-/74--/75	6/84	-/--
496	LSN 700T	Mercedes-Benz O305 307001 21 002328	BBA	4086/15	H57/41+12F	-/74--/75	7/84	-/--
497	LSP 080T	Mercedes-Benz O305 307001 21 002334	BBA	4085/23	H57/41+12F	-/74--/75	5/84	-/--
498	LST 175T	Mercedes-Benz O305 307001 21 002341	BBA	4086/9	H57/41+12F	-/74--/75	6/84	by 12/99
499	LST 182T	Mercedes-Benz O305 307001 21 002348	BBA	4086/13	H57/41+12F	-/74--/75	6/84	-/--
500	LST 214T	Mercedes-Benz O305 307001 21 002352	BBA	4086/3	H57/41+12F	-/74--/75	5/84	-/--
974	LSN 574T	Mercedes-Benz O305 307001 21 002358	BBA	4085/19	H57/41F+12	-/74--/75	5/84	-/--
975	LSL 919T	Mercedes-Benz O305 307001 21 000111	BBA	4085/25	H57/41F+12	-/74--/75	5/84	-/--
976	LSS 157T	Mercedes-Benz O305 307001 21 002416	BBA	4085/16	H57/41F+12	-/74--/75	5/84	-/--
977	LSH 502T	Mercedes-Benz O305 307001 21 002417	BBA	4085/3	H57/41F+12	-/74--/75	3/84	-/--
978	LSH 487T	Mercedes-Benz O305 307001 21 002418	BBA	4085/17	H57/41F+12	-/74--/75	4/84	-/--
979	LSH 495T	Mercedes-Benz O305 307001 21 002424	BBA	4085/4	H57/41F+12	-/74--/75	3/84	-/--
980	LST 049T	Mercedes-Benz O305 307001 21 002432	BBA	4085/11	H57/41F+12	-/74--/75	3/84	-/--
981	LST 055T	Mercedes-Benz O305 307001 21 002465	BBA	4085/6	H57/41F+12	-/74--/75	4/84	-/--
982	LST 063T	Mercedes-Benz O305 307001 21 002444	BBA	4085/12	H57/41F+12	-/74--/75	3/84	-/--
983	LST 354T	Mercedes-Benz O305 307001 21 002449	BBA	4085/14	H57/41F+12	-/74--/75	4/84	-/--
984	LSL 928T	Mercedes-Benz O305 307001 21 002454	BBA	4085/7	H57/41F+12	-/74--/75	3/84	-/--
985	LSL 941T	Mercedes-Benz O305 307001 21 002477	BBA	4085/9	H57/41F+12	-/74--/75	4/84	-/--
986	LSH 570T	Mercedes-Benz O305 307001 21 002482	BBA	4085/21	H57/41F+12	-/74--/75	6/84	-/--
987	LSH 563T	Mercedes-Benz O305 307001 21 002487	BBA	4085/2	H57/41F+12	-/74--/75	3/84	-/--
988	LSJ 320T	Mercedes-Benz O305 307001 21 002493	BBA	4085/1	H57/41F+12	-/74--/75	5/84	-/--
989	LSJ 352T	Mercedes-Benz O305 307001 21 002498	BBA	4085/18	H57/41F+12	-/74--/75	4/84	-/--
990	LSJ 398T	Mercedes-Benz O305 307001 21 000177	BBA	4085/22	H57/41F+12	-/74--/75	4/84	-/--
991	LSJ 410T	Mercedes-Benz O305 307001 21 000986	BBA	4085/24	H57/41F+12-/74--/75		5/84	-/--
992	LSJ 421T	Mercedes-Benz O305 307001 21 002513	BBA	4085/20	H57/41F+12	-/74--/75	4/84	-/--
993	LSJ 434T	Mercedes-Benz O305 307001 21 002522	BBA	4085/5	H57/41F+12	-/74--/75	3/84	-/--
994	LSJ 458T	Mercedes-Benz O305 307001 21 002531	BBA	4085/13	H57/41F+12	-74--/75	4/84	-/--
995	LSJ 469T	Mercedes-Benz O305 307001 21 002538	BBA	4086/4	H57/41F+12	-/74--/75	4/84	-/--
996	LSJ 483T	Mercedes-Benz O305 307001 21 002547	BBA	4085/8	H57/41F+12	-/74--/75	3/84	-/--
997	LSJ 535T	Mercedes-Benz O305 307001 21 002556	BBA	4085/15	H57/41F+12	-/74--/75	4/84	-/--
998	LSJ 574T	Mercedes-Benz O305 307001 21 002578	BBA	4085/10	H57/41F+12	-/74--/75	4/84	-/--

		Ford R1114	790576	BBA	3219/1	B--	8/76	8/76	-/--
		Isuzu BD732KT	141307	BBA	3517/1	B--	7/79	7/79	-/--
720	TJ 255.503	Hino	?	Craftsman		B62F+25	-/76	-/--	by2/88
721	TJ 15657	AEC Kudu	3S2RA1064	BBA	2914/5	B66F+19	4/73	4/73	by2/88
722	TJ 15707	AEC Kudu	3S2RA1066	BBA	2914/1	B66F+19	4/73	4/73	by2/88
723	TJ 15725	AEC Kudu	3S2RA1072	BBA	2914/2	B66F+19	4/73	4/73	by2/88
724	TJ 15732	AEC Kudu	3S2RA1073	BBA	2914/6	B66F+19	4/73	4/73	by2/88
725	TJ 15918	AEC Kudu	3S2RA1074	BBA	2914/4	B66F+19	4/73	4/73	by2/88
726	TJ 15993	AEC Kudu	3S2RA1075	BBA	2914/3	B66F+19	4/73	4/73	by2/88
1000	BBF 081T	Saurer U/F		Springfield		AB76F+69	-/78	-/78	by-/86
700	TJ 172.954	Saurer U/F	2567	Springfield		H100+2F	10/78	10/78	by-/86
701	CDN 881T	Saurer U/F	2617	Springfield		H55/38F	-/79	-/79	3/85
727		Saurer U/F		Springfield		B59F+36	-/80	-/80	by-/86
728		Saurer U/F		Springfield		B53F+55	-/80	-/80	by-/86
729		Saurer U/F		Springfield		B53F+55	-/80	-/80	by-/86
730		Saurer U/F		Springfield		B53F+55	-/80	-/80	by-/86
731	DHN 664T	Saurer U/F		Springfield		B53F+55	-/80	-/80	by-/86
732		Saurer U/F		Springfield		B53F+55	-/80	-/80	by-/86
733		Saurer U/F		Springfield		B53F+55	-/80	-/80	by-/86
734		Saurer U/F		Springfield		B53F+55	-/80	-/80	by-/86
735		Saurer U/F		Springfield		B53F+55	-/80	-/80	by-/86
736		Saurer U/F		Springfield		B53F+55	-/80	-/80	by-/86
737		Saurer U/F		Springfield		B53F+55	-/80	-/80	by-/86
738		Saurer U/F		Springfield		B53F+55	-/80	-/80	by-/86
739		Saurer U/F		Springfield		B53F+55	-/80	-/80	by-/86
740		Saurer U/F		Springfield		B53F+55	-/80	-/80	by-/86
741		Saurer U/F		Springfield		B53F+55	-/80	-/80	by-/86
501	TJ 199.118	Mercedes-Benz O305 307001 21 003990		BBA	3246/1	H50/40F+9	12/76	12/76	-/--
502	TJ 435.681	Mercedes-Benz O305 307001 21 006403		BBA	3361/14	H53/45F+11	6/78	6/78	-/--
503	TJ 435.682	Mercedes-Benz O305 307001 21 006407		BBA	3361/1	H53/45F+11	6/78	6/78	by12/99
504	TJ 435.683	Mercedes-Benz O305 307001 21 006408		BBA	3361/2	H53/45F+11	6/78	6/78	-/--
505	TJ 435.684	Mercedes-Benz O305 307001 21 006412		BBA	3361/7	H53/45F+11	6/78	6/78	-/--
506	TJ 435.685	Mercedes-Benz O305 307001 21 006413		BBA	3361/8	H53/45F+11	6/78	6/78	by12/99
507	TJ 435.686	Mercedes-Benz O305 307001 21 006417		BBA	3361/24	H53/45F+11	9/78	9/78	-/--
508	TJ 435.687	Mercedes-Benz O305 307001 21 006418		BBA	3361/3	H53/45F+11	6/78	6/78	by12/99
509	TJ 435.688	Mercedes-Benz O305 307001 21 006422		BBA	3361/4	H53/45F+11	6/78	6/78	-/--
510	TJ 435.689	Mercedes-Benz O305 307001 21 006423		BBA	3361/5	H53/45F+11	6/78	6/78	by12/99
511	TJ 435.690	Mercedes-Benz O305 307001 21 006427		BBA	3361/6	H53/45F+11	6/78	6/78	by12/99
512	TJ 435.691	Mercedes-Benz O305 307001 21 006428		BBA	3361/9	H53/45F+11	6/78	6/78	by12/99
513	TJ 435.692	Mercedes-Benz O305 307001 21 006432		BBA	3361/10	H53/45F+11	6/78	6/78	by12/99
514	TJ 435.693	Mercedes-Benz O305 307001 21 006433		BBA	3361/15	H53/45F+11	7/78	7/78	-/--
515	TJ 435.694	Mercedes-Benz O305 307001 21 006437		BBA	3361/16	H53/45F+11	6/78	6/78	-/--
516	TJ 435.695	Mercedes-Benz O305 307001 21 006438		BBA	3361/11	H53/45F+11	7/78	7/78	by12/99
517	TJ 435.696	Mercedes-Benz O305 307001 21 006443		BBA	3361/17	H53/45F+11	6/78	6/78	-/--
518	TJ 435.697	Mercedes-Benz O305 307001 21 006444		BBA	3361/18	H53/45F+11	7/78	7/78	by 5/09
519	TJ 435.698	Mercedes-Benz O305		BBA	3361/19	H53/45F+11	7/78	7/78	-/--

		307001 21 006448						
520	TJ 435.699	Mercedes-Benz O305	BBA	3361/12	H53/45F+11	6/78	6/78	-/--
		307001 21 006453						
521	TJ 435.700	Mercedes-Benz O305	BBA	3361/13	H53/45F+11	6/78	6/78	-/--
		307001 21 006454						
522	TJ 435.701	Mercedes-Benz O305	BBA	3361/25	H53/45F+11	9/78	9/78	by12/99
		307001 21 006477						
523	TJ 435.702	Mercedes-Benz O305	BBA	3361/20	H53/45F+11	7/78	7/78	-/--
		307001 21 006482						
524	TJ 435.703	Mercedes-Benz O305	BBA	3361/26	H53/45F+11	9/78	9/78	-/--
		307001 21 006483						
525	TJ 435.704	Mercedes-Benz O305	BBA	3361/27	H53/45F+11	7/78	7/78	by12/99
		307001 21 006486						
526	TJ 435.705	Mercedes-Benz O305	BBA	3439/1	H53/45F+11	12/78	12/78	-/--
		307001 21 006487						
527	TJ 435.706	Mercedes-Benz O305	BBA	3361/21	H53/45F+11	7/78	7/78	-/--
		307001 21 006491						
528	TJ 435.707	Mercedes-Benz O305	BBA	3361/28	H53/45F+11	9/78	9/78	-/--
		307001 21 006492						
529	TJ 435.708	Mercedes-Benz O305	BBA	3361/22	H53/45F+11	7/78	7/78	-/--
		307001 21 006496						
530	TJ 435.709	Mercedes-Benz O305	BBA	3361/29	H53/45F+11	9/78	9/78	-/--
		307001 21 006497						
531	TJ 435.710	Mercedes-Benz O305	BBA	3361/23	H53/45F+11	9/78	9/78	-/--
		307001 21 006500						
532	TJ 423.096	Mercedes-Benz O305	BBA	3361/31	H53/45F+11	9/78	9/78	-/--
		307001 61 006501						
533	TJ 423.325	Mercedes-Benz O305	BBA	3361/32	H53/45F+11	9/78	9/78	-/--
		307001 61 006505						
534	LSL 025T	Mercedes-Benz O305	BBA	3361/33	H53/45F+11	9/78	9/78	-/--
		307001 61 006506						
535	BGT 412T	Mercedes-Benz O305	Springfield		H53/44F+6	1/79	1/79	-/--
		307001 61 006511						
536	LSN 728T	Mercedes-Benz O305	BBA	3361/34	H53/45F+11	9/78	9/78	-/--
		307001 61 006512						
537	TJ 424.011	Mercedes-Benz O305	BBA	3361/35	H53/45F+11	9/78	9/78	-/--
		307001 61 006516						
538	TJ 424.187	Mercedes-Benz O305	BBA	3361/38	H53/45F+11	9/78	9/78	-/--
		307001 61 006517						
539	TJ 424.211	Mercedes-Benz O305	BBA	3361/36	H53/45F+11	9/78	9/78	-/--
		307001 61 006521						
540	TJ 424.615	Mercedes-Benz O305	BBA	3361/39	H53/45F+11	9/78	9/78	-/--
		307001 61 006522						
541	TJ 424.740	Mercedes-Benz O305	BBA	3361/37	H53/45F+11	9/78	9/78	-/--
		307001 61 006526						
542	TJ 424.905	Mercedes-Benz O305	BBA	3361/41	H53/45F+11	9/78	9/78	-/--
		307001 61 006527						
543	TJ 424.918	Mercedes-Benz O305	BBA	3361/40	H53/45F+11	9/78	9/78	-/--
		307001 61 006531						
544	BMG 720T	Mercedes-Benz O305	Springfield		H53/44F+6	1/79	1/79	-/--
		307001 61 006532						
545	BDF 754T	Mercedes-Benz O305	Springfield		H53/44F+6	12/78	12/78	-/--
		307001 61 006536						
546	BFD 323T	Mercedes-Benz O305	Springfield		H53/44F+6	1/79	1/79	by12/99
		307001 61 006537						
547	BZK 492T	Mercedes-Benz O305	BBA	3393/1	H53/45F+11	6/79	6/79	-/--
		307001 61 007277						
548	BZK 434T	Mercedes-Benz O305	BBA	3393/2	H53/45F+11	7/79	7/79	-/--
		307001 61 007278						
549	BRS 199T	Mercedes-Benz O305	BBA	3393/13	H53/45F+11	7/79	7/79	-/--
		307001 61 007286						
550	BZK 484T	Mercedes-Benz O305	BBA	3393/3	H53/45F+11	7/79	7/79	-/--
		307001 61 007287						
551	CBH 222T	Mercedes-Benz O305	BBA	3393/20	H53/45F+11	7/79	7/79	-/--

552	CBZ 774T	Mercedes-Benz O305 307001 61 007305	BBA	3393/21	H53/35F+11	7/79	7/79	-/--
553	CBT 347T	Mercedes-Benz O305 307001 61 007309	BBA	3393/4	H53/45F+11	7/79	7/79	-/--
554	CBP 664T	Mercedes-Benz O305 307001 61 007319	BBA	3393/5	H53/45F+11	7/79	7/79	-/--
555	BZT 581T	Mercedes-Benz O305 307001 61 007320	BBA	3393/6	H53/45F+11	6/79	6/79	-/--
556	BZK 460T	Mercedes-Benz O305 307001 61 007332	BBA	3393/7	H53/45F+11	6/79	6/79	-/--
557	BZT 556T	Mercedes-Benz O305 307001 61 007333	BBA	3393/8	H53/45F+11	6/79	6/79	-/--
558	BZT 565T	Mercedes-Benz O305 307001 61 007348	BBA	3393/9	H53/45F+11	7/79	7/79	-/--
559	BZZ 714T	Mercedes-Benz O305 307001 61 007349	BBA	3393/14	H53/45F+11	6/79	6/79	-/--
560	BZV 099T	Mercedes-Benz O305 307001 61 007399	BBA	3393/10	H53/45F+11	6/79	6/79	-/--
561	BZZ 723T	Mercedes-Benz O305 307001 61 007400	BBA	3393/15	H53/45F+11	7/79	7/79	-/--
562	BZK 476T	Mercedes-Benz O305 307001 61 007408	BBA	3393/11	H53/45F+11	6/79	6/79	-/--
563	CCP 789T	Mercedes-Benz O305 307001 61 007491	BBA	3393/16	H53/45F+11	7/79	7/79	-/--
564	CBP 679T	Mercedes-Benz O305 307001 61 007492	BBA	3393/22	H53/45F+11	7/79	7/79	by5/05
565	BZK 468T	Mercedes-Benz O305 307001 61 007504	BBA	3393/12	H53/45F+11	6/79	6/79	-/--
566	CBP 670T	Mercedes-Benz O305 307001 61 007505	BBA	3393/17	H53/45F+11	7/79	7/79	-/--
567	CBP 669T	Mercedes-Benz O305 307001 61 007522	BBA	3393/18	H53/45F+11	7/79	7/79	-/--
568	CBT 843T	Mercedes-Benz O305 307001 61 007523	BBA	3393/19	H53/45F+11	7/79	7/79	-/--
569	CBX 853T	Mercedes-Benz O305 307001 61 007532 307001 61 007533	BBA	3393/23	H53/45F+11	7/79	7/79	-/--

Re-registered:
TJ 344.905 (386) to LSJ 492T c1979.
TJ 425.701-8 (387-94) to LSL 300T, LSK 982T/40/895/4T, LSJ 509T, LSK 889T, LSJ 496T c1979.
TJ 425.709-17 (395-403) to LSH 709/691/723T, LSL 341T, LSN 813T, LST 337/42/31/19T c1979,
TJ 425.718-30 (404-16) to LSH 579/84/815/601/18/61/8/916/09/49/74T, LSJ 008T, LSH 971T c1979.
TJ 435.555-64 (417-26) to LSJ 009T, LSH 977/35/643/34/10/924T, GFB 530T, LSJ 377/545T c1979.
TJ 435.565-78 (427-40) to LSN 299/0T, LSJ 619T, LSL 846/78/4/0/68/5/3/678/57T, LSJ 671/592T c1979.
TJ 435.579-94 (441-56) to LSK 876T, LSJ 542/38/1/25/15/02/61/51/317/43/25/12/03/273T, LSL 832T c1979.
TJ 435.595-603 (457-65) to LSL 818/762T, LSN 349T, LSL 381T, LSJ 349/56/294T, LSS 179/69T c1979.
TJ 435.604-8 (466-70) to LSK 938/79/87, LSL 010/21T c1979.T
LSL 051/6/23/4T, LSJ 587T, LSN 254/43T (471-7) to FVH 059GP, FVF 891GP, FVH 060-2/36/9GP c1996.
LSN 160/33/073/661/53/332T (478-83) to FVH 043/7/72GP, HSF 438GP, FVH 054/73GP c1996.
LSN 316/08T, LSH 497/89T, LSS 227T (484-8) to FJD 045GP, FVH 053/8/66/74GP c1996.
LST 126T, LSS 207/0/187T, LSN 710/21T (490-5) to FVH 055/75/6/57GP, FJD 057GP, FHX 565GP c1996.
LSN 700T, LSP 080T, LST 175/82T (496-9) to FGG 432GP, FTZ 137GP, FGG 429GP, FXT 466GP c1996.
LST 214T, LSN 574T, LSL 919T (500, 974/5) to FTZ 155GP, FVB 036GP, FGD 923GP c1996.
LSS 157T, LSH 502/487/95T (976-9) to FHY 303GP, FVB 051GP, FVB 052/3GP c1996.
LST 049/55/63/354T, LSL 928T (980-4) to FGG 431GP, FXT 459GP, FVB 055/9/61GP c1996.
LSL 941T, LSH 570/63T, LSJ 320/52/98T (985-90) to FGD 915GP, FVB 063/6-8GP, FGD 902GP c1996.
LSJ 410/21/34/58/69/83/535/74T (991-8) to FVB 071/5/8GP, FGD 899GP, FVB 080/2/3/6GP c1996.
TJ 172.954 (700) to LST 083T c1979.
TJ 199.118 (501) to LSN 578T c1979, FLV 976GP c1996.
TJ 435.681 (502) to LSN 631T c1979, FGD 912GP c1996.
TJ 435.682 (503) to LSP 053T c1979.
TJ 435.683 (504) to LSP 066T c1979, HHY 945GP c1996.
TJ 435.684 (505) to LSH 485T c1979, FGD 904GP c1996.

TJ 435.685 (506) to LSH 501T c1979, FGD 980GP c1996.
TJ 435.686 (507) to LSH 486T c1979, FTZ 156GP c1996.
TJ 435.687 (508) to LSH 494T c1979, FGD 909GP. c1996.
TJ 435.688 (509) to LST 169T c1979, FRK 582GP c1996.
TJ 435.689 (510) to LSL 408T c1979, FGD 336GP c1996.
TJ 435.690 (511) to LSH 491T c1979, FGD 905GP c1996.
TJ 435.691 (512) to LSH 484T c1979.
TJ 435.692 (513) to LST 309T c1979, FGG 435GP c1990.
TJ 435.693 (514) to LSN 489T c1979, HSF 441GP c1996.
TJ 435.694 (515) to LSH 493T c1979, FTZ 159GP c1996.
TJ 435.695 (516) to LSL 822T c1979.
TJ 435.696 (517) to LSL 432T c1979, FRK 581GP c1996.
TJ 435.697 (518) to LSL 418T c1979, FRK 576GP c1996.
TJ 435.698 (519) to LSL 376T c1979, FRK 575GP c1996.
TJ 435.699 (520) to LSH 499T c1979, FRK 573GP c1996.
TJ 435.700 (521) to LSL 392T c1979, FRK 570GP c1996.
TJ 435.701 (522) to LSN 644T c1979.
TJ 435.702 (523) to LSN 648T c1979, FGD 922GP c1996.
TJ 435.703 (524) to LSN 671T c1979, FGG 424GP c1996.
TJ 435.704 (525) to FFL 900T 1/81.
TJ 435.705 (526) to BNM 026T 12/78, HLC 938GP c1996.
TJ 435.706 (527) to LSN 683T c1979, FVH 390GP c1996.
TJ 435.707 (528) to LSN 692T c1979, FJD 071GP c1996.
TJ 435.708 (529) to LSP 220T c1979, FVF 425GP c1996.
TJ 435.709 (530) to LSH 492T c1979, FVF 427GP c1996.
TJ 435.710 (531) to LSL 926T c1979, FVF 428GP c1996.
TJ 423.096 (532) to LSL 766T c1979, FVH 464GP c1996.
TJ 423.325 (533) to LSL 353T c1979.
TJ 423.325 (533) to FVH 065GP c1996.
LSL 025T (534) to FVH 066GP c1996.
BGT 412T (535) to FVF 894GP c1996.
LSN 728T (536) to FVF 421GP c1996.
TJ 424.011 (537) to LST 301T c1979, FVH 067GP c1996.
TJ 424.187 (538) to LSH 498T c1979, FVF 916GP c1996.
TJ 424.211 (539) to LSH 483T c1979, FJD 069GP c1996.
TJ 424.615 (540) to LSH 490T c1979, FLW 054GP c1996.
TJ 424.740 (541) to LST 289T c1979, FVH 068GP c1996.
TJ 424.905 (542) to LST 274T c1979, FVH 070GP c1996.
TJ 424.918 (543) to LST 265T c1979, FVH 071GP c1996.
BMG 720T (544) to HMP 665GP c1996.
BDF 754T (545) to FTZ 086GP c1996.
BZK 492T (547) to HKB 167GP c1996.
BZK 434T (548) to FYB 799GP c1996.
BRS 199T (549) to HLC 924GP c1996.
BZK 484T (550) to FJD 062GP c1996.
CBH 222T (551) to FVF 863GP c1996.
CBZ 774T (552) to FYB 798GP c1996.
CBT 347T (553) to FLW 050GP c1996.
CBP 664T (554) to FVF 874GP c1996.
BZT 581T (555) to FLW 048GP c1996.
BZK 460T (556) to FZS 734GP c1996.
BZT 556T (557) to FLW 042GP c1996.
BZT 565T (558) to FLW 026GP c1996.
BZZ 714T (559) to FLW 030GP c1996.
BZV 099T (560) to FLW 037GP c1996.
BZZ 723T (561) to FYB 797GP c1996.
BZK 476T (562) to FJD 068GP c1996.
CCP 789T (563) to FRH 968GP c1996.
CBP 679T (564) to FJD 060GP c1996.
BZK 468T (565) to FJD 066GP c1996.
CBP 670T (566) to FLW 033GP c1996.
CBP 669T (567) to FLW 032GP c1996.
CBT 843T (568) to FLW 019GP c1996.
CBX 853T (569) to FLW 023GP c1996.

Notes:

TJ 425.704 (390) recorded as H51F/31+6 in 3/76.
TJ 425.706 (392) recorded as H51F/30+6 in 3/76.
TJ 435.586 (448) rebuilt to open top by 2000.
TJ 435.593 (455) later re-registered DSG 149GP and rebuilt to open top for use as a tree cutter.
TJ 435.601 (463) rebuilt to open top by 2000.
LSL 051/6/23/4T, LSJ 587T, LSN 254/43/160/33/073/661/53T (471-82) rebodied as shown ex 191-7, 222, 199-202.
LSN 332/16/08T, LSH 497/89T, LSS 227T, ?, LST 126T, LSS 207/0T (483-92) rebodied as shown ex 203-5/37/07-12.
LSS 187T, LSN 710/21/00T, LSP 080T, LST 175/82T (493-9) rebodied as shown ex 238/14-6/42/18/9.
LSP 080T (497) rebuilt to open-top by 7/00 (as tree cutter) and extant 5/09.
LSP 080T (497) and LSJ 469T (995) have also been recorded with chassis numbers reversed.
LST 182T (499) rebuilt to open-top (PO57/41F) by 5/06.
LST 214T, LSN 574T, LSL 919T, LSS 157T, LSH 502/487/95T (500. 974-9) rebodied as shown ex 220/1, 198, 223-6.
LST 049/55/63/354T, LSL 928/41T, LSH 570/63T, LSJ 320/52/98T (980-90) rebodied as shown ex 227-36/06.
LSJ 410/21/34/58/69/83/535/74T (991-8) rebodied as shown ex 213/39-41/17/43-5.
TJ 255.503 (720) ex demonstrator.
TJ 199.118, 435.681-708 (501-31) were built as H96F but were reseated to H98F in 1979.
TJ 435.693 (514) rebuilt to open top by 7/00 (as tree cutter).
TJ 435.703, (524) rebuilt to open top by 5/06.
TJ 435.704 (525) has also been recorded with chassis number 021598. It seems likely that the original chassis was damaged and replaced with 307001 61 021598 in 1/81.
TJ 435.705 (526) The original body for 526 was BBA 3361/30 but this was irreparably damaged before delivery and replaced by BBA 3439/1 as shown.

Disposals:

TJ 344.889-95 (370-6): Roodepoort Municipality 55-61.
LSN 332T (483): OKI Printers, Johannesburg by 8/05, re-registered RYF 719GP.
CDN 881T (701): Germiston Municipality 40.
? (?) (total 4 Saurer U/F): Kempton Park Municipality.
TJ 435.697/701 (518/22): burnt out.

570	FBJ 308T	Mercedes-Benz O305 307001 61 022612	BBA	3698/1	H53/45F+11	1/81	1/81	-/--
571	FBG 164T	Mercedes-Benz O305 307001 61 022613	BBA	3698/2	H53/45F+11	1/81	1/81	-/--
572	FBG 248T	Mercedes-Benz O305 307001 61 022675	BBA	3698/3	H53/45F+11	1/81	1/81	-/--
573	FBG 220T	Mercedes-Benz O305 307001 61 022676	BBA	3698/4	H53/45F+11	1/81	1/81	-/--
574	FCH 196T	Mercedes-Benz O305 307001 61 022696	BBA	3698/5	H53/45F+11	1/81	1/81	by12/99
575	FBG 263T	Mercedes-Benz O305 307001 61 022697	BBA	3698/6	H53/45F+11	1/81	1/81	-/--
576	FBG 240T	Mercedes-Benz O305 307001 61 022717	BBA	3698/7	H53/45F+11	1/81	1/81	-/--
577	FBP 215T	Mercedes-Benz O305 307001 61 024238	BBA	3698/8	H53/45F+11	1/81	1/81	-/--
578	FCS 910T	Mercedes-Benz O305 307001 61 024284	BBA	3698/9	H53/45F+11	1/81	1/81	-/--
579	FBP 242T	Mercedes-Benz O305 307001 61 024331	BBA	3698/10	H53/45F+11	1/81	1/81	-/--
580	FBW 521T	Mercedes-Benz O305 307001 61 024556	BBA	3698/16	H53/45F+11	1/81	1/81	-/--
581	FBJ 327T	Mercedes-Benz O305 307001 61 024488	BBA	3698/11	H53/45F+11	2/81	2/81	-/--
582	FCD 048T	Mercedes-Benz O305 307001 61 024489	BBA	3698/14	H53/45F+11	1/81	1/81	-/--
583	FBP 285T	Mercedes-Benz O305 307001 61 024524	BBA	3698/12	H53/45F+11	1/81	1/81	-/--

584	FBP 259T	Mercedes-Benz O305 307001 61 024525	BBA	3698/15	H53/45F+11	1/81	1/81	-/--
585	FCD 101T	Mercedes-Benz O305 307001 61 024555	BBA	3698/13	H53/45F+11	1/81	1/81	-/--
586		Mercedes-Benz O305 307001 61 024598	BBA	3698/20	H53/45F+11	1/81	1/81	by 3/90
587	FBP 274T	Mercedes-Benz O305 307001 61 024599	BBA	3698/17	H53/45F+11	1/81	1/81	-/--
588	FBW 543T	Mercedes-Benz O305 307001 61 024636	BBA	3698/18	H53/45F+11	1/81	1/81	by12/99
589	FFH 075T	Mercedes-Benz O305 307001 61 024637	BBA	3698/19	H53/45F+11	2/81	2/81	by12/99
590	FKT 342T	Mercedes-Benz O305 307001 61 024679	BBA	3698/21	H53/41D+11	4/81	4/81	-/--
591	FMD 066T	Mercedes-Benz O305 307001 61 024722	BBA	3768/1	H53/45F+11	4/81	4/81	9/07
592	FMY 937T	Mercedes-Benz O305 307001 61 024723	BBA	3768/3	H53/45F+11	4/81	4/81	by12/99
593	FPP 788T	Mercedes-Benz O305 307001 61 024680	BBA	3768/2	H53/45F+11	6/81	6/81	by12/99
594	GSJ 956T	Mercedes-Benz O305 307001 61 029493	BBA	3915/6	H98F+13	5/82	5/82	-/--
595	GSK 011T	Mercedes-Benz O305 307001 61 029494	BBA	3915/1	H98F+13	5/82	5/82	9/07
596	GSV 316T	Mercedes-Benz O305 307001 61 029516	BBA	3915/2	H98F+13	6/82	6/82	-/--
597	GVK 336T	Mercedes-Benz O305 307001 61 029517	BBA	3915/11	H98F+13	6/82	6/82	-/--
598	GSK 014T	Mercedes-Benz O305 307001 61 029538x	BBA	3915/4	H98F+13	5/82	5/82	by12/99
599	GSV 293T	Mercedes-Benz O305 307001 61 029539	BBA	3915/4	H98F+13	5/82	5/82	by12/99
600	GSJ 950T	Mercedes-Benz O305 307001 61 029561	BBA	3915/5	H98F+13	6/82	6/82	by12/99
601	GSV 287T	Mercedes-Benz O305 307001 61 029562	BBA	3915/10	H98F+13	6/82	6/82	-/--
602	GTM 279T	Mercedes-Benz O305 307001 61 029584	BBA	3915/12	H98F+13	6/82	6/82	-/--
603	GTM 270T	Mercedes-Benz O305 307001 61 029836	BBA	3915/15	H98F+13	6/82	6/82	-/--
604	GSJ 938T	Mercedes-Benz O305 307001 61 029837	BBA	3915/7	H98F+13	7/82	7/82	-/--
605	GSY 684T	Mercedes-Benz O305 307001 61 029850	BBA	3915/8	H98F+13	6/82	6/82	by12/99
606	GTM 276T	Mercedes-Benz O305 307001 61 029851	BBA	3915/13	H98F+13	6/82	6/82	-/--
607	GSY 455T	Mercedes-Benz O305 307001 61 029864	BBA	3915/9	H98F+13	7/82	7/82	-/--
608	GTM 281T	Mercedes-Benz O305 307001 61 029865	BBA	3915/14	H98F+13	6/82	6/82	by12/99
609	GTM 251T	Mercedes-Benz O305 307001 61 029879	BBA	3915/16	H98F+13	6/82	6/82	-/--
610	GVK 349T	Mercedes-Benz O305 307001 61 029880	BBA	3915/17	H98F+13	6/82	6/82	by12/99
611	GYC 820T	Mercedes-Benz O305 307001 61 029894	BBA	3916/7	H98F+13	7/82	7/82	by12/99
612	GYJ 746T	Mercedes-Benz O305 307001 61 029895	BBA	3916/8	H98F+13	7/82	7/82	by12/99
613	GZL 377T	Mercedes-Benz O305 307001 61 029909	BBA	3916/9	H98F+13	8/82	8/82	-/--
614	GZL 378T	Mercedes-Benz O305 307001 61 029910	BBA	3916/10	H98F+13	8/82	8/82	-/--
615	GVK 324T	Mercedes-Benz O305 307001 61 029923	BBA	3915/19	H98F+13	6/82	6/82	-/--

616	GZL 375T	Mercedes-Benz O305 307001 61 029924	BBA	3916/11	H98F+13	7/82	7/82	-/--
617	GVK 374T	Mercedes-Benz O305 307001 61 029936	BBA	3915/20	H98F+13	7/82	7/82	-/--
618	GVK 339T	Mercedes-Benz O305 307001 61 029937	BBA	3915/21	H98F+13	7/82	7/82	-/--
619	GTM 271T	Mercedes-Benz O305 307001 61 029938	BBA	3915/18	H98F+13	7/82	7/82	-/--
620	GVT 467T	Mercedes-Benz O305 307001 61 029952	BBA	3915/22	H98F+13	6/82	6/82	-/--
621	GVK 325T	Mercedes-Benz O305 307001 61 029953	BBA	3915/23	H98F+13	6/82	6/82	by12/99
622	GVT 660T	Mercedes-Benz O305 307001 61 029965	BBA	3915/24	H98F+13	6/82	6/82	-/--
623	GVK 316T	Mercedes-Benz O305 307001 61 029966	BBA	3915/25	H98F+13	6/82	6/82	-/--
624	GVZ 229T	Mercedes-Benz O305 307001 61 029978	BBA	3916/1	H98F+13	7/82	7/82	-/--
625	GWF 581T	Mercedes-Benz O305 307001 61 029979	BBA	3916/2	H98F+13	7/82	7/82	9/07
626	GVZ 231T	Mercedes-Benz O305 307001 61 029992	BBA	3916/3	H98F+13	7/82	7/82	-/--
627	GWF 546T	Mercedes-Benz O305 307001 61 029993	BBA	3916/4	H98F+13	7/82	7/82	9/07
628	GXD 632T	Mercedes-Benz O305 307001 61 030005	BBA	3916/5	H98F+13	7/82	7/82	-/--
629	GYC 841T	Mercedes-Benz O305 307001 61 030006	BBA	3916/6	H98F+13	7/82	7/82	-/--
630	HBK 698T	Mercedes-Benz O305 307001 61 030175	BBA	3916/12	H98F+13	8/82	8/82	-/--
631	GZL 381T	Mercedes-Benz O305 307001 61 030189	BBA	3916/13	H98F+13	8/82	8/82	by12/99
632	HBK 689T	Mercedes-Benz O305 307001 61 030190	BBA	3916/18	H98F+13	8/82	8/82	by5/05
633	HBK 691T	Mercedes-Benz O305 307001 61 030216	BBA	3916/20	H98F+13	8/82	8/82	9/07
634	HBK 710T	Mercedes-Benz O305 307001 61 030217	BBA	3916/14	H98F+13	8/82	8/82	-/--
635	HBK 693T	Mercedes-Benz O305 307001 61 030230	BBA	3916/15	H98F+13	8/82	8/82	-/--
636	HBK 737T	Mercedes-Benz O305 307001 61 030231	BBA	3916/16	H98F+13	8/82	8/82	-/--
637	HBK 716T	Mercedes-Benz O305 307001 61 030245	BBA	3916/19	H98F+13	8/82	8/82	-/--
638	HBK 682T	Mercedes-Benz O305 307001 61 030246	BBA	3916/17	H98F+13	8/82	8/82	9/07
639	HHV 271T	Mercedes-Benz O305 307001 61 031510	BBA	3989/1	H98F+13	1/83	1/83	-/--
640	HHV 275T	Mercedes-Benz O305 307001 61 031549	BBA	3989/3	H98F+13	1/83	1/83	-/--
641	HHX 336T	Mercedes-Benz O305 307001 61 031530	BBA	3989/2	H98F+13	1/83	1/83	by12/99
642	HHX 343T	Mercedes-Benz O305 307001 61 031569	BBA	3989/4	H98F+13	1/83	1/83	9/07
643	HJB 083T	Mercedes-Benz O305 307001 61 031588	BBA	3989/5	H98F+13	1/83	1/83	-/--
644	HJF 744T	Mercedes-Benz O305 307001 61 031608	BBA	3989/6	H98F+13	1/83	1/83	-/--
645	JWJ 849T	Mercedes-Benz O305 307001 61 039427	BBA	4088/8	H98F+9	8/84	8/84	9/07
646	JWM 865T	Mercedes-Benz O305 307001 61 039449	BBA	4088/12	H98F+9	8/84	8/84	-/--
647	JWD 406T	Mercedes-Benz O305 307001 61 039472	BBA	4088/1	H98F+9	7/84	7/84	-/--

Alberton Municipality TDK 2718 (60) was one of the original batch of BBA bodied Leyland ERT2/1s placed in service when the operation commenced in February 1956, but was initially numbered 36. (Stewart J Brown)

Ten years later Alberton were still buying Leyland ERT2/1s with BBA bodywork, but the styling had changed considerably as seen on TDK 7690 (15), photographed in 1982. (Stewart J Brown)

TDK 10454 (106) was one of a batch of eleven Mercedes-Benz OH1517 with BBA bodies taken into stock in October 1970. Other similar buses were delivered to Alberton the following year. (Graham Shields)

In 1972 the Alberton fleet received its second batch of BBA bodied AEC Kudus, though they were badged as Leylands. The exact identity of TDK 17169 (117) is not known. (Andrew Johnson / Stan Hughes)

From its appearance TA 8675 (68) would appear to be a Leyland ERT2/1 with the standard style of BBA body, but no record has been found of it in official Benoni records. (Andrew Johnson / Stan Hughes)

1973 saw the arrival in Benoni of a batch of six Brockhouse bodied Mercedes Benz O302 buses of which TA 31644 (45) was an example. The same year also saw the arrival of eleven Brockhouse bodied Mercedes Benz OF1617 buses. (Stewart J Brown)

Contemporary with Benoni's 45 is this Mercedes Benz OF1117 with Transvaal Motor Body Builders 50 seat body. Boksburg's TB 25166 (25) was one of 27 broadly similar buses delivered between 1968 and 1972, some of which were longer vehicles. (Stewart J Brown)

In general the low mounted AEC radiator, as seen on Brakpan's TO 12665 (3), was found on the Ranger model which was less common that the Kudu model. The coachbuilder who produced the smart body is not recorded. (Andrew Johnson / Stan Hughes)

Nine AEC Regal IVs with standard BBA bodywork were taken into stock by Johannesburg in 1957/58. TJ 24274 (921) was the first of the series and was originally numbered 470, a number previously held by a Guy acquired with the Northern Bus Service company. (Andrew Johnson / Stan Hughes)

Johannesburg took delivery of a total of 30 Guy Arab IVs with three-axles, a Rolls-Royce engine and a BBA body. They also introduced a new style of bonnet, which became known as a Johannesburg front. TJ 161.248 (461) was one of the first batch of ten. (Alan Mortimer)

Around the same time as the Guys were being delivered some more standard AEC Regent Vs, also fitted with BBA bodies were arriving in large numbers. TJ 171.553 (244) was one of the batch of sixty delivered to Johannesburg in 1959. (Andrew Johnson / Stan Hughes)

Johannesburg trolleybuses have never carried registration numbers, only fleet numbers. Delivered in 1958 1639 (originally 639) was one of a batch of fifty BUT 9642T with BBA bodywork seating 73 with 19 standing. (John Squier)

As well as AEC Regal IVs, Johannesburg also bought a batch of 45 of the later AEC Regal VI model, all of which carried bodies made by Craftsman. TJ 243.229 (23) is one of the 1966 delivery. (Andrew Johnson / Stan Hughes)

The first rear engined double deckers in the Johannesburg fleet were a batch of fourteen Bristol VRL-LH6Ls with BBA bodywork. TJ 279.824 (324) is seen in the centre of Johannesburg. Some received Cummins engines and all were downseated in later years. (Alan Mortimer)

TJ 301.117 (46) was the first of a delivery of ten Craftsman 60 seater Daimler Roadliners. Never a particularly popular chassis both in the UK and overseas, they were not repeated in future Johannesburg orders. (Andrew Johnson / Stan Hughes)

1971 saw the start of many deliveries of Mercedes Benz O305 single deckers with Craftsman bodies, though some later deliveries carried Brockhouse or BBA bodies. TJ 345.546 (111) was one of those fitted with Craftsman 34 seater, dual entrance standee bodies. (Andrew Johnson / Stan Hughes)

In amongst the hoards of M-B O305s was a small batch of AEC Kudus for Johannesburg. TJ 15657 (721) was one of five delivered in April 1973 and was bodied by BBA. As was often the case, it carried Leyland identification, but also the Kudu badge in this case. (Andrew Johnson / Stan Hughes)

After taking large numbers of M-B O305s Johannesburg reverted to rear engined double deckers most being Daimler CRG6LX or Leyland FE30AGR, all with the standard BBA bodywork. TJ 435.604 (466) displays its brightly painted advertising livery. (Andrew Johnson / Stan Hughes)

In 1977 one of the earlier Johannesburg AEC Regent Vs received a totally new BBA body after the chassis had been extensively rebuilt. In its original form TJ 191.501 (999) dated from 1959, but the resultant bus looked very different from the original. (Andrew Johnson / Stan Hughes)

TJ 199.118 (501) was the forerunner of a large fleet of Mercedes Benz O305 fitted with BBA double deck bodies seating 96 or 98 passengers, though 501 initially only seated 90. Some of the double deckers were in fact rebodied Johannesburg single deckers from earlier years. (Andrew Johnson / Stan Hughes)

Kempton Park Bus Service was an independent company which sold out to Kempton Park Municipality in 1963. TCD 6003 (4) was a Leyland ERT2/1, originally fitted with BBA body, but by 1976 it had been rebodied with this stylish Springfield 65 seat body. (Graham Shields)

TCD 7818 (12) was a most unusual purchase by Kempton Park Municipality. It was a DAF with a 66 seat body by Trio. Later renumbered 16, it remained unique in the fleet. (Graham Shields)

Daimler Roadliners were found in a few fleets in South Africa, the Nigel Municipality being one of them. TDG 5409 (13) is one of a quartet purchased in 1967. They carried Transvaal Motor Body Builders bodies. (Daimler, via Jim Neale)

Later deliveries to Nigel included this Leyland, TDG 10943 (65), photographed in 1982, but for which details are lacking. It is quite possible that there were other similar buses purchased at the same time. (Stewart J Brown)

A number of municipalities in South Africa took deliveries of ECW bodied Bristol LWL6G buses. Roodepoort was one of them and in 1968 TU 6047 (6) was still active, though rarely saw service. Its twin, TU 6048 (7) had already been withdrawn. (Graham Shields)

Late 1956 saw the arrival of TU 6126 (9), an AEC Regal IV with Transvaal Motor Body Builders 66 seat body. The fleet was quite a mixed bag at this point, although later deliveries concentrated on AECs for some years. (Graham Shields)

Just six months after 9 was delivered, TU 6015 (10) was taken into stock. It was a Leyland ERT2/1 with Africa Body & Coach bodywork, the only such vehicle operated. For the next three years Roodepoort standardised on AEC Regal IVs. (Graham Shields)

TU 32644 (30) was another Leyland ERT2/1, but delivered some fourteen years after number 10. It was one of a small batch of five with Brockhouse 66 seat bodies, all of which entered service in 1972. (Stewart J Brown)

Springs Municipality was another which operated ECW bodied Bristol LWL6Gs in the early postwar years, twelve in all. TS 8196 (4) was one of the first batch of six, entering service in 1949 and seen here amid the palm trees at the bus station. (Graham Shields)

When Bristol chassis were no longer available Springs turned to the Guy Arab chassis, mostly Mark IV models, which it bought in large numbers. TS 13018 (39) was fitted with a full front body by Transvaal Motor Body Builders. (Stewart J Brown)

In 1967 and 1969 Springs took delivery of twenty Guy Warriors with Transvaal Motor Body Builders bodies. All passed to PUTCO when the Springs non-white operations passed to that operator. The newer vehicles remained to operate the whites-only services. (Graham Shields)

Springs Municipality was one of many who operated AEC Kudus, their entire fleet of thirty four being bodied by Transvaal Motor Body Builders. TS 18804 (17) was one of the last five delivered in 1967. (Stewart J Brown)

648	JWG 451T	Mercedes-Benz O305 307001 61 039494	BBA	4088/9	H98F+9	7/84	7/84	9/07
649	JWD 395T	Mercedes-Benz O305 307001 61 039495	BBA	4088/2	H98F+9	7/84	7/84	-/--
650	JWJ 830T	Mercedes-Benz O305 307001 61 039516	BBA	4088/10	H98F+9	8/84	8/84	9/07
651	JWD 399T	Mercedes-Benz O305 307001 61 039517	BBA	4088/3	H98F+9	7/84	7/84	9/07
652	JWJ 821T	Moroodco Bonz O305 307001 61 039537	BBA	4088/13	II90Г19	0/04	0/04	-/--
653	JWD 392T	Mercedes-Benz O305 307001 61 039538	BBA	4088/4	H98F+9	7/84	7/84	-/--
654	JWM 858T	Mercedes-Benz O305 307001 61 039557	BBA	4088/14	H98F+9	8/84	8/84	-/--
655	JWG 445T	Mercedes-Benz O305 307001 61 039558	BBA	4088/6	H98F+9	8/84	8/84	-/--
656	JWD 409T	Mercedes-Benz O305 307001 61 039576	BBA	4088/5	H98F+9	8/84	8/84	-/--
657	JWG 422T	Mercedes-Benz O305 307001 61 039577	BBA	4088/7	H98F+9	8/84	8/84	-/--
658	JWJ 809T	Mercedes-Benz O305 307001 61 039596	BBA	4088/11	H98F+9	8/84	8/84	-/--
659	JWM 849T	Mercedes-Benz O305 307001 61 039597	BBA	4088/15	H98F+9	8/84	8/84	-/--
660	JWS 374T	Mercedes-Benz O305 307001 61 039613	BBA	4089/1	H98F+9	8/84	8/84	-/--
661	JWW 921T	Mercedes-Benz O305 307001 61 039614	BBA	4089/2	H98F+9	8/84	8/84	-/--
662	JWW 914T	Mercedes-Benz O305 307001 61 039631	BBA	4089/3	H98F+9	8/84	8/84	9/07
663	JXG 592T	Mercedes-Benz O305 307001 61 039632	BBA	4089/4	H98F+9	8/84	8/84	9/07
664	JXD 632T	Mercedes-Benz O305 307001 61 039648	BBA	4089/5	H98F+9	8/84	8/84	9/07
665	JXC 257T	Mercedes-Benz O305 307001 61 039649	BBA	4089/6	H98F+9	8/84	8/84	-/--
666	JXH 232T	Mercedes-Benz O305 307001 61 039823	BBA	4089/11	H98F+9	8/84	8/84	-/--
667	JXC 229T	Mercedes-Benz O305 307001 61 039824	BBA	4089/7	H98F+9	8/84	8/84	9/07
668	JXT 515T	Mercedes-Benz O305 307001 61 039840	BBA	4089/15	H98F+9	9/84	9/84	-/--
669	JXG 597T	Mercedes-Benz O305 307001 61 039841	BBA	4089/8	H98F+9	8/84	8/84	-/--
670	JXH 225T	Mercedes-Benz O305 307001 61 039857	BBA	4089/9	H98F+9	8/84	8/84	-/-
671	JXH 372T	Mercedes-Benz O305 307001 61 039858	BBA	4089/10	H98F+9	8/84	8/84	-/--
672	JXH 358T	Mercedes-Benz O305 307001 61 039874	BBA	4089/12	H98F+9	8/84	8/84	-/--
673	JXT 523T	Mercedes-Benz O305 307001 61 039875	BBA	4089/13	H98F+9	9/84	9/84	9/07
674	JXT 517T	Mercedes-Benz O305 307001 61 039891	BBA	4089/14	H98F+9	9/84	9/84	9/07
690	DYZ 938T	Mercedes-Benz O305 307001 61 022262	Springfield		H52/45F+2	11/80		by12/99
691	FFC 224T	Mercedes-Benz O305 307001 61 022241	Springfield		H52/45F+2	1/81	1/81	-/--
692	FPH 760T	Mercedes-Benz O305 307001 61 022240	Springfield		H52/45F+2	6/81	6/81	-/--
693	FTF 455T	Mercedes-Benz O305 307001 61 022263	Springfield		H52/45F+2	6/81	6/81	-/--
694	FKH 602T	Mercedes-Benz O305 307001 61 022283	Springfield		H52/45F+2	3/81	3/81	-/--

695	FTV 811T	Mercedes-Benz O305 307001 61 022284	Springfield		H52/45F+2	7/81	7/81	-/--
696	FPZ 385T	Mercedes-Benz O305 307001 61 022633	Springfield		H52/45F+2	6/81	6/81	-/--
697	FNV 284T	Mercedes-Benz O305 307001 61 022634	Springfield		H52/45F+2	5/81	5/81	-/--
698	FMD 079T	Mercedes-Benz O305 307001 61 022654	Springfield		H52/45F+2	4/81	4/81	-/--
699	FMH 411T	Mercedes-Benz O305 307001 61 022655	Springfield		H52/45F+2	6/81	6/81	-/--
701	MHB 116T	Mercedes-Benz O305 307001 61 050527	BBA	4381/2	H57/41F+11	12/87	12/87	9/07
702	MKB 628T	Mercedes-Benz O305 307001 61 050543	BBA	4381/10	H57/41F+11	1/88	1/88	9/07
703	MFZ 579T	Mercedes-Benz O305 307001 61 050544	BBA	4381/4	H57/41F+11	12/87	12/87	9/07
704	MLX 718T	Mercedes-Benz O305 307001 61 050561	BBA	4382/1	H57/41F+11	1/88	1/88	9/07
705	MHB 115T	Mercedes-Benz O305 307001 61 050577	BBA	4381/5	H57/41F+11	12/87	12/87	9/07
706	MLX 729T	Mercedes-Benz O305 307001 61 050578	BBA	4382/2	H57/41F+11	1/88	1/88	9/07
707	MHF 873T	Mercedes-Benz O305 307001 61 050611	BBA	4381/6	H57/41F+11	12/87	12/87	C
708	MJW 704T	Mercedes-Benz O305 307001 61 050612	BBA	4381/7	H57/41F+11	1/88	1/88	-/--
709	MHB 117T	Mercedes-Benz O305 307001 61 050645	BBA	4381/1	H57/41F+11	12/87	12/87	9/07
710	MJW 737T	Mercedes-Benz O305 307001 61 050646	BBA	4381/8	H57/41F+11	1/88	1/88	9/07
711	MKD 945T	Mercedes-Benz O305 307001 61 050662	BBA	4381/9	H57/41F+11	1/88	1/88	-/--
712	MMB 648T	Mercedes-Benz O305 307001 61 050679	BBA	4382/3	H57/41F+11	1/88	1/88	9/07
713	MJZ 903T	Mercedes-Benz O305 307001 61 050680	BBA	4383/1	H57/41F+11	2/88	2/88	9/07
714	MFZ 578T	Mercedes-Benz O305 307001 61 050696	BBA	4381/3	H57/41F+11	1/88	1/88	9/07
715	MMF 727T	Mercedes-Benz O305 307001 61 050714	BBA	4382/4	H57/41F+11	2/88	2/88	9/07
716	MGB 194T	Mercedes-Benz O305 307001 61 050743	BBA	4382/5	H57/41F+11	2/88	2/88	-/--
717	MMZ 380T	Mercedes-Benz O305 307001 61 050744	BBA	4382/6	H57/41F+11	2/88	2/88	-/--
718	MLX 737T	Mercedes-Benz O305 307001 61 050759	BBA	4382/7	H57/41F+11	1/88	1/88	9/07
719	MLL 236T	Mercedes-Benz O305 307001 61 050760	BBA	4382/8	H57/41F+11	2/88	2/88	9/07
720	MJZ 868T	Mercedes-Benz O305 307001 61 050775	BBA	4382/9	H57/41F+11	3/88	3/88	9/07
721	MRN 134T	Mercedes-Benz O305 307001 61 050776	BBA	4383/2	H57/41F+11	4/88	4/88	9/07
722	MPL 679T	Mercedes-Benz O305 307001 61 050806	BBA	4383/4	H57/41F+11	4/88	4/88	9/07
723	MPL 669T	Mercedes-Benz O305 307001 61 050807	BBA	4383/3	H57/41F+11	3/88	3/88	-/--
724	MMB 741T	Mercedes-Benz O305 307001 61 050822	BBA	4382/10	H57/41F+11	2/88	2/88	9/07
725	MPL 416T	Mercedes-Benz O305 307001 61 050823	BBA	4383/5	H57/41F+11	3/88	3/88	9/07
726	MPR 241T	Mercedes-Benz O305 307001 61 050838	BBA	4383/6	H57/41F+11	3/88	3/88	-/--
727	MPL 658T	Mercedes-Benz O305 307001 61 050839	BBA	4383/7	H57/41F+11	3/88	3/88	-/--

728	MRN 127T	Mercedes-Benz O305 307001 61 050854	BBA	4383/8	H57/41F+11	5/88	5/88	9/07
729	MRV 429T	Mercedes-Benz O305 307001 61 050855	BBA	4383/9	H57/41F+11	4/88	4/88	9/07
730	MRY 177T	Mercedes-Benz O305 307001 61 050884	BBA	4383/10	H57/41F+11	5/88	5/88	9/07
731	NRL 897T	Mercedes-Benz O305 307001 26 000061	BBA	4488/1	H57/41F+10	12/89	12/89	9/07
732	NRL 928T	Mercedes-Benz O305 307001 26 000062	BBA	4488/2	H57/41F+10	12/80	12/80	-/--
733	NRN 238T	Mercedes-Benz O305 307001 26 000063	BBA	4488/3	H57/41F+10	12/89	12/89	-/--
734	NRP 323T	Mercedes-Benz O305 307001 26 000064	BBA	4488/4	H57/41F+10	12/89	12/89	9/07
735	NRP 329T	Mercedes-Benz O305 307001 26 000065	BBA	4488/5	H57/41F+10	12/89	12/89	9/07
736	NRV 278T	Mercedes-Benz O305 307001 26 000066	BBA	4488/6	H57/41F+10	12/89	12/89	by12/99
737	NSW 124T	Mercedes-Benz O305 307001 26 000067	BBA	4488/7	H57/41F+10	12/89	12/89	9/07
738	NSD 596T	Mercedes-Benz O305 307001 26 000068	BBA	4488/8	H57/41F+10	12/89	12/89	9/07
739	NSD 591T	Mercedes-Benz O305 307001 26 000069	BBA	4488/9	H57/41F+10	12/89	12/89	9/07
740	NSD 587T	Mercedes-Benz O305 307001 26 000070	BBA	4488/10	H57/41F+10	12/89	12/89	-/--
741	NSR 388T	Mercedes-Benz O305 307001 26 000071	BBA	4489/1	H57/41F+10	12/89	12/89	9/07
742	NSD 585T	Mercedes-Benz O305 307001 26 000072	BBA	4489/2	H57/41F+10	12/89	12/89	9/07
743	NSR 394T	Mercedes-Benz O305 307001 26 000073	BBA	4489/3	H57/41F+10	12/89	12/89	9/07
744	NSR 398T	Mercedes-Benz O305 307001 26 000074	BBA	4489/4	H57/41F+10	12/89	12/89	9/07
745	NSZ 603T	Mercedes-Benz O305 307001 26 000075	BBA	4489/5	H57/41F+10	12/89	12/89	-/--
746	NSZ 604T	Mercedes-Benz O305 307001 26 000076	BBA	4489/6	H57/41F+10	12/89	12/89	-/--
747	NSZ 606T	Mercedes-Benz O305 307001 26 000077	BBA	4489/7	H57/41F+10	12/89	12/89	-/--
748	NTH 770T	Mercedes-Benz O305 307001 26 000078	BBA	4489/8	H57/41F+10	1/90	1/90	-/--
749	NVJ 101T	Mercedes-Benz O305 307001 26 000079	BBA	4489/9	H57/41F+10	1/90	1/90	9/07
750	NVJ 102T	Mercedes-Benz O305 307001 26 000080	BBA	4489/10	H57/41F+10	1/90	1/90	9/07
800	NXZ 623T	Mercedes-Benz O305 307200 21 025125	?		H57/41F+10	-/81	3/90	-/--
801	MTW 901T	Mercedes-Benz O305 30700161044338	BBA	4268/1	H100F+9	6/86	1/88	9/07
802	NWM 151T	MAN 10.1704690042G045177	BBA	4462/1	B32F+18	12/88	3/90	4/90
	NXR 379T	Mercedes-Benz O811/42 688177618-----	?		B25F+12	3/90	4/90	by5/95
		Mercedes-Benz O305	BBA	4549/1	B--F	8/90	8/90	-/--

Re-registered:
FBJ 308T (570) to FJD 810GP c1996.
FBG 164T (571) to FJD 806GP c1996.
FBG 248T (572) to FRH 987GP c1996.
FBG 220T (573) to HLC 932GP c1996.
FBG 263T (575) to HLC 925GP c1996.
FBG 240T (576) to HLC 943GP c1996.
FBP 215T (577) to HLC 929GP c1996.
FCS 910T (578) to HLC 921GP c1996.

FBP 242T (579) to HLC 935GP c1996.
FBW 521T (580) to HLC 917GP c1996.
FBJ 327T (581) to FVX 854GP c1996.
FCD 048T (582) to HKX 435GP c1996.
FBP 285T (583) to HFC 455GP c1996.
FBP 259T (584) to HBC 080GP c1996.
FCD 101T (585) to FRK 567GP c1996.
FBP 274T (587) to FLV 971GP c1996.
FKT 342T (590) to HBC 113GP c1996.
FMD 066T (591) to FLV 968GP c1996.
FMY 937T (592) to FHY 311GP c1996.
GSJ 956T (594) to HBC 086GP c1996.
GSK 011T (595) to FLV 965GP c1996.
GSV 316T (596) to FHZ 638GP c1996.
GVK 336T (597) to FHX 137GP c1996.
GSK 014T (598) to FGG 412GP c1996.
GSV 293T (599) to FGG 413GP c1996.
GSJ 950T (600) to HBC 092GP c1996.
GSV 287T (601) to FRK 564GP c1996.
GTM 279T (602) to FHZ 563GP c1996.
GTM 270T (603) to FHZ 145GP c1996.
GSJ 938T (604) to FXT 463GP c1996.
GSY 684T (605) to FHZ 624GP c1996.
GTM 276T (606) to FHZ 173GP c1996.
GSY 455T (607) to FHY 309GP c1996.
GTM 281T (608) to FHZ 622GP c1996.
GTM 251T (609) to FHZ 154GP c1996.
GZL 377T (613) to FGG 440GP c1996.
GZL 378T (614) to HKZ 437GP c1996.
GVK 324T (615) to FHZ 132GP c1996.
GZL 375T (616) to FGG 428GP c1996.
GVK 374T (617) to FHZ 125GP c1996.
GVK 339T (618) to FHZ 129GP c1996.
GTM 271T (619) to FHZ 137GP c1996.
GVT 467T (620) to HFC 454GP c1996.
GVK 325T (621) to FHZ 619GP c1996.
GVT 660T (622) to FLV 495GP c1996.
GVK 316T (623) to FHY 307GP c1996.
GVZ 229T (624) to FLV 503GP c1996.
GWF 581T (625) to FRJ 002GP c1996.
GVZ 231T (626) to FLW 025GP c1996.
GWF 546T (627) to FLW 028GP c1996.
GXD 632T (628) to FRH 984GP c1996.
GYC 841T (629) to FRH 991GP c1996.
HBK 698T (630) to FVF 847GP c1996.
GZL 381T (631) to FVF 880GP c1996.
HBK 689T (632) to FVF 882GP c1996.
HBK 691T (633) to FVH 069GP c1996.
HBK 710T (634) to FZS 737GP c1996.
HBK 693T (635) to DGF 409GP c1996.
HBK 737T (636) to FVF 884GP c1996.
HBK 716T (637) to FVF 885GP c1996.
HBK 682T (638) to FVH 086GP c1996.
HHV 271T (639) to HKB 134GP c1996.
HHV 275T (640) to HJZ 389GP c1996.
HHX 343T (642) to HJZ 388GP c1996.
HJB 083T (643) to FJD 044GP c1996.
HJF 744T (644) to HJZ 387GP c1996.
JWJ 849T (645) to FVH 085GP c1996.
JWM 865T (646) to FVH 084GP c1996.
JWD 406T (647) to FVH 083GP c1996.
JWG 451T (648) to FVH 082GP c1996.
JWD 395T (649) to FVH 081GP c1996.
JWJ 830T (650) to FVH 080GP c1996.

JWD 399T (651) to FVH 079GP c1996.
JWJ 821T (652) to FVH 078GP c1996.
JWD 392T (653) to FVH 077GP c1996.
JWM 858T (654) to FVF 383GP c1996.
JWG 445T (655) to FVF 386GP c1996.
JWD 409T (656) to FVF 897GP c1996.
JWG 422T (657) to FVH 417GP c1996.
JWJ 809T (658) to FVF 873GP c1996.
JWM 849T (659) to FVF 871GP c1990.
JWS 374T (660) to FZS 735GP c1996.
JWW 921T (661) to HLC 937GP c1996.
JWW 914T (662) to FYB 770GP c1996.
JXG 592T (663) to FYB 788GP c1996.
JXD 632T (664) to FYB 868GP c1996.
JXC 257T (665) to FYB 722GP c1996.
JXH 232T (666) to FYB 787GP c1996.
JXC 229T (667) to FYB 775GP c1996.
JXT 515T (668) to FYB 783GP c1996.
JXG 597T (669) to FYB 781GP c1996.
JXH 225T (670) to FYB 779GP c1996.
JXH 372T (671) to FYB 778GP c1996.
JXH 358T (672) to FYB 776GP c1996.
JXT 523T (673) to FLW 031GP c1996.
JXT 517T (674) to FVF 864GP c1996.
FFC 224T (691) to HNY 122GP c1996.
FPH 760T (692) to FHZ 617GP c1996.
FTF 455T (693) to FRK 592GP c1996.
FKH 602T (694) to HBC 527GP c1996.
FTV 811T (695) to HHY 947GP c1996.
FPZ 385T (696) to FLV 492GP c1996.
FNV 284T (697) to FHY 308GP c1996.
FMD 079T (698) to HBC 096GP c1996.
FMH 411T (699) to NBM 753GP c1996.
MHB 116T (701) to FXT 460GP c1996.
MKB 628T (702) to FLV 537GP c1996.
MFZ 579T (703) to FLV 539GP c1996.
MLX 718T (704) to HFC 453GP c1996.
MHB 115T (705) to FLV 532GP c1996.
MLX 729T (706) to HFC 452GP c1996.
MHF 873T (707) to FLV 527GP c1996, withdrawn date unknown, reinstated -/09 : re-registered YBM
        925GP.
MJW 704T (708) to HFC 116GP c1996.
MHB 117T (709) to HBC 088GP c1996.
MJW 737T (710) to FLV 524GP c1996.
MKD 945T (711) to FLV 520GP c1996.
MMB 648T (712) to HBB 663GP c1996.
MJZ 903T (713) to FRK 562GP c1996.
MFZ 578T (714) to HFC 115GP c1996.
MMF 727T (715) to FRK 561GP c1996.
MGB 194T (716) to HFC 113GP c1996.
MMZ 380T (717) to HBC 094GP c1996.
MLX 737T (718) to HNY 125GP c1996.
MLL 236T (719) to FLV 515GP c1996.
MJZ 868T (720) to HNY 127GP c1996.
MRN 134T (721) to FVB 029GP c1996.
MPL 679T (722) to FGG 409GP c1996.
MPL 669T (723) to FLV 511GP c1996.
MMB 741T (724) to HNY 128GP c1996.
MPL 416T (725) to HNY 132GP c1996.
MPR 241T (726) to HBC 102GP c1996.
MPL 658T (727) to FLV 510GP c1996.
MRN 127T (728) to FHZ 142GP c1996.
MRV 429T (729) to FHY 317GP c1996.
MRY 177T (730) to FHY 313GP c1996.

NRL 897T (731) to HFC 112GP c1996.
NRL 928T (732) to HFC 109GP c1996.
NRN 238T (733) to FVB 033GP c1996.
NRP 323T (734) to HFC 108GP c1996.
NRP 329T (735) to FGG 425GP c1996.
NRV 278T (736) to FGD 329GP c1996.
NSW 124T (737) to HHY 951GP c1996.
NSD 596T (738) to HFC 118GP c1996.
NSD 591T (739) to HFC 103GP c1996.
NSD 587T (740) to HFY 154GP c1996, later to TSK 371GP c2006.
NSR 388T (741) to HJZ 385GP c1996.
NSD 585T (742) to HFY 153GP c1996.
NSR 394T (743) to HKB 157GP c1996.
NSR 398T (744) to HKB 158GP c1996.
NSZ 603T (745) to HKB 161GP c1996.
NSZ 604T (746) to HKB 164GP c1996.
NSZ 606T (747) to HKB 135GP c1996.
NTH 770T (748) to DGK 943GP c1996.
NVJ 101T (749) to HMP 657GP c1996.
NVJ 102T (750) to HMP 658GP c1996.

Notes:

GTM 270/81T, GVK 339T (603/8/18) rebuilt to open top by 5/06.

GTM 270T (603) was the vehicle repainted in a "Boks" livery for the triumphal tour of several South African cities by the victorious South African Rugby football team in October 2007. The 23 year old vehicle completed its 1500+ mile tour without experiencing any mechanical problems.

DYZ 938T, FFC 224T, FPH 760T, FKH 602T, FNV 284T, FMD 079T, FMH 411T (690-2/4/7-9) later noted as H93F+10.

FMH 411T (699) rebuilt to open top by 5/07 (tree cutter in 5/09).

MLL 236T (719) reported carrying chassis no. 307001 61 050759 in 10/04.

NXZ 623T (800) ex Trolleybus 800; Re-registered to FGG 416GP c1996.

MTW 901T (801) ex City Tramways 2030 (CA 585.457), new as a Mercedes-Benz demonstrator. Re-registered to FRK 593GP c1996.

NWM 151T (802) was built as a demonstrator for Durban Municipality. It demonstrated to JMT in 1990, later to Roodepoort Municipality and was acquired by JMT c2000, registered. LZM 676GP.

NXR 379T was on loan 4/90, perhaps a demonstrator.

Disposals:

FBG 263T (575): Giraffe Express, Sedgefield, Eastern Cape by 10/08.

FMD 066T (591): Algoa Bus, Port Elizabeth 9/09, named TATA.

NRV 278T (736): burnt out.

NVJ 102T (750): Algoa Bus, Port Elizabeth 3/08, named BIG BROTHER.

1	RYD 943T	ERF E6	71670	Mödling Citybus	B50F+33	8/93	8/93	by2/06
2	RYD 939T	ERF E6	71672	Mödling Citybus	B50F+33	8/93	8/93	by2/06
3	RYD 932T	ERF E6	71673	Mödling Citybus	B50F+33	8/93	8/93	by2/06
4	RYD 949T	ERF E6	70934	Mödling Citybus	B50F+33	9/93	9/93	by2/06
5	RYD 928T	ERF E6	70933	Mödling Citybus	B50F+33	9/93	9/93	by2/06
6	RYD 946T	ERF E6	71671	Mödling Citybus	B50F+33	8/93	8/93	by2/06
7	RYF 499T	MAN 16.240	36002591139	Mödling Citybus	B50F+37	7/93	7/93	by2/06
8	RYF 503T	MAN 16.240	36002571132	Mödling Citybus	B50F+37	7/93	7/93	by2/06
9	RYF 501T	MAN 16.240	36002581135	Mödling Citybus	B50F+37	7/93	7/93	-/--
10	RZY 304T	MAN 16.240	36002551119	Mödling Citybus	B50F+37	9/93	9/93	-/--
11	RZY 294T	MAN 16.240	36002561130	Mödling Citybus	B50F+37	9/93	9/93	-/--
12	SBZ 643T	MAN 16.240	72600160016	Mödling Citybus	B50F+22	10/93	10/93	-/--
13	SCG 041T	MAN 16.240	72600190777	Mödling Citybus	B50F+22	10/93	10/93	-/--
14	SCL 411T	MAN 16.240	72500200814	Mödling Citybus	B50F+22	11/93	11/93	-/--
15	SCV 416T	MAN 16.240	72600180774	Mödling Citybus	B50F+22	11/93	11/93	-/--
16	SDG 827T	MAN 16.240	72600170773	Mödling Citybus	B50F+22	11/93	11/93	-/--
17	SDM 236T	ERF	73535	Mödling Citybus	B49F+31	11/93	11/93	-/--
18	SDS 811T	ERF	73762	Mödling Citybus	B49F+31	12/93	12/93	-/--
19	SDS 647T	ERF	73761	Mödling Citybus	B49F+31	12/93	12/93	-/--
20	SDS 644T	ERF	73959	Mödling Citybus	B49F+31	12/93	12/93	-/--
21	SFB 686T	ERF	73396	Mödling Citybus	B49F+31	12/93	12/93	-/--

22	SGD 771T	ERF		73395	Mödling Citybus	B49F+31	1/94	1/94	
23	SGL 891T	ERF		73763	Mödling Citybus	B49F+31	1/94	1/94	
24	SGR 141T	ERF		73964	Mödling Citybus	B49F+31	2/94	2/94	
25	SGV 464T	ERF		73759	Mödling Citybus	B49F+31	2/94	2/94	
26	SGZ 000T	ERF		73963	Mödling Citybus	B49F+31	2/94	2/94	
27	SHG 807T	ERF		73097	Mödling Citybus	B49F+31	2/94	2/94	
28	SHN 794T	ERF		73536	Mödling Citybus	B49F+31	3/94	3/94	
29	SJP 533T	ERF		73099	Mödling Citybus	B49F+31	3/94	3/94	
30	SKV 776T	ERF		73537	Mödling Citybus	B40F+31	3/94	3/94	
31	SHT 565T	ERF		73393	Mödling Citybus	B49F+31	3/94	3/94	
32	SLJ 070T	ERF		74121	Mödling Citybus	B49F+31	3/94	3/94	
33	SLJ 074T	ERF		73100	Mödling Citybus	B49F+31	4/94	4/94	
34	SLR 361T	ERF		73760	Mödling Citybus	B49F+31	5/94	5/94	
35	SLZ 570T	ERF		73098	Mödling Citybus	B49F+31	5/94	5/94	
36	SMF 158T	ERF		73538	Mödling Citybus	B49F+31	5/94	5/94	
37	SMM 681T	ERF		73962	Mödling Citybus	B49F+31	6/94	6/94	
38	SMZ 503T	ERF		73394	Mödling Citybus	B49F+31	6/94	6/94	
39	SNH 988T	ERF		73960	Mödling Citybus	B49F+31	6/94	6/94	by12/99
40	SNR 851T	ERF		73961	Mödling Citybus	B49F+31	7/94	7/94	
41	SPK 349T	ERF		73758	Mödling Citybus	B49F+31	7/94	7/94	
42	SPK 339T	ERF		70359	Mödling Citybus	B49F+31	7/94	7/94	
43	SRN 632T	ERF	90086190074124	BBA	4720/1	B50F+37	7/94	7/94	
44	SRY 690T	ERF	90086190074126	BBA	4720/3	B50F+37	8/94	8/94	
45	SSK 038T	ERF	90086190074329	BBA	4720/4	B50F+37	9/94	9/94	by2/06
46	SSK 059T	ERF	90086190074330	BBA	4720/5	B50F+37	9/94	9/94	
47	SST 819T	ERF	90086190074331	BBA	4720/6	B50F+37	10/94	10/94	
48	SST 832T	ERF	90086190074332	BBA	4720/7	B50F+37	10/94	10/94	
49	SST 824T	ERF	90086190075749	BBA	4720/8	B50F+37	10/94	10/94	
50	SST 828T	ERF	90086190074125	BBA	4720/2	B50F+37	10/94	10/94	
51	STG 468T	ERF	90086190075750	BBA	4720/9	B50F+37	10/94	10/94	
52	STG 472T	ERF	90086190075751	BBA	4720/10	B50F+37	10/94	10/94	
53	STR 838T	ERF	90086190075752	BBA	4720/11	B50F+37	11/94	11/94	
54	STX 251T	ERF	90086190075753	BBA	4720/12	B50F+37	11/94	11/94	
55	STZ 224T	ERF	90086190075755	BBA	4720/14	B50F+37	11/94	11/94	
56	STZ 237T	ERF	90086190075754	BBA	4720/13	B50F+37	11/94	11/94	
57	SVR 384T	ERF	90086190075971	BBA	4720/15	B50F+37	12/94	12/94	
58	SVR 382T	ERF	90086190075972	BBA	4720/16	B50F+37	12/94	12/94	
59	SVV 216T	ERF	90086190075973	BBA	4720/17	B50F+37	12/94	12/94	
60	SVV 220T	ERF	90086190075974	BBA	4720/18	B50F+37	12/94	12/94	
61	SVY 208T	ERF	90086190075976	BBA	4720/20	B50F+37	12/94	12/94	
62	SVZ 255T	ERF	90086190075977	BBA	4720/21	B50F+37	12/94	12/94	
63	SWB 236T	ERF	90086190075978	BBA	4720/22	B50F+37	12/94	12/94	
64	SWB 497T	ERF	90086190076073	BBA	4720/23	B50F+37	12/94	12/94	
65	SWB 245T	ERF	90086190076074	BBA	4720/24	B50F+37	12/94	12/94	
66	SWC 769T	ERF	90086190075975	BBA	4720/19	B50F+37	12/94	12/94	
67	SXC 251T	ERF	90086190075075	BBA	4720/25	B50F+37	12/94	12/94	
68	SWB 419T	ERF	90086190076076	BBA	4720/26	B50F+37	12/94	12/94	by12/99
69	SWC 774T	ERF	90086190076070	BBA	4720/27	B50F+37	12/94	12/94	
70	SWC 256T	ERF	90086190076069	BBA	4720/28	B50F+37	12/94	12/94	
71	SWF 702T	ERF	90086190076071	BBA	4720/29	B50F+37	12/94	12/94	
72	SWF 699T	ERF	90086190076072	BBA	4720/30	B50F+37	12/94	12/94	
73	SXF 164T	ERF	90086190076187	BBA	4720/31	B50F+37	1/95	1/95	
74	SWT 944T	ERF	90086190076188	BBA	4720/32	B50F+37	1/95	1/95	
75	SWT 961T	ERF	90086190076189	BBA	4720/33	B50F+37	1/95	1/95	
76	SXP 299T	ERF	90086190076190	BBA	4720/34	B50F+37	1/95	1/95	
77	SXF 177T	ERF	90086190076191	BBA	4720/35	B50F+37	1/95	1/95	
78	SXX 866T	ERF	90086190076192	BBA	4720/36	B50F+37	2/95	2/95	by2/06
79	SXX 843T	ERF	90086190076193	BBA	4720/37	B50F+37	2/95	2/95	
80	SYR 694T	ERF	90086190076194	BBA	4720/38	B50F+37	2/95	2/95	
81	SZK 620T	ERF	90086190075756	BBA	4620/39	B50F+37	3/95	3/95	
82	SZK 619T	ERF	90086190076411	BBA	4720/40	B50F+37	3/95	3/95	
191	LSJ 371T	Mercedes-Benz O305 305220 20 000084		Durabuild		B57F+22	-/--	3/91	by5/05
192	LSM 022T	Mercedes-Benz O305		Durabuild		B57F+22	-/71	4/91	by2/06

193	LSH 921T	Mercedes-Benz O305 305220 20 001662	Durabuild			B57F+22	6/72	12/90	-/--
194	LST 200T	Mercedes-Benz O305 305220 20 001564	Durabuild			B57F+22	-/71	5/91	by5/05
200	THL 146T	Volvo B10M 305220 20 001673	BBA	4736/1	B49F+25	8/95	8/95	
201	THL 152T	Volvo B10M YV31M2F13SA042407	BBA	4737/1	B49F+25	8/95	8/95	
202	TJF 470T	Volvo B10M YV31M2F11S2043100	BBA	4737/2	B49F+25	8/95	8/95	
203	TJF 468T	Volvo B10M YV31M2F13S2043101	BBA	4737/3	B49F+25	8/95	8/95	
204	TJF 469T	Volvo B10M YV31M2F15S2043102	BBA	4737/4	B49F+25	8/95	8/95	
205	TJL 760T	Volvo B10M YV31M2F17S2043103	BBA	4738/1	B49F+25	9/95	9/95	
206	TJL 769T	Volvo B10M YV31M2F19S2043104	BBA	4738/2	B49F+25	9/95	9/95	
207	TJN 868T	Volvo B10M YV31M2F1012043105	BBA	4738/3	B49F+25	9/95	9/95	
208	TJN 859T	Volvo B10M YV31M2F12S2043106	BBA	4738/4	B49F+25	9/95	9/95	
209	TJW 588T	Volvo B10M YV31M2F114S043107	BBA	4738/5	B49F+25	9/95	9/95	
210	TKN 407T	Volvo B10M YV31M2F16S2043108	BBA	4739/1	B49F+25	9/95	9/95	
211	TKC 685T	Volvo B10M YV31M2F18S2043109	BBA	4739/2	B49F+25	9/95	9/95	
212	TKC 679T	Volvo B10M YV31M2F18S2043188	BBA	4739/3	B49F+25	9/95	9/95	
213	TKC 692T	Volvo B10M YV31M2F1XS2043189	BBA	4739/4	B49F+25	9/95	9/95	
214	TKN 354T	Volvo B10M YV31M2F16S2043190	BBA	4739/5	B49F+25	10/95	10/95	
215	TKN 367T	Volvo B10M YV31M2F16S2043191	BBA	4739/6	B49F+25	9/95	9/95	by 2/06
216	TKN 534T	Volvo B10M YV31M2F1XS2043192	BBA	4739/7	B49F+25	10/95	10/95	
217	TKN 420T	Volvo B10M YV31M2F11S2043193	BBA	4739/8	B49F+25	10/95	10/95	
218	TKN 542T	Volvo B10M YV31M2F13S2043194	BBA	4739/9	B49F+25	10/95	10/95	
219	TKN 452T	Volvo B10M YV31M2F15S2043195	BBA	4739/10	B49F+25	10/95	10/95	
220	TKV 160T	Volvo B10M YV31M2F17S2043196	BBA	4739/11	B49F+25	10/95	10/95	
221	TKV 172T	Volvo B10M YV31M2F19S2043197	BBA	4739/12	B49F+25	10/95	10/95	
222	TLJ 688T	Volvo B10M YV31M2F15SA042408	BBA	4740/1	B49F+25	10/95	10/95	
223	TLJ 729T	Volvo B10M YV31M2F17SA042409	BBA	4740/2	B49F+25	10/95	10/95	
224	TLJ 792T	Volvo B10M YV31M2F13SA042410	BBA	4740/3	B49F+25	10/95	10/95	
225	TLJ 683T	Volvo B10M YV31M2F17S2043649	BBA	4740/4	B49F+25	10/09	10/95	
226	TLK 628T	Volvo B10M YV31M2F13S2043650	BBA	4740/5	B49F+25	10/95	10/95	
227	TLJ 740T	Volvo B10M YV31M2F17S2043651	BBA	4740/6	B49F+25	10/95	10/95	
228	TLR 737T	Volvo B10M YV31M2F17S2043652	BBA	4740/7	B49F+25	10/95	10/95	
229	TLR 727T	Volvo B10M YV31M2F19S3043653	BBA	4740/8	B49F+25	10/95	10/95	

No	Reg	Model	VIN	Body	Fleet	Seating	Date1	Date2	Date3
			YV31M2F10S2043654						
230	TMF 154T	Volvo B10M		BBA	4740/9	B49F+25	11/95	11/95	
			YV31M2F12S2043655						
231	TMJ 087T	Volvo B10M		BBA	4740/10	B49F+25	11/95	11/95	
			YV31M2F14S2043656						
232	TML 861T	Volvo B10M		BBA	4740/11	B49F+25	11/95	11/95	
			YV31M2F16S2043657						
233	TML 856T	Volvo B10M		BBA	4740/12	B49F+25	11/95	11/95	
			YV31M2F18S2043658						
234	TML 787T	Volvo B10M		BBA	4741/1	B49F+25	11/95	11/95	
			YV31M2F16S2043902						
235	TMM 915T	Volvo B10M		BBA	4741/2	B49F+25	11/95	11/95	
			YV31M2F16S2043903						
236	TMM 902T	Volvo B10M		BBA	4741/3	B49F+25	11/95	11/95	
			YV31M2F1XS2043904						
237	TMM 892T	Volvo B10M		BBA	4741/4	B49F+25	11/95	11/95	
			YV31M2F1XS2043905						
238	TMS 198T	Volvo B10M		BBA	4741/5	B49F+25	11/95	11/95	
			YV31M2F11S2043906						
239	TMW 236T	Volvo B10M		BBA	4741/6	B49F+25	12/95	12/95	
			YV31M2F13S2043907						
240	TMW 240T	Volvo B10M		BBA	4741/7	B49F+25	12/95	12/95	
			YV31M2F15S2043908						
241	TMX 013T	Volvo B10M		BBA	4741/8	B49F+25	12/95	12/95	9/07
			YV31M2F1XS2043909						
242	TMX 022T	Volvo B10M		BBA	4741/9	B49F+25	12/95	12/95	
			YV31M2F13S2043910						
243	TNG 626T	Volvo B10M		BBA	4741/10	B49F+25	12/95	12/95	9/07
			YV31M2F15S2043911						
244	TNG 623T	Volvo B10M		BBA	4741/11	B49F+25	12/95	12/95	
			YV31M2F11T2044085						
245	TNJ 145T	Volvo B10M		BBA	4741/12	B49F+25	12/95	12/95	
			YV31M2F17T2044088						
246	TPF 338T	Volvo B10M		BBA	4742/1	B49F+25	12/95	12/95	
			YV31M2F15T2044090						
247	TPF 342T	Volvo B10M		BBA	4742/2	B49F+25	12/95	12/95	
			YV31M2F13T2044086						
248	TPR 716T	Volvo B10M		BBA	4742/4	B49F+25	12/95	12/95	
			YV31M2F19T2044089						
249	TPR 707T	Volvo B10M		BBA	4742/3	B49F+25	12/95	12/95	
			YV31M2F15T2044087						
250	TRP 460T	Volvo B10M		BBA	4742/5	B49F+25	1/96	1/96	
			YV31M2F17T2044091						
251	TRR 418T	Volvo B10M		BBA	4742/6	B49F+25	2/96	2/96	
			YV31M2F19T2044092						
252	TRX 640T	Volvo B10M		BBA	4742/7	B49F+25	2/96	2/96	
			YV31M2F10T2044093						
253	TRX 635T	Volvo B10M		BBA	4742/8	B49F+25	2/96	2/96	
			YV31M2F14T2044095						
254	TRZ 538T	Volvo B10M		BBA	4742/9	B49F+25	2/96	2/96	
			YV31M2F16T2044096						
255	TSL 723T	Volvo B10M		BBA	4742/10	B49F+25	2/96	2/96	
			YV31M2F12T2044094						
256	TSL 728T	Volvo B10M		BBA	4742/11	B49F+25	2/96	2/96	
			YV31M2F18T2044097						
257	TSX 119T	Volvo B10M		BBA	4742/12	B49F+25	3/96	3/96	
			YV31M2F1XT2044098						
258	TSX 126T	Volvo B10M		BBA	4743/1	B49F+25	3/96	3/96	
			YV31M2F11T2044099						
259	TTD 139T	Volvo B10M		BBA	4743/2	B49F+25	3/96	3/96	
			YV31M2F14T2044100						
260	TTD 148T	Volvo B10M		BBA	4743/3	B49F+25	3/96	3/96	
			YV31M2F16T2044101						
261	TTD 181T	Volvo B10M		BBA	4743/4	B49F+25	3/96	3/96	

262	TTD 173T	Volvo B10M	YV31M2F18T2044102	BBA	4743/5	B49F+25	3/96	3/96	by5/05
263	TTD 163T	Volvo B10M	YV31M2F1XT2044104	BBA	4743/6	B49F+25	3/96	3/96	
264	TTS 939T	Volvo B10M	YV31M2F1XT2044103	BBA	4743/7	B49F+25	4/96	4/96	
265	TTL 340T	Volvo B10M	YV31M2F12T2044323	BBA	4743/8	B49F+25	4/96	4/96	
266	TTL 335T	Volvo B10M	YV31M2F14T2044324	BBA	4743/9	B49F+25	4/96	4/96	by2/06
267	TTL 327T	Volvo B10M	YV31M2F1XT2044327	BBA	4743/10	B49F+25	4/96	4/96	
268	TTL 343T	Volvo B10M	YV31M2F11T2044328	BBA	4743/11	B49F+25	4/96	4/96	
269	TVC 901T	Volvo B10M	YV31M2F13T2044329	BBA	4743/12	B49F+25	4/96	4/96	
270	TVD 228T	Volvo B10M	YV31M2F16T2044325	BBA	4744/1	B49F+25	4/96	4/96	
271	TVD 904T	Volvo B10M	YV31M2F18T2044326	BBA	4744/2	B49F+25	4/96	4/96	
272	TVC 910T	Volvo B10M	YV31M2F1XT2044330	BBA	4744/3	B49F+25	4/96	4/96	
273	TTV 462T	Volvo B10M	YV31M2F10T2044563	BBA	4744/5	B49F+25	4/96	4/96	
274	TTV 439T	Volvo B10M	YV31M2F12T2044564	BBA	4744/5	B49F+25	4/96	4/96	
275	TVC 905T	Volvo B10M	YV31M2F14T2044565	BBA	4744/6	B49F+25	4/96	4/96	
276	TXP 560T	Volvo B10M	YV31M2F1XT2044568	BBA	4744/7	B49F+25	6/96	6/96	
277	TXP 573T	Volvo B10M	YV31M2F15T2044566	BBA	4744/8	B49F+25	6/96	6/96	
278	TXP 553T	Volvo B10M	YV31M2F18T2044567	BBA	4744/9	B49F+25	6/96	6/96	
279	TXP 561T	Volvo B10M	YV31M2F14T2044569	BBA	4745/11	B49F+25	6/96	6/96	
280	TXP 566T	Volvo B10M	YV31M2F18T2044780	BBA	4745/12	B49F+25	6/96	6/96	
281	TXT 595T	Volvo B10M	YV31M2F1XT2044781	BBA	4746/5	B49F+25	6/96	6/96	
282	TXT 623T	Volvo B10M	YV31M2F11T2044572	BBA	4746/6	B49F+25	6/96	6/96	
283	TXT 614T	Volvo B10M	YV31M2F12T2044774	BBA	4746/2	B49F+25	6/96	6/96	
284	TXT 607T	Volvo B10M	YV31M2F1XT2044778	BBA	4746/3	B49F+25	6/96	6/96	
285	TXT 635T	Volvo B10M	YV31M2F11T2044779	BBA	4746/4	B49F+25	6/96	6/96	
286	TXT 629T	Volvo B10M	YV31M2F11T2044782	BBA	4746/1	B49F+25	6/96	6/96	
287	TYP 855T	Volvo B10M	YV31M2F13T2044783	BBA	4746/7	B49F+25	7/96	7/96	
288	TYP 854T	Volvo B10M	YV31M2F18T2044777	BBA	4746/9	B49F+25	7/96	7/96	
289	TYP 858T	Volvo B10M	YV31M2F11T2044331	BBA	4746/8	B49F+25	7/96	7/96	
			YV31M2F15T2044784						

Re-registered:
RYD 943T (1) to FVB 093GB c1996.
RYD 939T (2) to FTY 512GP c1996.
RYD 932T (3) to HBB 662GP c1996.
RYD 949T (4) to FTY 519GP c1996.
RYD 928T (5) to FGD 903GP c1996.

RYD 946T (6) to FTY 523GP c1996.
RYF 499T (7) to FTY 531GP c1996.
RYF 503T (8) to HBB 630GP c1996.
RYF 501T (9) to HBC 531GP c1996.
RZY 304T (10) to HBC 534GP c1996.
RZY 294T (11) to HBB 635GP c1996.
SBZ 643T (12) to FLV 988GP c1996.
SCG 041T(13) to HFC 478GP c1996.
SCL 411T (14) to HFC 477GP o1006.
SCV 416T (15) to HHY 921GP c1996.
SDG 827T (16) to HBC 553GP c1996.
SDM 236T (17) to HBB 660GP c1996.
SDS 811T (18) to HFC 476GP c1996.
SDS 647T (19) to HKX 546GP c1996.
SDS 644T (20) to HBB 658GP c1996.
SFB 686T (21) to HFC 475GP c1996.
SGD 771T (22) to FXT 477GP c1996.
SGL 891T (23) to DZW 036GP c1996., to SLG 982GP c2005.
SGR 141T (24) to DZW 038GP c1996, to SLG 975GP c2005.
SGV 464T (25) to DZW 033GP c1996.
SGZ 000T (26) to HBC 558GP c1996.
SHG 807T (27) to HFD 156GP c1996.
SHN 794T (28) to HBB 647GP c1996.
SJP 533T (29) to HBB 648GP c1996.
SKV 776T (30) to FRL 159GP c1996.
SHT 565T (31) to HBC 556GP c1996.
SLJ 070T (32) to FHZ 573GP c1996.
SLJ 074T (33) to FHZ 570GP c1996.
SLR 361T (34) to FLV 501GP c1996.
SLZ 570T (35) to FRL 157GP c1996.
SMF 158T (36) to FLV 476GP c1996.
SMM 681T (37) to FRK 635GP c1996.
SMZ 503T (38) to FRK 631GP c1996.
SNR 851T (40) to FTZ 104GP c1996.
SPK 349T (41) to FRK 621GP c1996.
SPK 339T (42) to FRK 620GP c1996.
SRN 632T (43) to FXT 475GP c1996.
SRY 690T (44) to HBC 550GP c1996.
SSK 038T (45) to HBC 651GP c1996.
SSK 059T (46) to HBC 116GP c1996.
SST 819T (47) to HFC 470GP c1996.
SST 832T (48) to HFC 469GP c1996.
SST 824T (49) to HFC 465GP c1996.
SST 828T (50) to HFC 463GP c1996.
STG 468T (51) to HFC 462GP c1996.
STG 472T (52) to HFC 460GP c1996.
STR 838T (53) to HFC 457GP c1996.
STX 251T (54) to HHY 923GP c1996.
STZ 224T (55) to HHY 925GP c1996.
STZ 237T (56) to HHY 926GP c1996.
SVR 384T (57) to HKX 549GP c1996.
SVR 382T (58) to HKX 884GP c1996.
SVV 216T (59) to HKX 886GP c1996.
SVV 220T (60) to HKX 889GP c1996.
SVY 208T (61) to HKX 892GP c1996.
SVZ 255T (62) to HKX 893GP c1996.
SWB 236T (63) to HKZ 388GP c1996.
SWB 497T (64) to HHY 927GP c1996.
SWB 245T (65) to HKZ 392GP c1996.
SWC 769T (66) to HKZ 393GP c1996.
SXC 251T (67) to HKZ 396GP c1996.
SWC 774T (69) to HKZ 397GP c1996.
SWC 256T (70) to HKZ 403GP c1996.
SWF 702T (71) to HKZ 399GP c1996.

SWF 699T (72) to HKZ 407GP c1996.
SXF 164T (73) to HMP 655GP c1996.
SWT 944T (74) to HMP 652GP c1996.
SWT 961T(75) to HMP 664GP c1996.
SXP 299T (76) to HMP 648GP c1996.
SXF 177T (77) to HLC 636GP c1996.
SXX 866T (78) to FJD 048GP c1996.
SXX 843T (79) to FJD 049GP c1996.
SYR 694T (80) to FRH 995GP c1996.
SZK 620T (81) to KKZ 993GP c1996.
SZK 619T (82) to KKZ 991GP c1996.
LSJ 371T (191) to FXT 474GP c1996.
LSM 022T (192) to HHY 138GP (or HFY 138GP) c1996.
LSH 921T (193) to HFC 456GP c1996.
LST 200T (194) to FLV 981GP c1996.
THL 146T (200) to FYC 121GP c1996.
THL 152T (201) to FYB 808GP c1996.
TJF 470T (202) to FYB 806GP c1996.
TJF 468T (203) to FYB 804GP c1996.
TJF 469T (204) to FYB 802GP c1996.
TJL 760T (205) to FZS 746GP c1996.
TJL 769T (206) to FZT 077GP c1996.
TJN 868T (207) to FZT 071GP c1996.
TJN 859T (208) to FZT 083GP c1996.
TJW 588T (209) to FZT 074GP c1996.
TKN 407T (210) to FRH 981GP c1996.
TKC 685T (211) to FZS 736GP c1996.
TKC 679T (212) to FZS 739GP c1996.
TKC 692T (213) to FJD 059GP c1996.
TKN 354T (214) to HFY 135GP c1996.
TKN 367T (215) to HFY 133GP c1996.
TKN 534T (216) to FRJ 007GP c1996.
TKN 420T (217) to HFY 143GP c1996.
TKN 542T (218) to HFY 136GP c1996.
TKN 452T (219) to HFY 142GP c1996.
TKV 160T (220) to HFY 139GP c1996.
TKV 172T (221) to HFY 144GP c1996.
TLJ 688T (222) to FVF 904GP c1996.
TLJ 729T (223) to HFY 145GP c1996.
TLJ 792T (224) to FVF 898GP c1996.
TLJ 683T (225) to HFY 147GP c1996.
TLK 628T (226) to HFY 152GP c1996.
TLJ 740T (227) to HFY 149GP c1996.
TLR 737T (228) to HKB 141GP c1996.
TLR 727T (229) to HKB 142GP c1996.
TMF 154T (230) to FJD 052GP c1996.
TMJ 087T (231) to FJD 054GP c1996.
TML 861T (232) to FJB 056GP c1996.
TML 856T (233) to HKB 145GP c1996.
TML 787T (234) to HKB 147GP c1996.
TMM 915T (235) to HKB 148GP c1996.
TMM 902T (236) to HKB 149GP c1996.
TMM 892T (237) to HKB 151GP c1996.
TMS 198T (238) to HHY 941GP c1996.
TMW 236T (239) to HKZ 414GP c1996.
TMW 240T (240) to HKZ 416GP c1996.
TMX 013T (241) to HKZ 419GP c1996.
TMX 022T (242) to HKZ 422GP c1996.
TNG 626T (243) to HKZ 425GP c1996.
TNG 623T (244) to HKZ 428GP c1996.
TNJ 145T (245) to HKZ 431GP c1996.
TPF 338T (246) to HNY 115GP c1996.
TPF 342T (247) to HNY 117GP c1996.
TPR 716T (248) to HNY 120GP c1996.

TPR 707T (249) to HNY 121GP c1996.
TRP 460T (250) to DZW 041GP c1996.
TRR 418T (251) to DZW 050GP c1996.
TRX 640T (252) to DZW 027GP c1996.
TRX 635T (253) to DZW 029GP c1996.
TRZ 538T (254) to DZW 030GP c1996.
TSL 723T (255) to FGD 874GP c1996.
TSL 728T (256) to FGG 410GP c1996.
TCX 110T (257) to FCD 338GP c1996.
TSX 126T (258) to FGD 332GP c1996.
TTD 139T (259) to FGD 897GP c1996.
TTD 148T (260) to FGG 422GP c1996.
TTD 181T (261) to FGD 343GP c1996.
TTD 173T (262) to FGD 875GP c1996.
TTD 163T (263) to FGG 419GP c1996.
TTS 939T (264) to FHZ 608GP c1996.
TTL 340T (265) to FHZ 594GP c1996.
TTL 335T (266) to FHZ 614GP c1996.
TTL 327T (267) to FHZ 599GP c1996.
TTL 343T (268) to FHZ 604GP c1996.
TVC 901T (269) to FHZ 592GP c1996.
TVD 228T (270) to FHZ 609GP c1996.
TVD 904T (271) to FHZ 588GP c1996.
TVC 910T (272) to FHX 127GP c1996.
TTV 462T (273) to FHZ 577GP c1996.
TTV 439T (274) to FHZ 578GP c1996.
TVC 905T (275) to FHZ 583GP c1996.
TXP 560T (276) to FRK 603GP c1996.
TXP 573T (277) to FRK 607GP c1996.
TXP 553T (278) to FRK 619GP c1996.
TXP 561T (279) to FRK 617GP c1996.
TXP 566T (280) to FRK 615GP c1996.
TXT 595T (281) to FRK 614GP c1996.
TXT 623T (282) to FRK 612GP c1996.
TXT 614T (283) to FRK 611GP c1996.
TXT 607T (284) to FRK 608GP c1996.
TXT 635T (285) to FRH 976GP c1996.
TXT 629T (286) to FRH 977GP c1996.
TYP 855T (287) to FVF 912GP c1996.
TYP 854T (288) to FVF 908GP c1996.
TYP 858T (289) to FJD 061GP c1996.

Notes:
1-6 were ERF Super Trailblazer E6.
1-30 were later B47F+37.
17-82 were ERF Super Trailblazer.
31-82 were later B49F+30.
LSJ 371T (191) rebodied as shown ex ? This chassis no. not previously recorded.
LSM 022T (192) rebodied as show ex 107.
LSH 921T (193) rebodied as shown ex 103; noted in use as a driving tuition vehicle in 5/07.
LST 200T (194) rebodied as shown ex 108.

Disposals:
SNH 988T (39): burnt out.
SWB 419T (68): burnt out.
TTD 173T (262): stolen.

083	JWR 513GP	AMC		AMC	B--	by-/00	by-/00
M001	KVT 758GP	AMC	ABA594S0298E50099	AMC	B30F+14	6/00	8/01
M002	KVZ 764GP	AMC	ABA594S0298G50117	AMC	B30F+14	6/00	8/01
M003	KVZ 760GP	AMC	ABA594S0298G50116	AMC	B30F+14	6/00	8/01
M004	KVT 767GP	AMC	ABA594S0298G50112	AMC	B30F+14	6/00	8/01
M005	KVT 771GP	AMC	ABA594S0298G50109	AMC	B30F+14	6/00	8/01

M006	KVZ 759GP	AMC	ABA594S0298G50112	AMC	B30F+14	6/00	8/01
M007	KVT 763GP	AMC	ABA594S0298E50098	AMC	B30F+14	6/00	8/01
M008	KVT 768GP	AMC	ABA594S0298G50110	AMC	B30F+14	6/00	8/01
M009	KVT 769GP	AMC	ABA594S0298E50095	AMC	B30F+14	6/00	8/01
M010	KVT 766GP	AMC	ABA594S0298G50121	AMC	B30F+14	6/00	8/01
M011	KWH 043GP	AMC	ABA594S0298G50127	AMC	B30F+14	6/00	8/01
M012	KVT 764GP	AMC	ABA594S0298G50111	AMC	B30F+14	6/00	8/01
M013	KWH 056GP	AMC	ABA594S0298G50114	AMC	B30F+14	6/00	8/01
M014	KWK 778GP	AMC	ABA594S0298G50118	AMC	B30F+14	6/00	8/01
M015	LCT 607GP	AMC	ABA594S0298E50048	AMC	B30F+14	6/00	8/01
M016	KWH 037GP	AMC	ABA594S0298G50125	AMC	B30F+14	6/00	8/01
M017	KVT 757GP	AMC	ABA594S0298G50113	AMC	B30F+14	6/00	8/01
M018	KWK 775GP	AMC	ABA594S0298G50126	AMC	B30F+14	6/00	8/01
M019	KWH 054GP	AMC	ABA594S0298G50128	AMC	B30F+14	6/00	8/01
M020	KWK 776GP	AMC	ABA594S0298G50131	AMC	B30F+14	6/00	8/01
M021	KWH 057GP	AMC	ABA594S0298G50115	AMC	B30F+14	6/00	8/01
M022	KWJ 070GP	AMC	ABA594S0298G50124	AMC	B30F+14	6/00	8/01
M023	KWH 039GP	AMC	ABA594S0298G50123	AMC	B30F+14	6/00	8/01
M024	KWH 041GP	AMC	ABA594S0298G50119	AMC	B30F+14	6/00	8/01
M025	KWH 055GP	AMC	ABA594S0298G50132	AMC	B30F+14	6/00	8/01

Notes:
M001-25 were leased from Afinta Motor Corporation.

New vehicles subsequent to the change of entity to Metrobus:

10102	NFY 906GP	Volvo B7L YV3S2G61X1A001522	Marcopolo	118034	H43/27F	12/01	12/01
10202	NFY 921GP	Volvo B7L YV3S2G6132A001637	Marcopolo	119969	H43/27F	12/01	12/01
10302	NFZ 037GP	Volvo B7L YV3S2G6152A001641	Marcopolo	119972	H43/27F	12/01	12/01
10402	NFZ 040GP	Volvo B7L YV3S2G6192A001643	Marcopolo	119975	H43/27F	12/01	12/01
10502	NHB 569GP	Volvo B7L YV3S2G6102A001644	Marcopolo	119978	H43/27F	12/01	12/01
10602	NFZ 067GP	Volvo B7L YV3S2G6192A001660	Marcopolo	119981	H43/27F	12/01	12/01
10702	NHB 563GP	Volvo B7L YV3S2G6162A001700	Marcopolo	119984	H43/27F	12/01	12/01
10802	NHB 604GP	Volvo B7L YV3S2G61X2A001747	Marcopolo	119987	H43/27F	12/01	12/01
10902	NHB 579GP	Volvo B7L YV3S2G6102A001742	Marcopolo	119990	H43/27F	12/01	12/01
11002	NHC 139GP	Volvo B7L YV3S2G6152A001753	Marcopolo	119993	H43/27F	12/01	12/01
11102	NHB 591GP	Volvo B7L YV3S2G6162A001745	Marcopolo	119996	H43/27F	12/01	12/01
11202	NHB 594GP	Volvo B7L YV3S2G6182A001746	Marcopolo	119999	H43/27F	12/01	12/01
11302	NHC 137GP	Volvo B7L YV3S2G6132A001752	Marcopolo	120001	H43/27F	12/01	12/01
11402	NHB 587GP	Volvo B7L YV3S2G6122A001743	Marcopolo	120003	H43/27F	12/01	12/01
11502	NHC 179GP	Volvo B7L YV3S2G61X2A001814	Marcopolo	120005	H43/27F	12/01	12/01
11602	NHC 187GP	Volvo B7L YV3S2G6132A001816	Marcopolo	120007	H43/27F	12/01	12/01
11702	NHC 141GP	Volvo B7L YV3S2G6162A001762	Marcopolo	120009	H43/27F	12/01	12/01
11802	NHC 151GP	Volvo B7L YV3S2G61X2A001764	Marcopolo	120011	H43/27F	12/01	12/01
11902	NHC 155GP	Volvo B7L YV3S2G6192A001769	Marcopolo	120113	H43/27F	12/01	12/01

12002	NHC 171GP	Volvo B7L YV3S2G6192A001772	Marcopolo	120015	H43/27F	12/01	12/01
12102	NHC 178GP	Volvo B7L YV3S2G6142A001775	Marcopolo	120017	H43/27F	1/02	1/02
12202	NJT 823GP	Volvo B7L YV3S2G6182A001777	Marcopolo	120019	H43/27F	1/02	1/02
12302	NJT 812GP	Volvo B7L YV3S2G61X2A001781	Marcopolo	120021	H43/27F	1/02	1/02
12402	NJX 517GP	Volvo B7L YV3S2G6172A001768	Marcopolo	120023	H43/27F	1/02	1/02
12502	NJV 256GP	Volvo B7L YV3S2G6122A001774	Marcopolo	120025	H43/27F	1/02	1/02
12602	NJT 767GP	Volvo B7L YV3S2G6112A001801	Marcopolo	120027	H43/27F	1/02	1/02
12701	NJT 783GP	Volvo B7L YV3S2G6152A001798	Marcopolo	120029	H43/27F	1/02	1/02
12802	NJT 771GP	Volvo B7L YV3S2G61X2A001800	Marcopolo	120031	H43/27F	1/02	1/02
12902	NJT 780GP	Volvo B7L YV3S2G6172A001804	Marcopolo	120033	H43/27F	1/02	1/02
13002	NJT 808GP	Volvo B7L YV3S2G6122A001791	Marcopolo	120035	H43/27F	1/02	1/02
13102	NJT 793GP	Volvo B7L YV3S2G6182A001794	Marcopolo	120037	H43/27F	1/02	1/02
13202	NJT 785GP	Volvo B7L YV3S2G6112A001796	Marcopolo	120039	H43/27F	1/02	1/02
13302	NJT 773GP	Volvo B7L YV3S2G6122A001824	Marcopolo	120041	H43/27F	1/02	1/02
13402	NJT 772GP	Volvo B7L YV3S2G6162A001826	Marcopolo	120043	H43/27F	1/02	1/02
13502	NKW 067GP	Volvo B7L YV3S2G6182A001830	Marcopolo	120045	H43/27F	1/02	1/02
13602	NKW 070GP	Volvo B7L YV3S2G6112A001832	Marcopolo	120047	H43/27F	1/02	1/02
13702	NKW 058GP	Volvo B7L YV3S2G6182A001827	Marcopolo	120049	H43/27F	1/02	1/02
13802	NKW 073GP	Volvo B7L YV3S2G6132A001833	Marcopolo	120051	H43/27F	1/02	1/02
13902	NKW 410GP	Volvo B7L YV3S2G6152A001865	Marcopolo	120053	H43/27F	1/02	1/02
14002	NKW 421GP	Volvo B7L YV3S2G6192A001867	Marcopolo	120055	H43/27F	1/02	1/02
14102	NKW 733GP	Volvo B7L YV3S2G6122A001869	Marcopolo	120057	H43/27F	1/02	1/02
14202	NKV 742GP	Volvo B7L YV3S2G6122A001872	Marcopolo	120059	H43/27F	1/02	1/02
14302	NKV 712GP	Volvo B7L YV3S2G6152A001879	Marcopolo	120061	H43/27F	2/02	2/02
14402	NKV 737GP	Volvo B7L YV3S2G61X2A001876	Marcopolo	120063	H43/27F	2/02	2/02
14502	NLP 357GP	Volvo B7L YV3S2G61X2A001893	Marcopolo	120065	H43/27F	2/02	2/02
14602	NLP 365GP	Volvo B7L YV3S2G6192A001898	Marcopolo	120067	H43/27F	2/02	2/02
14702	NLP 364GP	Volvo B7L YV3S2G6172A001897	Marcopolo	120069	H43/27F	2/02	2/02
14802	NLP 352GP	Volvo B7L YV3S2G6162A001891	Marcopolo	120071	H43/27F	2/02	2/02
14902	NLP 360GP	Volvo B7L YV3S2G6132A001895	Marcopolo	120073	H43/27F	2/02	2/02
15002	NLP 349GP	Volvo B7L YV3S2G6182A001875	Marcopolo	120075	H43/27F	2/02	2/02
15102	NLP 369GP	Volvo B7L YV3S2G6162A001938	Marcopolo	120077	H43/27F	2/02	2/02

15202	NLP 371GP	Volvo B7L YV3S2G6142A001940	Marcopolo	120079	H43/27F	2/02	2/02
15302	NLP 372GP	Volvo B7L YV3S2G6182A001942	Marcopolo	120081	H43/27F	2/02	2/02
15402	NLY 582GP	Volvo B7L YV3S2G6112A001944	Marcopolo	120083	H43/27F	2/02	2/02
15502	NLY 519GP	Volvo B7L YV3S2G6152A001915	Marcopolo	120085	H43/27F	2/02	2/02
15602	NLY 514GP	Volvo B7L YV3S2G6122A001905	Marcopolo	120087	H43/27F	2/02	2/02
15702	NLY 522GP	Volvo B7L YV3S2G6172A001916	Marcopolo	120089	H43/27F	2/02	2/02
15802	NLY 287GP	Volvo B7L YV3S2G6132A001900	Marcopolo	120091	H43/27F	2/02	2/02
15902	NLY 512GP	Volvo B7L YV3S2G6102A001904	Marcopolo	120093	H43/27F	2/02	2/02
16002	NLY 517GP	Volvo B7L YV3S2G6132A001914	Marcopolo	120095	H43/27F	2/02	2/02
16102	NLY 529GP	Volvo B7L YV3S2G6192A001920	Marcopolo	120097	H43/27F	2/02	2/02
16202	NLY 534GP	Volvo B7L YV3S2G6122A001922	Marcopolo	120099	H43/27F	2/02	2/02
16302	NLY 538GP	Volvo B7L YV3S2G6162A001924	Marcopolo	121001	H43/27F	2/02	2/02
16402	NLY 551GP	Volvo B7L YV3S2G6132A001928	Marcopolo	120105	H43/27F	2/02	2/02
16502	NLY 548GP	Volvo B7L YV3S2G61X2A001926	Marcopolo	120105	H43/27F	2/02	2/02
16602	NJZ 698GP	Volvo B7R YV3R6B5171A002795	Marcopolo	500310	B60F	3/02	3/02
16702	NKN 484GP	Volvo B7R YV3R6B51722003182	Marcopolo	500311	B60F	3/02	3/02
16802	NKN 478GP	Volvo B7R YV3R6B51222003185	Marcopolo	500314	B60F	3/02	3/02
16902	NKN 469GP	Volvo B7R YV3R6B51822003188	Marcopolo	500317	B60F	3/02	3/02
17002	NJZ 695GP	Volvo B7R YV3R6B51222003817	Marcopolo	500320	B60F	3/02	3/02
17102	NKN 488GP	Volvo B7R YV3R6B51222003820	Marcopolo	500323	B60F	3/02	3/02
17202	NLP 314GP	Volvo B7R YV3R6B51822003823	Marcopolo	500326	B60F	3/02	3/02
17302	NLP 319GP	Volvo B7R YV3R6B51722003926	Marcopolo	500329	B60F	3/02	3/02
17402	NLP 328GP	Volvo B7R YV3R6B51222003929	Marcopolo	500332	B60F	3/02	3/02
17502	NLX 807GP	Volvo B7R YV3R6B51222003932	Marcopolo	500335	B60F	3/02	3/02
20102	NFY 915GP	Volvo B7L YV3S2G6111A001635	Marcopolo	119967	H43/27F	12/01	12/01
20202	NFZ 032GP	Volvo B7L YV3S2G6172A001640	Marcopolo	119970	H43/27F	12/01	12/01
20302	NFZ 031GP	Volvo B7L YV3S2G6172A001639	Marcopolo	119973	H43/27F	12/01	12/01
20402	NFY 908GP	Volvo B7L YV3S2G61X1A001634	Marcopolo	119976	H43/27F	12/01	12/01
20502	NFZ 046GP	Volvo B7L YV3S2G6122A001659	Marcopolo	119979	H43/27F	12/01	12/01
20602	NFZ 055GP	Volvo B7L YV3S2G6112A001698	Marcopolo	119982	H43/27F	12/01	12/01
20702	NHB 568GP	Volvo B7L YV3S2G6162A001701	Marcopolo	119985	H43/27F	12/01	12/01
20802	NFZ 064GP	Volvo B7L YV3S2G6172A001754	Marcopolo	119988	H43/27F	12/01	12/01

20902 NHB 589GP	Volvo B7L YV3S2G6142A001744	Marcopolo	119991	H43/27F	12/01	12/01
21002 NHB 613GP	Volvo B7L YV3S2G6112A001750	Marcopolo	119994	H43/27F	12/01	12/01
21102 NHC 136GP	Volvo B7L YV3S2G6112A001751	Marcopolo	119997	H43/27F	12/01	12/01
21202 NHB 608GP	Volvo B7L YV3S2G6112A001748	Marcopolo	120000	H43/27F	12/01	12/01
21302 NHB 574GP	Volvo B7L YV3S2G6102A001739	Marcopolo	120002	H43/27F	12/01	12/01
21402 NFZ 060GP	Volvo B7L YV3S2G6172A001740	Marcopolo	120004	H43/27F	12/01	12/01
21502 NHC 183GP	Volvo B7L YV3S2G6112A001815	Marcopolo	120006	H43/27F	12/01	12/01
21602 NHC 189GP	Volvo B7L YV3S2G6152A001817	Marcopolo	120008	H43/27F	12/01	12/01
21702 NHC 146GP	Volvo B7L YV3S2G6182A001763	Marcopolo	120010	H43/27F	12/01	12/01
21802 NHC 152GP	Volvo B7L YV3S2G6152A001767	Marcopolo	120012	H43/27F	12/01	12/01
21902 NHC 159GP	Volvo B7L YV3S2G6172A001771	Marcopolo	120014	H43/27F	12/01	12/01
22002 NHC 175GP	Volvo B7L YV3S2G6102A001773	Marcopolo	120016	H43/27F	1/02	1/02
22102 NJT 825GP	Volvo B7L YV3S2G6162A001776	Marcopolo	120018	H43/27F	1/02	1/02
22202 NJT 819GP	Volvo B7L YV3S2G61X2A001778	Marcopolo	120020	H43/27F	1/02	1/02
22302 NJV 613GP	Volvo B7L YV3S2G6122A001760	Marcopolo	120022	H43/27F	1/02	1/02
22402 NJX 516GP	Volvo B7L YV3S2G6152A001770	Marcopolo	120024	H43/27F	1/02	1/02
22502 NJT 816GP	Volvo B7L YV3S2G6112A001779	Marcopolo	120026	H43/27F	1/02	1/02
22602 NJT 814GP	Volvo B7L YV3S2G6182A001780	Marcopolo	120028	H43/27F	1/02	1/02
22702 NJT 782GP	Volvo B7L YV3S2G6172A001799	Marcopolo	120030	H43/27F	1/02	1/02
22802 NJT 765GP	Volvo B7L YV3S2G6152A001803	Marcopolo	120032	H43/27F	1/02	1/02
22902 NJT 801GP	Volvo B7L YV3S2G6142A001792	Marcopolo	120034	H43/27F	1/02	1/02
23002 NJT 798GP	Volvo B7L YV3S2G6162A001793	Marcopolo	120036	H43/27F	1/02	1/02
23102 NJT 790GP	Volvo B7L YV3S2G61X2A001795	Marcopolo	120038	H43/27F	1/02	1/02
23202 NJT 766GP	Volvo B7L YV3S2G6132A001802	Marcopolo	120040	H43/27F	1/02	1/02
23302 NND 522GP	Volvo B7L YV3S2G6112A001829	Marcopolo	120042	H43/27F	1/02	1/02
23402 NKW 721GP	Volvo B7L YV3S2G61X2A001828	Marcopolo	120044	H43/27F	1/02	1/02
23502 NKW 068GP	Volvo B7L YV3S2G61X2A001831	Marcopolo	120046	H43/27F	1/02	1/02
23602 NKW 726GP	Volvo B7L YV3S2G6142A001825	Marcopolo	120048	H43/27F	1/02	1/02
23702 NKW 406GP	Volvo B7L YV3S2G6152A001834	Marcopolo	120050	H43/27F	1/02	1/02
23802 NKW 002GP	Volvo B7L YV3S2G6142A001761	Marcopolo	120052	H43/27F	1/02	1/02
23902 NKW 419GP	Volvo B7L YV3S2G6172A001866	Marcopolo	120054	H43/27F	1/02	1/02
24002 NKW 481GP	Volvo B7L YV3S2G6102A001868	Marcopolo	120056	H43/27F	1/02	1/02

24102 NKW 748GP	Volvo B7L YV3S2G6192A001870	Marcopolo	120058	H43/27F	1/02	1/02
24202 NKV 733GP	Volvo B7L YV3S2G6112A001877	Marcopolo	120060	H43/27F	1/02	1/02
24302 NKV 724GP	Volvo B7L YV3S2G6132A001878	Marcopolo	120062	H43/27F	2/02	2/02
24402 NKV 739GP	Volvo B7L YV3S2G6162A001874	Marcopolo	120064	H43/27F	2/02	2/02
24502 NKV 719GP	Volvo B7L YV3S2G6112A001894	Marcopolo	120066	H43/27F	2/02	2/02
24602 NLP 346GP	Volvo B7L YV3S2G6102A001871	Marcopolo	120068	H43/27F	2/02	2/02
24702 NLP 367GP	Volvo B7L YV3S2G6102A001899	Marcopolo	120070	H43/27F	2/02	2/02
24802 NLP 361GP	Volvo B7L YV3S2G6152A001896	Marcopolo	120072	H43/27F	2/02	2/02
24902 NLP 355GP	Volvo B7L YV3S2G6182A001892	Marcopolo	120074	H43/27F	2/02	2/02
25002 NLP 348GP	Volvo B7L YV3S2G6142A001873	Marcopolo	120076	H43/27F	2/02	2/02
25102 NLP 370GP	Volvo B7L YV3S2G6182A001939	Marcopolo	120078	H43/27F	2/02	2/02
25202 NLY 577GP	Volvo B7L YV3S2G6162A001941	Marcopolo	120080	H43/27F	2/02	2/02
25302 NLY 579GP	Volvo B7L YV3S2G61X2A001943	Marcopolo	120082	H43/27F	2/02	2/02
25402 NLY 528GP	Volvo B7L YV3S2G6122A001919	Marcopolo	120084	H43/27F	2/02	2/02
25502 NLY 510GP	Volvo B7L YV3S2G6172A001902	Marcopolo	120086	H43/27F	2/02	2/02
25602 NLY 527GP	Volvo B7L YV3S2G6102A001918	Marcopolo	120088	H43/27F	2/02	2/02
25702 NLY 508GP	Volvo B7L YV3S2G6152A001901	Marcopolo	120090	H43/27F	2/02	2/02
25802 NLY 511GP	Volvo B7L YV3S2G6192A001903	Marcopolo	120092	H43/27F	2/02	2/02
25902 NLY 515GP	Volvo B7L YV3S2G6142A001906	Marcopolo	120094	H43/27F	2/02	2/02
26002 NLY 523GP	Volvo B7L YV3S2G6192A001917	Marcopolo	120096	H43/27F	2/02	2/02
26102 NLY 531GP	Volvo B7L YV3S2G6102A001921	Marcopolo	120098	H43/27F	2/02	2/02
26202 NLY 535GP	Volvo B7L YV3S2G6142A001923	Marcopolo	120100	H43/27F	2/02	2/02
26302 NLY 550GP	Volvo B7L YV3S2G6112A001927	Marcopolo	120102	H43/27F	2/02	2/02
26402 NLY 547GP	Volvo B7L YV3S2G6182A001925	Marcopolo	120105	H43/27F	2/02	2/02
26502 NLY 598GP	Volvo B7L YV3S2G6152A001963	Marcopolo	120107	H43/27F	2/02	2/02
26602 NLY 595GP	Volvo B7L YV3S2G6112A001961	Marcopolo	120108	H43/27F	2/02	2/02
26702 NLY 611GP	Volvo B7L YV3S2G6192A001965	Marcopolo	120109	H43/27F	2/02	2/02
26802 NLY 596GP	Volvo B7L YV3S2G6132A001962	Marcopolo	120110	H43/27F	3/02	3/02
26902 NLY 591GP	Volvo B7L YV3S2G6132A001959	Marcopolo	120111	H43/27F	3/02	3/02
27002 NLY 589GP	Volvo B7L YV3S2G6112A001958	Marcopolo	120112	H43/27F	3/02	3/02
27102 NLY 615GP	Volvo B7L YV3S2G6122A001967	Marcopolo	120113	H43/27F	3/02	3/02
27202 NLY 604GP	Volvo B7L YV3S2G6172A001964	Marcopolo	120114	H43/27F	3/02	3/02

27302 NLY 593GP	Volvo B7L YV3S2G61X2A001960	Marcopolo	120115	H43/27F	3/02	3/02
27402 NLY 614GP	Volvo B7L YV3S2G6102A001966	Marcopolo	120116	H43/27F	3/02	3/02
27502 NKW 723GP	Volvo B7L YV3S2G6132A001797	Marcopolo	120103	H43/27F	3/02	3/02
27602 NKN 493GP	Volvo B7R YV3R6B51322003180	Marcopolo	500309	B60F	2/02	2/02
27702 NKN 482GP	Volvo B7R YV3R6B51922003183	Marcopolo	500312	D00Г	2/02	2/02
27802 NKN 475GP	Volvo B7R YV3R6B51422003186	Marcopolo	500315	B60F	2/02	2/02
27902 NJZ 696GP	Volvo B7R YV3R6B51X32003189	Marcopolo	500318	B60F	2/02	2/02
28002 NKN 466GP	Volvo B7R YV3R6B51422003818	Marcopolo	500321	B60F	2/02	2/02
28102 NLP 281GP	Volvo B7R YV3R6B51422003821	Marcopolo	500324	B60F	2/02	2/02
28202 NLP 315GP	Volvo B7R YV3R6B51X22003824	Marcopolo	500327	B60F	3/02	3/02
28302 NLP 326GP	Volvo B7R YV3R6B51922003927	Marcopolo	500330	B60F	3/02	3/02
28402 NLP 330GP	Volvo B7R YV3R6B51922003930	Marcopolo	500333	B60F	3/02	3/02
28502 NLX 812GP	Volvo B7R YV3R6B51422003933	Marcopolo	500336	B60F	3/02	3/02
28602 NLX 847GP	Volvo B7R YV3R6B51X22003936	Marcopolo	500339	B60F	3/02	3/02
28702 NLX 858GP	Volvo B7R YV3R6B51322003938	Marcopolo	500341	B60F	3/02	3/02
28802 NLX 974GP	Volvo B7R YV3R6B51122003940	Marcopolo	500343	B60F	3/02	3/02
28902 NLY 007GP	Volvo B7R YV3R6B51422004001	Marcopolo	500345	B60F	3/02	3/02
29002 NLY 066GP	Volvo B7R YV3R6B51822004003	Marcopolo	500347	B60F	4/02	4/02
29102 NLY 183GP	Volvo B7R YV3R6B51122004005	Marcopolo	500349	B60F	4/02	4/02
29202 NLY 190GP	Volvo B7R YV3R6B51522004007	Marcopolo	500351	B60F	4/02	4/02
29302 NLY 199GP	Volvo B7R YV3R6B51922004009	Marcopolo	500359	B60F	4/02	4/02
29402 NLY 203GP	Volvo B7R YV3R6B51722004011	Marcopolo	500355	B60F	4/02	4/02
29502 NLY 206GP	Volvo B7R YV3R6B51022004013	Marcopolo	500357	B60F	4/02	4/02
30102 NFY 919GP	Volvo B7L YV3S2G6112A001636	Marcopolo	119971	H43/27F	10/01	10/01
30202 NFY 923GP	Volvo B7L YV3S2G6152A001638	Marcopolo	119968	H43/27F	10/01	10/01
30302 NFZ 039GP	Volvo B7L YV3S2G6172A001642	Marcopolo	119974	H43/27F	10/01	10/01
30402 NFZ 044GP	Volvo B7L YV3S2G6122A001645	Marcopolo	119977	H43/27F	10/01	10/01
30502 NFZ 051GP	Volvo B7L YV3S2G6102A001661	Marcopolo	119980	H43/27F	10/01	10/01
30602 NFZ 056GP	Volvo B7L YV3S2G6132A001699	Marcopolo	119986	H43/27F	10/01	10/01
30702 NFZ 057GP	Volvo B7L YV3S2G61X2A001702	Marcopolo	119983	H43/27F	10/01	10/01
30802 NFZ 061GP	Volvo B7L YV3S2G6132A001749	Marcopolo	119989	H43/27F	10/01	10/01
30902 NHB 577GP	Volvo B7L YV3S2G6192A001741	Marcopolo	119992	H43/27F	10/01	10/01

31002	NHB 571GP	Volvo B7L	YV3S2G6192A001738	Marcopolo	119995	H43/27F	10/01	10/01		
31102	NKN 487GP	Volvo B7R	YV3R6B51522003181	Marcopolo	500301	B60F	2/02	2/02		
31202	NKN 481GP	Volvo B7R	YV3R6B51022003184	Marcopolo	500313	B60F	2/02	2/02		
31302	NKN 473GP	Volvo B7R	YV3R6B51622003187	Marcopolo	500316	B60F	3/02	3/02		
31402	NKN 468GP	Volvo B7R	YV3R6B51022003816	Marcopolo	500319	B60F	3/02	3/02		
31502	NKN 496GP	Volvo B7R	YV3R6B51622003819	Marcopolo	500322	B60F	3/02	3/02		
31602	NLP 283GP	Volvo B7R	YV3R6B51622003822	Marcopolo	500325	B60F	3/02	3/02		
31702	NLP 317GP	Volvo B7R	YV3R6B51122003825	Marcopolo	500328	B60F	3/02	3/02		
31802	NLP 327GP	Volvo B7R	YV3R6B51022003928	Marcopolo	500331	B60F	3/02	3/02		
31902	NLX 783GP	Volvo B7R	YV3R6B51022003931	Marcopolo	500334	B60F	5/02	5/02		
32002	NLX 817GP	Volvo B7R	YV3R6B51622003934	Marcopolo	500337	B60F	3/02	3/02		
32102	NLX 824GP	Volvo B7R	YV3R6B51822003935	Marcopolo	500338	B60F	4/02	4/02		
32202	NLX 854GP	Volvo B7R	YV3R6B51122003937	Marcopolo	500340	B60F	4/02	4/02		
32302	NLX 970GP	Volvo B7R	YV3R6B51522003939	Marcopolo	500342	B60F	4/02	4/02		
32402	NLX 984GP	Volvo B7R	YV3R6B51X22004000	Marcopolo	500344	B60F	4/02	4/02		
32502	NLY 012GP	Volvo B7R	YV3R6B51X22004002	Marcopolo	500346	B60F	4/02	4/02		
32602	NLY 071GP	Volvo B7R	YV3R6B51X22004004	Marcopolo	500348	B60F	4/02	4/02		
32702	NLY 187GP	Volvo B7R	YV3R6B51322004006	Marcopolo	500350	B60F	4/02	4/02		
32802	NLY 193GP	Volvo B7R	YV3R6B51722004008	Marcopolo	500352	B60F	4/02	4/02		
32902	NLY 201GP	Volvo B7R	YV3R6B51522004010	Marcopolo	500354	B60F	4/02	4/02		
33002	NLY 209GP	Volvo B7R	YV3R6B51922004012	Marcopolo	500356	B60F	4/02	4/02		

Notes:

The double-decker Volvos have bodies styled Viale. Fifteen of these have been erroneously reported as fitted with chair lifts. This is not the case. A number (not confirmed as fifteen) are equipped with a "bus-to-pavement" extension flap to ease boarding by disabled passengers. Body numbers are prefixed "BUSUCFBMN2B" and are suffixed "POLO".

The single-decker Volvos have bodies styled Torino. Body numbers are prefixed "BUSUCFBSN26" and are suffixed "POLO".

301	DJJ 292GP	ERF Trailblazer E6	65268	BBL	?	B50F+12	10/90	12/03	by 2/07
302	FVY 104GP	Mercedes-Benz OF1617	24 200501	Craftsman		B62F+16	-/76	12/03	
303	FVF 213GP	Mercedes-Benz O305	307001 61 030950	BBA	3917/1	H98F+16	6/82	12/03	by 2/07
304	FPN 641GP	ERF Super Trailblazer	72097	BBL	1642/1	B60F+12	-/94	12/03	
305	DYC 860GP	ERF Trailblazer E6	65269	BBL	1370/1	B50F+12	-/90	12/03	by 2/07
306	FPN 642GP	ERF Super Trailblazer	72098	BBL	1642/2	B60F+12	-/91	12/03	
307	DYC 861GP	ERF Super Trailblazer	66618	BBL	1370/2	B65F+16	-/91	12/03	
308	FTV 429GP	Volvo B10M	YV31M2F1XT2044570	BBA	4745/1	B49F+25	4/96	12/03	by 2/07
310	FTV 430GP	Volvo B10M	YV31M2F1XT2044571	BBA	4745/2	B49F+25	4/96	12/03	by 2/07

311	FTV 432GP	Volvo B10M	BBA	4745/4	B49F+25	5/96	12/03	
		YV31M2F15T2044770						
312	FTV 432GP	Mercedes-Benz O317K	Craftsman		B62F+18	-/72	12/03	-/--
		317240 24 2000502						
313	FTV 433GP	Nissan CB20N 00462	De Haan		B64F+15	4/79	12/03	-/--
314	FTV 434GP	Volvo B10M	BBA	4745/3	B49F+25	4/96	12/03	
		YV31M2F19T2044769						
315	FVF 215GP	Volvo B10M	BBA	4745/5	B49F+25	5/96	12/03	
		YV31M2F17T2044771						
316	FVF 216GP	Volvo B10M	BBA	4745/9	B49F+25	5/96	12/03	
		YV31M2F10T2044773						
317	FVY 109GP	ERF Super Trailblazer 66617	BBL	?	B65F+16	-/91	12/03	
318	FVF 218GP	Volvo B10M	BBA	4745/10	B49F+25	5/96	12/03	
		YV31M2F16T2044776						
320	FVF 219GP	Volvo B10M	BBA	4745/7	B49F+25	5/96	12/03	
		YV31M2F1XT2044775						
321	FVF 223GP	Volvo B10M	BBA	4745/8	B49F+25	5/96	12/03	
		YV31M2F13T2044332						
323	CZD 264GP	Leyland Victory 2 ADE	BBL (?)		B59F+16	-/84	12/03	by11/06
		JVTB 820149						
324	FTV 437GP	Nissan CB20N 00461	De Haan		B65F+16	6/79	12/03	by11/06
326	CZD 263GP	Mercedes-Benz 1621						
		355098 64 647302	BBL (?)		B65F+22	8/81	12/03	by11/06
327	FTV 438GP	Mercedes-Benz 1621						
		355098 64 647303	BBL (?)		B65F+16	4/81	12/03	by11/06
330	FVF 225GP	Volvo B10M	BBA	4745/6	B49F+25	5/96	12/03	
		YV31M2F1579004772						
336	FVY 115GP	Nissan CB20ND 00361	BBL (?)		B65F+16	6/78	12/03	
338	FTV 451GP	Mercedes-Benz OF1617	Busmark		B65F+21	4/80	12/03	by11/06
		355098 64 619903						
339	FVF 226GP	Mercedes-Benz OF1617	Busmark		B65F+24	5/80	12/03	
		355098 64 619571						
340	FVF 228GP	Mercedes-Benz OF1617	Busmark		B65F+24	5/80	12/03	by11/06
		355098 64 619570						
341	FVF 229GP	Mercedes-Benz OF1617	Busmark		B65F+24	5/80	12/03	by11/06
		355098 64 619569						
342	FVF 208GP	Mercedes-Benz OF1621	BBL (?)		B52D	3/81	12/03	by11/06
		355098 64 674304						
343	CXL 019GP	Mercedes-Benz OF1621	BBL (?)		B52D	7/81	12/03	by11/06
		355098 64 674305						
344	CZD 262GP	Mercedes-Benz OF1624	BBL (?)		B65F+16	8/82	12/03	by11/06
		397047 64 855652						
345	FVY 117GP	Mercedes-Benz OF1624	BBL (?)		B65F+22	6/82	12/03	by11/06
		397047 64 855653						
346	CXL 016GP	Mercedes-Benz OF1624	BBL (?)		B65F+22	-/83	12/03	by11/06
		397047 64 936636						
347	CXL 015GP	Mercedes-Benz OF1624	BBL (?)		B65F+22	-/83	12/03	by11/06
		397047 64 936637						
348	CXL 014GP	Mercedes-Benz O305	BBA	4051/1	H98F+16	7/83	12/03	by11/06
		307001 61 032450						
349	CXL 017GP	Mercedes-Benz O305	BBA	4051/2	H98F+12	7/83	12/03	by11/06
		307001 61 032451						
350	CXL 018GP	Mercedes-Benz O305	BBA	4051/3	H98F+12	7/83	12/03	
		307001 61 032723						
352	FVF 214GP	Mercedes-Benz 613	Miller		B26F+8	-/84	12/03	by11/06
		310404 60 587694						
353	FVY 118GP	Leyland Victory2 ADE	BBL (?)		B60F+16	6/84	12/03	by11/06
		JVTB820128						
354	FTV 452GP	Mercedes-Benz O305	BBA	4194/1	H57/41F+16	4/85	12/03	
		307001 61 041111						
355	FVY 119GP	ERF Trailblazer E6 66616	BBL (?)		B66F+12	11/90	12/03	by11/06
356	FVF 231GP	Leyland TRC/3R 8401146	BBL (?)		B58F+27	5/88	12/03	by11/06
357	FVF 232GP	Leyland TRC/3R 8500247	BBL (?)		B58F+27	5/88	12/03	by11/06
358	FVF 234GP	Leyland TRC/3R 8400981	BBL (?)		B58F+27	5/88	12/03	by11/06

359	FVF 235GP	Mercedes-Benz O305 307001 61 030838	BBA	3926/3	B54F+37	7/82	12/03	by11/06
360	FVF 236GP	Mercedes-Benz O305 307001 61 030874	BBA	3926/4	B54F+37	8/82	12/03	by11/06
361	FVF 238GP	Mercedes-Benz O305G 307101 21 007907	?		AB61D+62	5/79	12/03	-/--
362	FVF 211GP	Leyland TRCTL11/3R8300704	BBA	4129/1	B61F+16	3/85	12/03	by11/06
363	DNS 942GP	Leyland TRC/3R 8401048	Santini		B61F+16	10/87	12/03	by11/06
364	FVF 210GP	Leyland TRC/3R 8400979	Santini		B61F+15	3/88	12/03	by11/06
365	DNS 946GP	Leyland TRC/3R 8500325	Santini		B66F+16	10/88	12/03	by11/06
366	DNS 949GP	Leyland TRC/3R 8500326	Santini		B66F+16	10/89	12/03	by11/06
367	DYC 862GP	Leyland TRC/3R 8500327	Santini		B66F+16	12/88	12/03	by11/06
368	DJJ 293GP	Mercedes-Benz O305 307001 61 049430	BBA	4440/1	H98F+29	9/88	12/03	by11/06
369	DJJ 294GP	Mercedes-Benz O305 307001 61 049460	BBA	4440/2	H98F+29	9/88	12/03	
370	CZD 261GP	Leyland TRC/3R 8500328	Santini		B66F+16	889	12/03	by11/06
371	DNS 950GP	Mercedes-Benz O305 307001 26 000081	BBA	4495/1	H98F+16	10/89	12/03	9/07
372	DNS 951GP	Mercedes-Benz O305 307001 26 000082	BBA	4495/2	H98F+16	11/89	12/03	
373	DNS 952GP	Mercedes-Benz O305 307001 26 000083	BBA	4495/3	H98F+16	11/89	12/03	
374	DRJ 423GP	Mercedes-Benz O305 307001 26 000087	BBA	4567/1	H98F+16	12/90	12/03	
375	DRJ 424GP	Mercedes-Benz O305 307001 26 000088	BBA	4567/2	H98F+16	12/90	12/03	
376	FCL 467GP	Mercedes-Benz O305 307012 61 033207	BBA	3952/21	B60F+12	2/83	12/03	
377	DYC 863GP	Mercedes-Benz O305 307012 61 032947	BBA	3952/18	B60F+12	2/83	12/03	
379	DRJ 425GP	Mercedes-Benz O305 307012 61 032978	BBA	3952/22	B60F+12	2/83	12/03	
380	FCL 466GP	Mercedes-Benz O305 307012 61 035290	BBA	4012/5	B60F+12	7/83	12/03	
381	FCL 465GP	Mercedes-Benz O305 307012 61 035259	BBA	4012/3	B60F+12	6/83	12/03	
382	DYC 855GP	Mercedes-Benz O305 307110 61 035258	BBA	4012/2	B60F+12	6/83	12/03	
383	FCL 463GP	Mercedes-Benz O305 307012 61 035275	BBA	4012/4	B60F+12	7/83	12/03	
384	FCL 462GP	Mercedes-Benz O305 307012 61 035242	BBA	4012/1	B60F+12	6/83	12/03	
385	DYC 856GP	Mercedes-Benz O305 307001 61 038864	BBA	4076/5	B60F+12	6/84	12/03	
386	FCL 461GP	Mercedes-Benz O305 307001 61 038900	BBA	4076/7	B60F+12	7/84	12/03	
387	DYC 857GP	Mercedes-Benz O305 307001 61 038843	BBA	4076/2	B60F+12	6/84	12/03	
388	DYC 859GP	Mercedes-Benz O305 307001 61 038863	BBA	4076/4	B60F+12	6/84	12/03	
389	DNS 954GP	Mercedes-Benz O305 307001 61 038844	BBA	4076/3	B61F+12	6/84	12/03	
390	DYC 858GP	Mercedes-Benz O305 307001 61 038882	BBA	4076/6	B61F+12	7/84	12/03	
391	DYC 865GP	Mercedes-Benz O305 307001 61 033825	BBA	4076/1	B62F+12	6/84	12/03	
392	DNS 955GP	Mercedes-Benz O305 307001 61 042453	BBA	4158/2	C45F+12	6/85	12/03	
393	DNS 956GP	Mercedes-Benz O305 307001 61 042452	BBA	4158/1	B60F+12	6/85	12/03	by 11/06
394	DNS 957GP	Mercedes-Benz O305 307001 61 042495	BBA	4158/4	C45F+12	6/85	12/03	by 11/06

Notes:

301-394 ex Roodepoort 1-94 (not all numbers used). These vehicles were recorded with R suffixes to their
fleet numbers but these were not carried.
FVF 235/6GP (359/60) were new to Benoni Municipality.
FVF 210GP , DYC 862GP (364/7) also quoted as C49F.
FCL 467GP, DYC 863GP (376/7) were new to Pretoria Municipality 524/5.
DRJ 425GP, FCL 466/5GP, DYC 855GP (379-82) were new to Pretoria Municipality 527-30.
FCL 463/2GP, DYC 856GP, FCL 461GP (383-6) were new to Pretoria Municipality 531/2/41/2.
DYC 857/9GP, DNS 954GP, DYC 858/65GP (387-91) were new to Pretoria Municipality 543 7.
DNS 955-7GP (392-4) were new to Pretoria Municipality 551-3.
Vehicles were re-registered as follows prior to c1996:
DJJ 292GP (301) ex NVN 654T
FVY 104GP (302) ex LRT 370T and TU 32756 prior to c1979.
FVF 213GP (303) ex GXC 777T.
FPN 641GP (304) ex SHZ 097T.
DYC 860GP (305) ex NVS 157T.
FPN 642GP (306) ex SJB 408T.
DYC 861GP (307) ex PLP 223T.
FTV 429GP (308) ex TWL747T.
FTV 430GP (310) ex TWL735T.
FTV 432GP (311) ex TWL725T.
FVY 107GP (312) ex LRT 284T and TU 32755 prior to c1979.
FTV 433GP (313) ex CBK 726T.
FTV 434GP (314) ex TWV 137T.
FVF 215GP (315) ex TXK 401T.
FVF 216GP (316) ex TXK 402T.
FVY 109GP (317) ex PLP 198T.
FVF 218GP (318) ex TXK 406T.
FVF 219GP (320) ex TXK 398T.
FVF 223GP (321) ex TXK 403T.
CZD 264GP (323) ex JYN 326T.
FTV 437GP (324) ex CBK 734T.
CZD 263GP (326) ex FML 508T.
FTV 438GP (327) ex FML 486T.
FVF 225GP (330) ex TXK 399T.
FVY 115GP (336) ex LRR 659T and TU 6112 prior to c1979.
FTV 449GP (337) ex CBK 755T.
FTV 451GP (338) ex DJM 286T.
FVF 226GP (339) ex DKK 164T.
FVF 228GP (340) ex DKW 989T.
FVF 229GP (341) ex DLJ 248T.
FVF 208GP (342) ex FMS 178T.
CXL 019GP (343) ex FMS 161T.
CZD 262GP (344) ex GTF 782T.
FVY 117GP (345) ex GZT 065T.
CXL 016GP (346) ex HYY 199T.
CXL 015GP (347) ex HYY 202T.
CXL 014GP (348) ex HYY 211T.
CXL 017GP (349) ex HYY 220T.
CXL 018GP (350) ex HYY 221T.
FVF 214GP (352) ex JNP 386T.
FVY 118GP (353) ex JFM 835T.
FTV 452GP (354) ex KKC 322T.
FVY 119GP (355) ex PJH 915T.
FVF 231GP (356) ex MTN 201T.
FVF 232GP (357) ex MTN 203T.
FVF 234GP (358) ex MTN 206T.
FVF 235GP (359) ex FVZ 794T.
FVF 236GP (360) ex FVZ 795T.
FVF 238GP (361) ex CGP 778T.
FVF 211GP (362) ex KJT 190T.
DNS 942GP (363) ex MFV 607T.
FVF 210GP (364) ex MRR 323T.
DNS 946GP (365) ex NBV 743T.

DNS 949GP (366) ex NCC 029T.
DYC 862GP (367) ex NDV 559T.
DJJ 293GP (368) ex MYT 788T.
DJJ 294GP (369) ex MYT 787T.
CZD 261GP (370) ex NNY 227T.
DNS 950GP (371) ex NTB 944T.
DNS 951GP (372) ex NTB 924T.
DNS 952GP (373) ex NTB 929T.
DRJ 423GP (374) ex PKJ 213T.
DRJ 424GP (375) ex PJY 978T.
FCL 467GP (376) ex HTG 186T.
DYC 863GP (377) ex HTG 182T.
DYV 853GP (378) ex HTG 177T.
DRJ 425GP (379) ex HVT 930T.
FCL 466GP (380) ex HYH 360T.
FCL 465GP (381) ex HYK 395T.
DYC 855GP (382) ex HYK 428T
FCL 463GP (383) ex HYK 403T.
FCL 462GP (384) ex HYK 415T.
DYC 856GP (385) ex JWZ 781T.
FCL 461GP (386) ex JWZ 788T.
DYC 857GP (387) ex JWZ 799T.
DYC 859GP (388) ex JWZ 790T.
DNS 954GP (389) ex JXD 188T.
DYC 858GP (390) ex JXN 705T.
DYC 865GP (391) ex JXW 437T.
DNS 955GP (392) ex KLV 652T.
DNS 956GP (393) ex KLV 639T.
DNS 957GP (394) ex KLV 662T.

Disposals:

FTV 433GP (313): WJ De Beer Motors Roodepoort, Florida.

4001	VCP 387GP	Mercedes Benz 9BM3821886B476645	Marcopolo	501662	B21FL+56	9/06	9/06
4002	VCP 409GP	Mercedes Benz 9BM3821886B479363	Marcopolo	501663	B21FL+56	9/06	9/06
4003	VCP 426GP	Mercedes Benz 9BM3821886B483335	Marcopolo	501664	B21FL+56	9/06	9/06
4004	VCP 419GP	Mercedes Benz 9BM3821886B482884	Marcopolo	501665	B21FL+56	9/06	9/06
4005	VCT 447GP	Mercedes Benz 9BM3821886B482465	Marcopolo	501667	B21FL+56	9/06	9/06
4006	VCT 487GP	Mercedes Benz 9BM3821886B482515	Marcopolo	501666	B21FL+56	9/06	9/06
4007	VCB 255GP	Mercedes Benz 9BM3821886B482030	Marcopolo	501661	B60F+0	9/06	9/06
4008	VBZ 842GP	Mercedes Benz 9BM3821886B479190	Marcopolo	501632	B60F+0	9/06	9/06
4009	VCB 045GP	Mercedes Benz 9BM3821886B479197	Marcopolo	501633	B60F+0	9/06	9/06
4010	VCB 096GP	Mercedes Benz 9BM3821886B480779	Marcopolo	501634	B60F+0	9/06	9/06
4011	VCB 055GP	Mercedes Benz 9BM3821886B481022	Marcopolo	501635	B60F+0	9/06	9/06
4012	VCB 083GP	Mercedes Benz 9BM3821886B481059	Marcopolo	501636	B60F+0	9/06	9/06
4013	VCB 192GP	Mercedes Benz 9BM3821886B481254	Marcopolo	501637	B60F+0	9/06	9/06
4014	VBZ 887GP	Mercedes Benz 9BM3821886B481261	Marcopolo	501638	B60F+0	9/06	9/06
4015	VBZ 861GP	Mercedes Benz 9BM3821886B481286	Marcopolo	501639	B60F+0	9/06	9/06
4016	VCB 217GP	Mercedes Benz	Marcopolo	501640	B60F+0	9/06	9/06

		9BM3821886B481477					
4017	VBZ 824GP	Mercedes Benz	Marcopolo	501641	B60F+0	9/06	9/06
		9BM3821886B481502					
4018	VCB 173GP	Mercedes Benz	Marcopolo	501642	B60F+0	9/06	9/06
		9BM3821886B482547					
4019	VCB 139GP	Mercedes Benz	Marcopolo	501643	B60F+0	9/06	9/06
		9BM3821886B481955					
4020	VBZ 950GP	Mercedes Benz	Marcopolo	501644	B60F+0	9/06	9/06
		9BM3821886B482052					
4021	VCB 153GP	Mercedes Benz	Marcopolo	501645	B60F+0	9/06	9/06
		9BM3821886B482066					
4022	VCB 233GP	Mercedes Benz	Marcopolo	501646	B60F+0	7/06	7/06
		9BM3821886B482073					
4023	VCB 120GP	Mercedes Benz	Marcopolo	501647	B60F+0	7/06	7/06
		9BM3821886B482079					
4024	VCB 103GP	Mercedes Benz	Marcopolo	501648	B60F+0	7/06	7/06
		9BM3821886B482091					
4025	VCB 273GP	Mercedes Benz	Marcopolo	501649	B60F+0	8/06	8/06
		9BM3821886B482094					
4026	VCB 020GP	Mercedes Benz	Marcopolo	501650	B60F+0	8/06	8/06
		9BM3821886B480815					
4027	VCB 183GP	Mercedes Benz	Marcopolo	501651	B60F+0	8/06	8/06
		9BM3821886B481246					
4028	VCB 166GP	Mercedes Benz	Marcopolo	501652	B60F+0	8/06	8/06
		9BM3821886B481004					
4029	VCB 290GP	Mercedes Benz	Marcopolo	501653	B60F+0	8/06	8/06
		9BM3821886B481513					
4030	VCB 382GP	Mercedes Benz	Marcopolo	501654	B60F+0	8/06	8/06
		9BM3821886B481243					
4031	VBZ 908GP	Mercedes Benz	Marcopolo	501655	B60F+0	8/06	8/06
		9BM3821886B482001					
4032	VCH 172GP	Mercedes Benz	Marcopolo	501656	B60F+0	8/06	8/06
		9BM3821886B481537					
4033	VCB 148GP	Mercedes Benz	Marcopolo	501657	B60F+0	8/06	8/06
		9BM3821886B480800					
4034	VCB 283GP	Mercedes Benz	Marcopolo	501658	B60F+0	8/06	8/06
		9BM3821886B482878					
4035	VCB 201GP	Mercedes Benz	Marcopolo	501659	B60F+0	8/06	8/06
		9BM3821886B481234					
4036	VCT 421GP	Mercedes Benz	Marcopolo	501660	B60F+0	8/06	8/06
		9BM3821886B481497					
4037	VHT 484GP	Mercedes Benz	Marcopolo	501716	B60F+0	10/06	10/06
		9BM3821886B481996					
4038	VJF 343GP	Mercedes Benz	Marcopolo	501717	B60F+0	10/06	10/06
		9BM3821886B482413					
4039	VHT 174GP	Mercedes Benz	Marcopolo	501718	B60F+0	10/06	10/06
		9BM3821886B481269					
4040	VHT 097GP	Mercedes Benz	Marcopolo	501719	B60F+0	10/06	10/06
		9BM3821886B480763					
4041	VHT 114GP	Mercedes Benz	Marcopolo	501720	B60F+0	10/06	10/06
		9BM3821886B481489					
4042	VHT 161GP	Mercedes Benz	Marcopolo	501721	B60F+0	10/06	10/06
		9BM3821886B481042					
4043	VHT 197GP	Mercedes Benz	Marcopolo	501722	B60F+0	10/06	10/06
		9BM3821886B488740					
4044	VHT 361GP	Mercedes Benz	Marcopolo	501723	B60F+0	10/06	10/06
		9BM3821886B488739					
4045	VHT 362GP	Mercedes Benz	Marcopolo	501724	B60F+0	10/06	10/06
		9BM3821886B488738					
4046	VHT 367GP	Mercedes Benz	Marcopolo	501725	B60F+0	10/06	10/06
		9BM3821886B488983					
4047	VHT 373GP	Mercedes Benz	Marcopolo	501726	B60F+0	10/06	10/06
		9BM3821886B499984					
4048	VHT 317GP	Mercedes Benz	Marcopolo	501727	B60F+0	10/06	1006

				9BM3821886B488985						
4049	VHT 172GP	Mercedes Benz			Marcopolo	501728	B60F+0	10/06	1006	
				9BM3821886B489223						
4050	VHT 126GP	Mercedes Benz			Marcopolo	501729	B60F+0	10/06	1006	
				9BM3821886B489456						
4051	VHT 146GP	Mercedes Benz			Marcopolo	501730	B60F+0	10/06	1006	
				9BM3821886B489222						
4052	VHT 105GP	Mercedes Benz			Marcopolo	501731	B60F+0	10/06	1006	
				9BM3821886B489457						
4053	VHT 209GP	Mercedes Benz			Marcopolo	501732	B60F+0	10/06	1006	by5/09
				9BM3821886B489458						
4054	VHT 188GP	Mercedes Benz			Marcopolo	501733	B60F+0	10/06	1006	
				9BM3821886B489724						
4055	VHT 352GP	Mercedes Benz			Marcopolo	501734	B60F+0	10/06	1006	
				9BM3821886B489224						
4056	VJD 329GP	Mercedes Benz			Marcopolo	501735	B60F+0	10/06	1006	
				9BM3821886B489725						
4057	VHT 446GP	Mercedes Benz			Marcopolo	501736	B60F+0	10/06	1006	
				9BM3821886B489726						
4058	VHT 440GP	Mercedes Benz			Marcopolo	501737	B60F+0	10/06	1006	
				9BM3821886B489727						
4059	VHT 376GP	Mercedes Benz			Marcopolo	501738	B60F+0	10/06	1006	
				9BM3821886B489728						
4060	VHT 378GP	Mercedes Benz			Marcopolo	501739	B60F+0	10/06	1006	
				9BM3821886B489729						
4061	VHT 441GP	Mercedes Benz			Marcopolo	501740	B60F+0	10/06	1006	
				9BM3821886B489924						
4062	VHT 370GP	Mercedes Benz			Marcopolo	501741	B60F+0	10/06	1006	
				9BM3821886B489925						
4063	VHT 347GP	Mercedes Benz			Marcopolo	501742	B60F+0	10/06	1006	
				9BM3821886B489927						
4064	VHT 135GP	Mercedes Benz			Marcopolo	501743	B60F+0	10/06	1006	
				9BM3821886B489928						
4065	VHT 480GP	Mercedes Benz			Marcopolo	501744	B60F+0	10/06	1006	
				9BM3821886B489923						
4066	VJF 345GP	Mercedes Benz			Marcopolo	501745	B60F+0	10/06	1006	
				9BM3821886B489730						
4067	VJR 020GP	Mercedes Benz			Marcopolo	501746	B60F+0	10/06	1006	
				9BM3821886B490290						
4068	VJR 019GP	Mercedes Benz			Marcopolo	501747	B60F+0	10/06	1006	
				9BM3821886B489926						
4069	VJR 027GP	Mercedes Benz			Marcopolo	501748	B60F+0	10/06	1006	
				9BM3821886B489929						
4070	VJR 026GP	Mercedes Benz			Marcopolo	501749	B60F+0	10/06	1006	
				9BM3821886B490293						
4071	VJR 028GP	Mercedes Benz			Marcopolo	501750	B60F+0	10/06	1006	
				9BM3821886B490292						
4072	VJR 022GP	Mercedes Benz			Marcopolo	501751	B60F+0	1006	1006	
				9BM3821886B490356						
4073	VJR 024GP	Mercedes Benz			Marcopolo	501752	B60F+0	1006	1006	
				9BM3821886B490358						
4074	VJR 025GP	Mercedes Benz			Marcopolo	501753	B60F+0	1006	1006	
				9BM3821886B490357						
4075	VJP 992GP	Mercedes Benz			Marcopolo	501754	B60F+0	1006	1006	
				9BM3821886B490597						
4076	VJR 017GP	Mercedes Benz			Marcopolo	501755	B60F+0	10/06	1006	
				9BM3821886B490291						
4077	VJP 995GP	Mercedes Benz			Marcopolo	501756	B60F+0	10/06	10/06	
				9BM3821886B490598						
4078	VJP 998GP	Mercedes Benz			Marcopolo	501757	B60F+0	10/06	10/06	
				9BM3821886B490601						
4079	VJP 980GP	Mercedes Benz			Marcopolo	501758	B60F+0	10/06	10/06	
				9BM3821886B490355						
4080	VJP 972GP	Mercedes Benz			Marcopolo	501759	B60F+0	10/06	10/06	

			9BM3821886B490600					
4081	VJP 969GP	Mercedes Benz		Marcopolo	501760	B60F+0	10/06	10/06
			9BM3821886B490602					
4082	VJP 977GP	Mercedes Benz		Marcopolo	501761	B60F+0	10/06	10/06
			9BM3821886B490596					
4083	VJP 983GP	Mercedes Benz		Marcopolo	501762	B60F+0	10/06	10/06
			9BM3821886B490595					
4084	VJP 975GP	Mercedes Benz		Marcopolo	501763	B60F+0	11/06	11/06
			9BM3821886B490604					
4085	VJR 030GP	Mercedes Benz		Marcopolo	501764	B60F+0	11/06	11/06
			9BM3821886B490603					
4086	VJR 031GP	Mercedes Benz		Marcopolo	501765	B60F+0	11/06	11/06
			9BM3821886B490340					
4087	VJR 034GP	Mercedes Benz		Marcopolo	501766	B60F+0	110/6	11/06
			9BM3821886B490343					
4088	VJR 033GP	Mercedes Benz		Marcopolo	501767	B60F+0	110/6	11/06
			9BM3821886B490344					
4089	VJR 008GP	Mercedes Benz		Marcopolo	501768	B60F+0	110/6	11/06
			9BM3821886B490345					
4090	VJR 002GP	Mercedes Benz		Marcopolo	501769	B60F+0	11/06	11/06
			9BM3821886B490599					
4091	VJR 007GP	Mercedes Benz		Marcopolo	501770	B60F+0	11/06	11/06
			9BM3821886B490342					
4092	VJR 012GP	Mercedes Benz		Marcopolo	501771	B60F+0	11/06	11/06
			9BM3821886B490760					
4093	VJR 010GP	Mercedes Benz		Marcopolo	501772	B60F+0	11/06	11/06
			9BM3821886B490759					
4094	VJR 013GP	Mercedes Benz		Marcopolo	501773	B60F+0	11/06	11/06
			9BM3821886B490761					
4095	VJR 015GP	Mercedes Benz		Marcopolo	501774	B60F+0	11/06	11/06
			9BM3821886B490762					
4096	VJR 006GP	Mercedes Benz		Marcopolo	501775	B60F+0	11/06	11/06
			9BM3821886B490341					
4097	VLC 403GP	Mercedes Benz		Marcopolo	501776	B60F+0	11/06	11/06
			9BM3821886B491373					
4098	VLC 381GP	Mercedes Benz		Marcopolo	501777	B60F+0	11/06	11/06
			9BM3821886B491333					
4099	VLC 389GP	Mercedes Benz		Marcopolo	501778	B60F+0	110/6	11/06
			9BM3821886B491372					
4100	VLC 154GP	Mercedes Benz		Marcopolo	501779	B60F+0	11/06	11/06
			9BM3821886B491805					
4101	VLC 411GP	Mercedes Benz		Marcopolo	501780	B60F+0	11/06	11/06
			9BM3821886B491374					
4102	VLC 372GP	Mercedes Benz		Marcopolo	501781	B60F+0	11/06	11/06
			9BM3821886B491332					
4103	VLC 158GP	Mercedes Benz		Marcopolo	501782	B60F+0	11/06	11/06
			9BM3821886B491808					
4104	VLC 397GP	Mercedes Benz		Marcopolo	501783	B60F+0	11/06	11/06
			9BM3821886B491371					
4105	VLC 165GP	Mercedes Benz		Marcopolo	501784	B60F+0	11/06	11/06
			9BM3821886B491807					
4106	VLC 173GP	Mercedes Benz		Marcopolo	501785	B60F+0	11/06	11/06
			9BM3821886B491506					
4107	VLC 347GP	Mercedes Benz		Marcopolo	501786	B60F+0	11/06	11/06
			9BM3821886B491952					
4108	VLC 196GP	Mercedes Benz		Marcopolo	501787	B60F+0	11/06	11/06
			9BM3821886B492187					
4109	VLC 217GP	Mercedes Benz		Marcopolo	501788	B60F+0	11/06	11/06
			9BM3821886B491503					
4110	VLC 209GP	Mercedes Benz		Marcopolo	501789	B60F+0	11/06	11/06
			9BM3821886B491954					
4111	VLC 205GP	Mercedes Benz		Marcopolo	501790	B60F+0	11/06	11/06
			9BM3821886B492185					
4112	VLC 187GP	Mercedes Benz		Marcopolo	501791	B60F+0	11/06	11/06

		9BM3821886B492186						
4113	VLC 181GP	Mercedes Benz	Marcopolo	501792	B60F+0	11/06	11/06	
		9BM3821886B491951						
4114	VLC 120GP	Mercedes Benz	Marcopolo	501793	B60F+0	11/06	11/06	
		9BM3821886B492661						
4115	VLC 137GP	Mercedes Benz	Marcopolo	501794	B60F+0	11/06	11/06	
		9BM3821886B492663						
4116	VLC 080GP	Mercedes Benz	Marcopolo	501795	B60F+0	11/06	11/06	
		9BM3821886B492425						
4117	VLC 147GP	Mercedes Banz	Marcopolo	501796	B60F+0	11/06	11/06	
		9BM3821886B492665						
4118	VLC 112GP	Mercedes Benz	Marcopolo	501797	B60F+0	11/06	11/06	
		9BM3821886B492660						
4119	VLC 125GP	Mercedes Benz	Marcopolo	501798	B60F+0	11/06	11/06	
		9BM3821886B490662						
4120	VLC 358GP	Mercedes Benz	Marcopolo	501799	B60F+0	11/06	11/06	
		9BM3821886B492188						
4121	VLC 088GP	Mercedes Benz	Marcopolo	501800	B60F+0	12/06	12/06	
		9BM3821886B492424						
4122	VLC 106GP	Mercedes Benz	Marcopolo	501801	B60F+0	12/06	12/06	
		9BM3821886B492418						
4123	VLC 056GP	Mercedes Benz	Marcopolo	501802	B60F+0	12/06	12/06	
		9BM3821886B492886						
4124	VLC 100GP	Mercedes Benz	Marcopolo	501803	B60F+0	12/06	12/06	
		9BM3821886B492419						
4125	VLC 072GP	Mercedes Benz	Marcopolo	501804	B60F+0	12/06	12/06	
		9BM3821886B492889						
4126	VLC 048GP	Mercedes Benz	Marcopolo	501805	B60F+0	12/06	12/06	
		9BM3821886B492888						
X100	TVL 481GP	Mercedes-Benz	Brasa	68162047	C45FT	6/07	6/07	
		9BM6340615B458012						
X101	TVN 083GP	Mercedes-Benz	Brasa	68162046	C45FT	6/07	6/07	
		9BM6340615B457498						

Notes:
TVL 481GP, TVN 083GP (X100/1) have body numbers preceded by BUSRGFBUN and followed by POLO.

Disposal:
VHT 209GP (4053): burnt out.

Trolleybuses

Vehicle on Demonstration from Guy Motors Ltd, Wolverhampton 11/30 – 11/32

?	TJ 12732	Guy BTX60	BTX23579	Guy		H66R	7/30	11/30	11/32

Notes:
TJ 12732 is reported to have been an unregistered demonstrator with JMT but it carried this registration when it arrived in Cape Town. Originally a Guy demonstrator this trolleybus was sold to City Tramways. Seating has also been reported as H31/28R.

1		Sunbeam MF2	13035	MCCW	H36/24R+12	9/36	9/36	by9/59
2		Sunbeam MF2	13036	MCCW	H36/24R+12	9/36	9/36	by9/59
3		Sunbeam MF2	13037	MCCW	H36/24R+12	9/36	9/36	by9/59
4		Sunbeam MF2	13038	MCCW	H36/24R+12	9/36	9/36	by9/59
5		Sunbeam MF2	13039	MCCW	H36/24R+12	9/36	9/36	by9/59
6		Sunbeam MF2	13040	MCCW	H36/24R+12	9/36	9/36	by9/59
7		Sunbeam MF2	13041	MCCW	H36/24R+12	9/36	9/36	by9/59
8		Sunbeam MF2	13042	MCCW	H36/24R+12	9/36	9/36	by9/59
9		Sunbeam MF2	13043	MCCW	H36/24R+12	9/36	9/36	by9/59
10		Sunbeam MF2	13044	MCCW	H36/24R+12	9/36	9/36	by9/59
11		Sunbeam MF2	13045	MCCW	H36/24R+12	9/36	9/36	by9/59
12		AEC 661T	661T089	MCCW	H36/24R+12	9/36	9/36	by9/59

13	AEC 661T	661T080	MCCW		H36/24R+12	9/36	9/36	by9/59
14	AEC 661T	661T088	MCCW		H36/24R+12	9/36	9/36	by9/59
15	AEC 661T	661T079	MCCW		H36/24R+12	9/36	9/36	by9/59
16	AEC 661T	661T086	MCCW		H36/24R+12	9/36	9/36	by9/59
17	AEC 661T	661T087	MCCW		H36/24R+12	9/36	9/36	by9/59
18	AEC 661T	661T081	MCCW		H36/24R+12	9/36	9/36	by9/59
19	AEC 661T	661T084	MCCW		H36/24R+12	9/36	9/36	by9/59
20	AEC 661T	661T082	MCCW		H36/24R+12	9/36	9/36	by9/59
21	AEC 661T	661T085	MCCW		H36/24R+12	9/36	9/36	by9/59
22	AEC 661T	661T083	MCCW		H36/24R+12	9/36	9/36	by9/59
23	AEC 661T	661T203	MCCW		H34/26D	4/38	4/38	by9/59
24	AEC 661T	661T205	MCCW		H34/26D	4/38	4/38	by9/59
25	AEC 661T	661T204	MCCW		H34/26D	4/38	4/38	by9/59
26	AEC 661T	661T207	MCCW		H34/26D	4/38	4/38	by9/59
27	AEC 661T	661T206	MCCW		H34/26D	4/38	4/38	by9/59
28	AEC 661T	661T202	MCCW		H34/26D	4/38	4/38	by9/59
29	AEC 661T	661T201	MCCW		H34/26D	4/38	4/38	by9/59
30	AEC 661T	661T200	MCCW		H34/26D	4/38	4/38	by9/59
31	Sunbeam MF2	13061	MCCW		H34/26D	4/38	4/38	by9/59
32	Sunbeam MF2	13062	MCCW		H34/26D	4/38	4/38	by9/59
33	Sunbeam MF2	13063	MCCW		H34/26D	4/38	4/38	by9/59
34	Sunbeam MF2	13064	MCCW		H34/26D	4/38	4/38	by9/59
35	Sunbeam MF2	13065	MCCW		H34/26D	4/38	4/38	by9/59
36	Sunbeam MF2	13066	MCCW		H34/26D	4/38	4/38	by9/59
37	Sunbeam MF2	13067	MCCW		H34/26D	4/38	4/38	by9/59
38	Sunbeam MF2	13068	MCCW		H34/26D	4/38	4/38	by9/59
539	Sunbeam W4-BTH	50406	MCCW/BBA	M156	H34/26D	7/48	7/48	by3/76
540	Sunbeam W4-BTH	50412	MCCW/BBA	M157	H34/26D	7/48	7/48	by3/76
541	Sunbeam W4-BTH	50414	MCCW/BBA	M158	H34/26D	7/48	7/48	by3/76
542	Sunbeam W4-BTH	50419	MCCW/BBA	M159	H34/26D	7/48	7/48	by3/76
543	Sunbeam W4-BTH	50410	MCCW/BBA	M160	H34/26D	7/48	7/48	by12/62
544	Sunbeam W4-BTH	50415	MCCW/BBA	M161	H34/26D	7/48	7/48	by3/76
545	Sunbeam W4-BTH	50409	MCCW/BBA	M162	H34/26D	7/48	7/48	by12/62
546	Sunbeam W4-BTH	50416	MCCW/BBA	M163	H34/26D	8/48	8/48	by3/76
547	Sunbeam W4-BTH	50426	MCCW/BBA	M164	H34/26D	8/48	8/48	by3/76
548	Sunbeam W4-BTH	50427	MCCW/BBA	M165	H34/26D	8/48	8/48	by12/62
549	Sunbeam W4-BTH	50411	MCCW/BBA	M166	H34/26D	8/48	8/48	by12/62
550	Sunbeam W4-BTH	50417	MCCW/BBA	M167	H34/26D	8/48	8/48	by12/62
551	Sunbeam W4-BTH	50424	MCCW/BBA	M168	H34/26D	8/48	8/48	by12/62
552	Sunbeam W4-BTH	50425	MCCW/BBA	M169	H34/26D	8/48	8/48	by3/76
553	Sunbeam W4-BTH	50404	MCCW/BBA	M170	H34/26D	8/48	8/48	by12/62
554	Sunbeam W4-BTH	50407	MCCW/BBA	M171	H34/26D	8/48	8/48	by3/76
555	Sunbeam W4-BTH	50408	MCCW/BBA	M172	H34/26D	8/48	8/48	by12/62
556	Sunbeam W4-BTH	50421	MCCW/BBA	M173	H34/26D	8/48	8/48	by12/62
557	Sunbeam W4-BTH	50405	MCCW/BBA	M174	H34/26D	8/48	8/48	by12/62
558	Sunbeam W4-BTH	50413	MCCW/BBA	M175	H34/26D	8/48	8/48	by3/76
559	Sunbeam W4-BTH	50418	MCCW/BBA	M176	H34/26D	9/48	9/48	by3/76
560	Sunbeam W4-BTH	50423	MCCW/BBA	M177	H34/26D	9/48	9/48	by12/62
561	Sunbeam W4-BTH	50420	MCCW/BBA	M178	H34/26D	9/48	9/48	by3/76
562	Sunbeam W4-BTH	50422	MCCW/BBA	M179	H34/26D	9/48	9/48	by12/62
563	Sunbeam W4-BTH	50403	MCCW		H34/26D	7/48	7/48	by3/76
564	BUT 964T/EE	964T001	MCCW		H40/31D+13	2/48	2/48	by3/76
565	BUT 964T/EE	964T002	MCCW/BBA	M111	H40/31D+13	3/48	3/48	by3/76
566	BUT 964T/EE	964T003	MCCW/BBA	M112	H40/31D+13	4/48	4/48	by3/76
567	BUT 964T/EE	964T004	MCCW/BBA	M113	H40/31D+13	4/48	4/48	by3/76
568	BUT 964T/EE	964T012	MCCW/BBA	M114	H40/31D+13	4/48	4/48	by3/76
569	BUT 964T/EE	964T013	MCCW/BBA	M115	H40/31D+13	4/48	4/48	by3/76
570	BUT 964T/EE	964T014	MCCW/BBA	M116	H40/31D+13	4/48	4/48	by3/76
571	BUT 964T/EE	964T006	MCCW/BBA	M117	H40/31D+13	4/48	4/48	by3/76
572	BUT 964T/EE	964T007	MCCW/BBA	M118	H40/31D+13	4/48	4/48	by3/76
573	BUT 964T/EE	964T008	MCCW/BBA	M119	H40/31D+13	4/48	4/48	by3/76
574	BUT 964T/EE	964T009	MCCW/BBA	M120	H40/31D+13	4/48	4/48	by3/76
575	BUT 964T/EE	964T021	MCCW/BBA	M121	H40/31D+13	4/48	4/48	by3/76
576	BUT 964T/EE	964T022	MCCW/BBA	M122	H40/31D+13	4/48	4/48	by3/76

577	BUT 964T/EE	964T023	MCCW/BBA	M123	H40/31D+13	5/48	5/48	by3/76
578	BUT 964T/EE	964T010	MCCW/BBA	M124	H40/31D+13	5/48	5/48	by3/76
579	BUT 964T/EE	964T011	MCCW/BBA	M125	H40/31D+13	5/48	5/48	by3/76
580	BUT 964T/EE	964T036	MCCW/BBA	M126	H40/31D+13	5/48	5/48	by3/76
581	BUT 964T/EE	964T037	MCCW/BBA	M127	H40/31D+13	5/48	5/48	by3/76
582	BUT 964T/EE	964T020	MCCW/BBA	M128	H40/31D+13	5/48	5/48	by3/76
583	BUT 964T/EE	964T015	MCCW/BBA	M129	H40/31D+13	5/48	5/48	by3/76
584	BUT 964T/EE	964T032	MCCW/BBA	M130	H40/31D+13	5/48	5/48	by3/76
585	BUT 964T/EE	964T019	MCCW/BBA	M131	H40/31D+13	5/48	5/48	by3/76
586	BUT 964T/EE	964T016	MCCW/BBA	M132	H40/31D+13	5/48	5/48	by3/76
587	BUT 964T/EE	964T028	MCCW/BBA	M133	H40/31D+13	5/48	5/48	by3/76
588	BUT 964T/EE	964T024	MCCW/BBA	M134	H40/31D+13	5/48	5/48	by3/76
589	BUT 964T/EE	964T026	MCCW/BBA	M135	H40/31D+13	5/48	5/48	by3/76
590	BUT 964T/EE	964T027	MCCW/BBA	M136	H40/31D+13	5/48	5/48	by3/76
591	BUT 964T/EE	964T017	MCCW/BBA	M137	H40/31D+13	6/48	6/48	by3/76
592	BUT 964T/EE	964T031	MCCW/BBA	M138	H40/31D+13	6/48	6/48	by3/76
593	BUT 964T/EE	964T029	MCCW/BBA	M139	H40/31D+13	6/48	6/48	by3/76
594	BUT 964T/EE	964T030	MCCW/BBA	M140	H40/31D+13	6/48	6/48	by3/76
595	BUT 964T/EE	964T018	MCCW/BBA	M141	H40/31D+13	6/48	6/48	by3/76
596	BUT 964T/EE	964T025	MCCW/BBA	M142	H40/31D+13	6/48	6/48	by3/76
597	BUT 964T/EE	964T033	MCCW/BBA	M143	H40/31D+13	6/48	6/48	by3/76
598	BUT 964T/EE	964T034	MCCW/BBA	M144	H40/31D+13	6/48	6/48	by3/76
599	BUT 964T/EE	964T035	MCCW/BBA	M145	H40/31D+13	6/48	6/48	by3/76
600	BUT 964T/EE	964T038	MCCW/BBA	M146	H40/31D+13	6/48	6/48	-/74
601	BUT 964T/EE	964T039	MCCW/BBA	M147	H40/31D+13	6/48	6/48	by3/76
602	BUT 964T/EE	964T041	MCCW/BBA	M148	H40/31D+13	6/48	6/48	by3/76
603	BUT 964T/EE	964T042	MCCW/BBA	M149	H40/31D+13	6/48	6/48	by3/76
604	BUT 964T/EE	964T046	MCCW/BBA	M150	H40/31D+13	7/48	7/48	by3/76
605	BUT 964T/EE	964T047	MCCW/BBA	M151	H40/31D+13	7/48	7/48	by3/76
606	BUT 964T/EE	964T048	MCCW/BBA	M152	H40/31D+13	7/48	7/48	by3/76
607	BUT 964T/EE	964T049	MCCW/BBA	M153	H40/31D+13	7/48	7/48	by3/76
608	BUT 964T/EE	964T052	MCCW/BBA	M154	H40/31D+13	7/48	7/48	by3/76
609	BUT 964T/EE	964T005	BMS		H40/31D+13	3/48	3/48	by3/76
610	BUT 964T/EE	964T053	BMS		H40/31D+13	4/48	4/48	by3/76
611	BUT 964T/EE	964T043	BMS		H40/31D+13	4/48	4/48	by3/76
612	BUT 964T/EE	964T040	BMS		H40/31D+13	4/48	4/48	by3/76
613	BUT 964T/EE	964T050	BMS		H40/31D+13	5/48	5/48	by3/76
614	BUT 964T/EE	964T044	BMS		H40/31D+13	5/48	5/48	-/--
615	BUT 964T/EE	964T059	BMS		H40/31D+13	5/48	5/48	-/--
616	BUT 964T/EE	964T057	BMS		H40/31D+13	5/48	5/48	-/--
617	BUT 964T/EE	964T055	BMS		H40/31D+13	6/48	6/48	by3/76
618	BUT 964T/EE	964T045	BMS		H40/31D+13	6/48	6/48	-/--
619	BUT 964T/EE	964T056	BMS		H40/31D+13	6/48	6/48	-/--
620	BUT 964T/EE	964T054	BMS		H40/31D+13	6/48	6/48	-/--
621	BUT 964T/EE	964T060	BMS		H40/31D+13	6/48	6/48	-/--
622	BUT 964T/EE	964T051	BMS		H40/31D+13	8/48	8/48	-/--
623	BUT 964T/EE	964T058	BMS		H40/31D+13	4/49	4/49	-/--
624	BUT 9642T	9642T613	BBA	172/1	H43/30D+19	5/58	5/58	by -/82
625	BUT 9642T	9642T614	BBA	172/2	H43/30D+19	5/58	5/58	-/--
626	BUT 9642T	9642T615	BBA	172/3	H43/30D+19	5/58	5/58	-/--
627	BUT 9642T	9642T616	BBA	172/4	H43/30D+19	5/58	5/58	by -/82
628	BUT 9642T	9642T617	BBA	172/5	H43/30D+19	5/58	5/58	-/--
629	BUT 9642T	9642T618	BBA	172/6	H43/30D+19	5/58	5/58	by -/82
630	BUT 9642T	9642T619	BBA	172/7	H43/30D+19	5/58	5/58	-/--
631	BUT 9642T	9642T620	BBA	172/8	H43/30D+19	5/58	5/58	-/--
632	BUT 9642T	9642T621	BBA	172/9	H43/30D+19	5/58	5/58	by -/82
633	BUT 9642T	9642T622	BBA	172/10	H43/30D+19	5/58	5/58	-/--
634	BUT 9642T	9642T623	BBA	172/11	H43/30D+19	5/58	5/58	-/--
635	BUT 9642T	9642T624	BBA	172/12	H43/30D+19	6/58	6/58	-/--
636	BUT 9642T	9642T625	BBA	172/13	H43/30D+19	7/58	7/58	-/--
637	BUT 9642T	9642T626	BBA	172/14	H43/30D+19	7/58	7/58	by -/82
638	BUT 9642T	9642T627	BBA	172/15	H43/30D+19	7/58	7/58	by -/82
639	BUT 9642T	9642T628	BBA	172/16	H43/30D+19	6/58	6/58	-/--
640	BUT 9642T	9642T629	BBA	172/17	H43/30D+19	7/58	7/58	-/--

641	BUT 9642T	9642T630	BBA	172/18	H43/30D+19	7/58	7/58	-/--
642	BUT 9642T	9642T632	BBA	172/19	H43/30D+19	7/58	7/58	by -/82
643	BUT 9642T	9642T631	BBA	172/20	H43/30D+19	6/58	6/58	by -/82
644	BUT 9642T	9642T633	BBA	172/21	H43/30D+19	7/58	7/58	by -/82
645	BUT 9642T	9642T634	BBA	172/22	H43/30D+19	7/58	7/58	-/--
646	BUT 9642T	9642T635	BBA	172/23	H43/30D+19	7/58	7/58	-/--
647	BUT 9642T	9642T636	BBA	172/24	H43/30D+19	8/58	8/58	by -/82
648	BUT 9642T	0642T637	BBA	172/25	H43/30D+19	6/58	6/58	by -/82
649	BUT 9642T	9642T638	BBA	172/26	H43/30D+19	6/58	6/58	11/86
650	BUT 9642T	9642T639	BBA	172/27	H43/30D+19	6/58	6/58	by -/82
651	BUT 9642T	9642T640	BBA	172/28	H43/30D+19	7/58	7/58	-/--
652	BUT 9642T	9642T641	BBA	172/29	H43/30D+19	8/58	8/58	by -/82
653	BUT 9642T	9642T642	BBA	172/30	H43/30D+19	8/58	8/58	-/--
654	BUT 9642T	9642T643	BBA	172/31	H43/30D+19	5/58	5/58	by -/82
655	BUT 9642T	9642T644	BBA	172/32	H43/30D+19	6/58	6/58	-/--
656	BUT 9642T	9642T645	BBA	172/33	H43/30D+19	6/58	6/58	-/--
657	BUT 9642T	9642T646	BBA	172/34	H43/30D+19	7/58	7/58	-/--
658	BUT 9642T	9642T647	BBA	172/35	H43/30D+19	6/58	6/58	-/--
659	BUT 9642T	9642T648	BBA	172/36	H43/30D+19	7/58	7/58	-/--
660	BUT 9642T	9642T649	BBA	172/37	H43/30D+19	7/58	7/58	-/--
661	BUT 9642T	9642T650	BBA	172/38	H43/30D+19	6/58	6/58	-/--
662	BUT 9642T	9642T651	BBA	172/39	H43/30D+19	6/58	6/58	-/--
663	BUT 9642T	9642T652	BBA	172/40	H43/30D+19	6/58	6/58	by -/82
664	BUT 9642T	9642T653	BBA	172/41	H43/30D+19	8/58	8/58	-/--
665	BUT 9642T	9642T654	BBA	172/42	H43/30D+19	8/58	8/58	-/--
666	BUT 9642T	9642T655	BBA	172/43	H43/30D+19	9/58	9/58	-/--
667	BUT 9642T	9642T656	BBA	172/44	H43/30D+19	8/58	8/58	-/--
668	BUT 9642T	9642T657	BBA	172/45	H43/30D+19	8/58	8/58	-/--
669	BUT 9642T	9642T658	BBA	172/46	H43/30D+19	8/58	8/58	-/--
670	BUT 9642T	9642T659	BBA	172/47	H43/30D+19	9/58	9/58	-/--
671	BUT 9642T	9642T660	BBA	172/48	H43/30D+19	9/58	9/58	-/--
672	BUT 9642T	9642T661	BBA	172/49	H43/30D+19	9/58	9/58	-/--
673	BUT 9642T	9642T662	BBA	172/50	H43/30D+19	9/58	9/58	-/--
674	Alfa Romeo	C15062	BBA	176/1	H51/34D+25	12/58	12/58	by-/82
675	Alfa Romeo	C15064	BBA	176/2	H51/34D+25	12/58	12/58	by-/82
676	Alfa Romeo	C15073	BBA	176/3	H51/34D+25	10/58	10/58	by-/82
677	Alfa Romeo	C15084	BBA	176/4	H51/34D+25	11/58	11/58	by-/82
678	Alfa Romeo	C15092	BBA	176/5	H51/34D+25	12/58	12/58	by-/82
679	Alfa Romeo	C15080	BBA	176/6	H51/34D+25	11/58	11/58	by-/82
680	Alfa Romeo	C15085	BBA	176/7	H51/34D+25	11/58	11/58	by-/82
681	Alfa Romeo	C15070	BBA	176/8	H51/34D+25	11/58	11/58	by-/82
682	Alfa Romeo	C15082	BBA	176/9	H51/34D+25	11/58	11/58	by-/82
683	Alfa Romeo	C15091	BBA	176/10	H51/34D+25	-/58	-/58	by-/82
684	Alfa Romeo	C15077	BBA	176/11	H51/34D+25	10/58	10/58	by-/82
685	Alfa Romeo	C15078	BBA	176/12	H51/34D+25	11/58	11/58	by-/82
686	Alfa Romeo	C15066	BBA	176/13	H51/34D+25	11/58	11/58	by-/82
687	Alfa Romeo	C15081	BBA	176/14	H51/34D+25	10/58	10/58	by-/82
688	Alfa Romeo	C15083	BBA	176/15	H51/34D+25	11/58	11/58	by-/82
689	Alfa Romeo	C15063	BBA	176/16	H51/34D+25	10/58	10/58	by-/82
690	Alfa Romeo	C15061	BBA	176/17	H51/34D+25	11/58	11/58	by-/82
691	Alfa Romeo	C15075	BBA	176/18	H51/34D+25	11/58	11/58	by-/82
692	Alfa Romeo	C15079	BBA	176/19	H51/34D+25	11/58	11/58	by-/82
693	Alfa Romeo	C15065	BBA	176/20	H51/34D+25	11/58	11/58	by-/82
694	Sunbeam S7A	TFD74072	BBA	177/1	H51/34D+22	2/59	2/59	-/--
695	Sunbeam S7A	TFD74073	BBA	177/2	H51/34D+22	2/59	2/59	by-/82
696	Sunbeam S7A	TFD74071	BBA	177/3	H51/34D+22	2/59	2/59	-/--
697	Sunbeam S7A	TFD74075	BBA	177/4	H51/34D+22	2/59	2/59	-/--
698	Sunbeam S7A	TFD74077	BBA	177/5	H51/34D+22	2/59	2/59	-/--
699	Sunbeam S7A	TFD74078	BBA	177/6	H51/34D+22	2/59	2/59	by3/76
700	Sunbeam S7A	TFD74074	BBA	177/7	H51/34D+22	2/59	2/59	-/--
701	Sunbeam S7A	TFD74076	BBA	177/8	H51/34D+22	12/58	12/58	by3/76
702	Sunbeam S7A	TFD74079	BBA	177/9	H51/34D+22	1/59	1/59	by-/82
703	Sunbeam S7A	TFD74080	BBA	177/10	H51/34D+22	2/59	2/59	by-/82
704	Sunbeam S7A	TFD74081	BBA	177/11	H51/34D+22	12/58	12/58	by3/76

705	Sunbeam S7A	TFD74082	BBA	177/12	H51/34D+22	1/59	1/59	-/--
706	Sunbeam S7A	TFD74083	BBA	177/13	H51/34D+22	1/59	1/59	by-/82
707	Sunbeam S7A	TFD74084	BBA	177/14	H51/34D+22	1/59	1/59	-/--
708	Sunbeam S7A	TFD74085	BBA	177/15	H51/34D+22	1/59	1/59	-/--
709	Sunbeam S7A	TFD74086	BBA	177/16	H51/34D+22	1/59	1/59	by3/76
710	Sunbeam S7A	TFD74087	BBA	177/17	H51/34D+22	1/59	1/59	by-/82
711	Sunbeam S7A	TFD74088	BBA	177/18	H51/34D+22	12/58	12/58	-/--
712	Sunbeam S7A	TFD74089	BBA	177/19	H51/34D+22	1/59	1/59	-/--
713	Sunbeam S7A	TFD74090	BBA	177/20	H51/34D+22	4/59	4/59	-/--
800	Mercedes-Benz O305	?			H49/45F	-/81	-/81	-/86
		307200 21 025125						
801	Quest 80 E1	STE-001	BBA	3745/1	H43/40F	5/81	5/81	-/86
802	Springfield	Springfield			H49/40F+11	-/81	-/81	-/86
803	Springfield	Springfield			H91F	-/81	-/81	-/86
804	Springfield	Springfield			H91F	-/81	-/81	-/86
805	Springfield	Springfield			AB79D	-/81	-/81	-/86
806	Springfield	Springfield			AB79D	-/81	-/81	-/86

Notes:

1-11 later renumbered 501-11. Seating has also been recorded as H34/30D.
12 Seating also been reported as H34/30D.
12-22 later renumbered 512-22.
23-30 and 31-8 also recorded as H36/24D+12 (most likely) and H34/30D.
23-30 later renumbered 523-30
31-8 later renumbered 531-8.
564-623 carried chassis numbers prefixed 964T. AEC later listed them as 9641T.
563/4 allocated BBA body numbers M155, M110 but were fully built by MCCW.
577/9/88/93, 601 rebuilt to H39/28D+13 for one man operation in 1969.
587/93 & 601 renumbered 1578/93, 1601 in 1978.
609-23 the source for the chassis number information cannot be traced and after rebodying only the
following vehicles carried chassis numbers, some of which differed from those previously
given. The new numbers are as follows:
616: 9641T057 (no change), 618: 9641T053, 619: 9641T040, 623: 9641T059.
611-5 rebodied by Brockhouse c1962/3. Only 614/5 carried body numbers: 08028 and 0828 respectively.
616-23 rebodied by Brockhouse H43/30D+19 in 1960.
620-2/4-73/94-8, 700/3/5/8/10-3 renumbered 1620-2/4-73/94-8, 1700/3/5/8/10-3 in 1978.
626-48 modified for one man operation in 1969.
The following trolleybuses were ordered as below but not delivered due to World War II:

AEC 664T	664T830-47	MCCW	Diverted to LPTB 1747-64.
AEC 664T	664T848-59	MCCW	Cancelled.
Sunbeam MF2	13082-96	Weymann	Diverted to Bradford 693-702 and Nottingham 447-51.
Sunbeam MF2	13097-106	Massey	Diverted to St. Helens 157-66.

Disposals:

600: James Hall Museum of Transport, La Rochelle, Johannesburg.
649 (as 1649): James Hall Museum of Transport 11/86 (no longer on the Museum's web site).
800: converted to bus 800 and registered NXZ 623T.
801-5: scrapped.
806 to be donated to the James Hall Museum of Transport – not on website.

KEMPTON PARK BUS SERVICE, KEMPTON PARK

Kempton Park Bus Service was an independent company which passed to Kempton Park Municipality in 1963.

		Leyland ECPO2/1R	564776	BBA	150/2	B50F	6/56	6/56	-/--
		Leyland ECPO2/1R	565279	BBA	151/3	B50F	9/56	9/56	-/--
5	TCD 6004	Leyland PSUC1/3	?	AB&C		B55F	-/56	-/56	-/63
		Albion PF101B	64555C	BBA	243/1	B47F	9/57	9/57	-/--
		Albion PF101B	64555B	BBA	243/2	B47F	11/57	11/57	-/--
8	TCD 6008	Leyland PSUC1/3	?	BBA	?	B55F	-/57	-/57	-/63
6	TCD 2001	Leyland ERT2/1	573746	BBA	270/10	B49F+12	5/58	5/58	-/63

1	TCD 6001	Leyland ERT2/1	581994	BBA	284/1	B56F	8/58	8/58	-/63
2	TCD 6002	Leyland ERT2/1	581995	BBA	284/2	B53F	9/58	9/58	-/63
4	TCD 6003	Leyland ERT2/1	582459	BBA	327/1	B51F	5/59	5/59	-/63
7	TCD 6010	Leyland 14B/1XL	593081	BBA	372/1	B54F	7/60	7/60	-/63
9	TCD 6012	Leyland 14B/1XL	593082	BBA	372/2	B54F	7/60	7/60	-/63
17	TCD 6009	Leyland 14B/1XL	593182	BBA	373/3	B54F	8/60	8/60	-/63
11	TCD 6011	Leyland 14B/1XL	601486	BBA	373/2	B54F	8/60	8/60	-/63
3	TCD 6014	Leyland ERT2/1	?	DBA	?	B63F	-/61	-/61	-/63
		Leyland ERT2/1	622576	BBA	1821/1	DP--F	3/63	3/63	-/63
		Leyland ERT2/1	622577	BBA	1821/2	DP--F	3/63	3/63	-/63

Disposals:
TCD 6009-6012 (17/7/11/9) were Leyland VoortrekkeR models, a special PSV design for South Africa.
TCD 6004/8, 2001, 6001-3/10/2 (5, 8, 6, 1, 2, 4, 7, 9): Kempton Park Municipality 5, 8, 6, 1, 2, 4, 7, 9.
TCD 6009/11/4.?, ? (17, 11, 3, ?, ? (Leyland ERT2/1 622576/7): Kempton Park Municipality 17, 11, 3, ?, ?.

KEMPTON PARK MUNICIPALITY

Formed in 1963 when the Municipality acquired the local independent, Kempton Park Bus Service. Fleet size increased to 40 in 1984. Non white services (total 12 buses) were sold to PUTCO c1986.

1	TCD 6001	Leyland ERT2/1	581994	BBA	284/1	B56F	8/58	-/63	-/--
2	TCD 6002	Leyland ERT2/1	581995	BBA	284/2	B53F	9/58	-/63	-/--
3	TDC 6014	Leyland ERT2/1	?	BBA	?	B63F	-/61	-/63	-/--
4	TCD 6003	Leyland ERT2/1	582459	BBA	327/1	B51F	5/59	-/63	-/--
5	TCD 6004	Leyland PSUC1/3	?	AB&C		B55F	-/56	-/63	-/--
6	TCD 2001	Leyland ERT2/1	573746	BBA	270/10	B49F+12	5/58	-/63	-/--
7	TCD 6010	Leyland 14B/1XL	593081	BBA	372/1	B54F	7/60	-/63	-/--
8	TCD 6008	Leyland PSUC1/3	?	BBA	?	B55F	-/57	-/63	-/--
9	TCD 6012	Leyland 14B/1XL	593082	BBA	372/2	B54F	7/60	-/63	-/--
10	TCD 6058	AEC Kudu	?	TMBB		B65F	-/67?	-/67?	-/--
11	TCD 6011	Leyland 14B/1XL	601486	BBA	373/2	B54F	8/60	-/63	-/--
17	TCD 6009	Leyland 14B/1XL	593182	BBA	373/3	B54F	8/60	-/63	-/--
		Leyland ERT2/1	622576	BBA	1821/1	DP--F	3/63	-/63	-/--
		Leyland ERT2/1	622577	BBA	1821/2	DP--F	3/63	-/63	-/--
12	TCD 7818	DAF	?	Trio		B66F	-/65	-/65	-/--
12	TCD 3006	AEC Kudu	?	TMBB		B65F	-/66	-/66	-/--
13	TCD 3048	AEC Kudu	?	TMBB		B64F	-/66	-/66	-/--
14	TCD 6013	AEC Kudu	?	TMBB		B64F	-/66	-/66	-/--
16	TCD 6425	AEC Kudu	?	TMBB		B61F	-/69--/70	-/69--/70	-/--
	TCD 6415	AEC Kudu	?	TMBB		B61F	-/69--/70	-/69--/70	-/--
	TCD 6504	AEC Kudu	?	TMBB		B61F	-/69--/70	-/69--/70	-/--
221	TCD 4993	Bussing Konsul II	?	Springfield		B60F	-/70	-/70	-/--
222	TCD 3708	Bussing Konsul II	?	Springfield		B60F	-/70	-/70	-/--
223	TCD 2483	Leyland ERT2/1	?	TMBB		B--F	-/72	-/72	-/--
224	TCD 63359	Leyland ERT2/1	?	TMBB		B--F	-/72	-/72	-/--
225	TCD 21186	Leyland ERT2/1	?	TMBB		B--F	-/72	-/72	-/--
		Mercedes-Benz OF1617	?	Brockhouse		B--F	-/73	-/73	-/--
3		Saurer	?	?		B--F	by-/78	by-/78	-/--
30		MAN	?	?		AB---	by-/78	by-/78	-/--
		Nissan CB20N	01889	BBA	3883/1	B--F	2/82	2/82	-/--
		Nissan CB20N	01892	BBA	3883/2	B--F	2/82	2/82	-/--
		Nissan CB20N	01897	BBA	3883/3	B--F	2/82	2/82	-/--
		Nissan CB20N	01891	BBA	3883/4	B--F	2/82	2/82	-/--
		Saurer U/F (total 4)	?	Springfield		B53F+55	-/80	by-/86	-/--
		Leyland	?	BBA		AB---	by-/87	by-/87	-/--
		Leyland Tiger	?	?		?	by-/87	by-/87	-/--
38	TCD 1179	Leyland ERT	?	?		B--	-/--	-/--	-/--
43	TCD 2885	Leyland ERT	?	?		B--	-/--	-/--	-/--

Notes:

TCD 6001/3 (1/4) ex Kempton Park Bus Service 1/4. Both rebodied Springfield B65F at an unknown date.
TCD 6002/14/03/4, 2001, 6010/08/12/1/09 (2-9, 11, 17) ex Kempton Park Bus Service 2-9, 11, 17.
TCD 6009-12 (17/7/11/9) were Leyland VoortrekkeR models, a special PSV design for South Africa.
TCD 7818 (12) later renumbered 16.
?, ? (?, ?) (Leyland ERT2/1 622576/7) ex Kempton Park Bus Service.
? (?) (4 Saurer) ex Johannesburg MT.

NIGEL MUNICIPALITY

Fleet total 1984: 59 buses, 1 coach (as Nigel Town Council).

		Ford tractor unit	?	BMS	AB---	by3/44	by3/44	-/--
		Albion CX9	58035A	?	B---	3/46	3/46	-/--
		Albion CX9	58035B	?	B---	3/46	3/46	-/--
		AEC Regal	O6624245	TMBB	B---	1/47	1/47	-/--
		AEC Regal	O6625591	TMBB	B---	5/47	5/47	-/--
		AEC Regal	O6625590	TMBB	B---	10/47	10/47	-/--
		AEC Regal	O6625595	TMBB	B---	10/47	10/47	-/--
		AEC Regal	O6625597	TMBB	B---	10/47	10/47	-/--
		AEC Regal	O6625596	TMBB	B---	11/47	11/47	-/--
		Daimler CVG5XSD	13352	?	B---	-/47	-/47	-/--
4	TDG 3694	AEC Regal IV	9822E1845	Brockhouse	B57F	11/55	11/55	-/--
5	TDG 3695	AEC Regal IV	9822E1846	Brockhouse	B57F	11/55	11/55	-/--
6	TDG 3696	AEC Regal IV	9822E1847	Brockhouse	B57F	11/55	11/55	-/--
14	TDG 3552	Daimler D650HS	?	Brockhouse	B--F	-/--	-/--	-/--
15	TDG 3697	Daimler D650HS	?	Brockhouse	B--F	-/--	-/--	-/--
16		Daimler D650HS	?	Brockhouse	B--F	-/--	-/--	-/--
17	TDG 3760	Daimler D650HS	?	Brockhouse	B--F	-/--	-/--	-/--
		Daimler D650HS	25543	Brockhouse	B--F	-/56	-/56	-/--
		Daimler D650HS	25544	Brockhouse	B--F	-/56	-/56	-/--
8		Daimler D650HS	25549	?	B--F	-/56	-/56	-/--
9		Daimler D650HS	25691	?	B---	-/57	-/57	-/--
20		Daimler D650HS	25692	?	B---	-/57	-/57	-/--
20	TDG 3880	Ford Thames	?	?	B---	-/--	-/--	-/--
21	TDG 6144	AEC Ranger	M4RA3289	AB&C	B---	3/61	3/61	-/--
22	TDG 3511	Mercedes-Benz LIB5075	?	?	B---	-/--	-/--	-/--
23	TDG 6671	Ford Thames	?	?	B---	-/--	-/--	-/--
24	TDG 6672	Ford Thames	?	?	B---	-/--	-/--	-/--
25		Ford Thames	?	?	B---	-/--	-/--	-/--
26		Ford Thames	?	?	B---	-/--	-/--	-/--
27		Ford Thames	?	?	B---	-/--	-/--	-/--
28		Ford Thames	?	?	B---	-/--	-/--	-/--
29	TDG 7228	Ford Thames	?	?	B---	-/--	-/--	-/--
30	TDG 7229	Ford Thames	?	?	B---	-/--	-/--	-/--
31		Ford Thames	?	?	B---	-/--	-/--	-/--
32		Ford Thames	?	?	B---	-/--	-/--	-/--
33		Mercedes-Benz	?	?	B---	-/--	-/--	-/--
34		Mercedes-Benz	?	?	B---	-/--	-/--	-/--
		Mercedes-Benz LPO322/51	?	?	B---	c-/61	c-/61	-/--
		Mercedes-Benz LPO322/51	?	?	B---	c-/61	c-/61	-/--
		Mercedes-Benz LPO322/51	?	?	B---	c-/61	c-/61	-/--
		Mercedes-Benz LPO322/51	?	?	B---	c-/61	c-/61	-/--
2	TDG7541	AEC Reliance 2HMU3RA2937	AB&C		B---	6/61	6/61	-/--
3	TDG7542	AEC Reliance 2HMU3RA2936	AB&C		B---	6/61	6/61	-/--
14		AEC Reliance 2HMU2RA3891	?		B---	-/62	-/62	-/--
7		AEC Reliance 2HMU2RA3893	?		B---	-/62	-/62	-/--
36	TDG7547	AEC Reliance 2HMU3RA4098	?		B---	-/62	-/62	-/--
37	TDG7548	AEC Reliance 2HMU3RA4096	?		B---	-/62	-/62	-/--
38	TDG7549	AEC Reliance 2HMU3RA4097	?		B---	-/62	-/62	-/--

39		?	17052			B---	-/--	-/--	-/--
1		Mercedes-Benz 319	?	Craftsman		B---	-/63	-/63	-/--
12		Ford 570E	351257	BBA	2077/1	B---	3/64	3/64	-/--
25		Ford 570E	351436	BBA	2077/2	B---	4/64	4/64	-/--
26		Ford 570E	351440	BBA	2077/3	B---	4/64	4/64	-/--
27		Ford 570E	351495	BBA	2077/4	B---	4/64	4/64	-/--
28		Ford 570E	351879	BBA	2077/5	B---	4/64	4/64	-/--
29		Ford 570E	351910	BBA	2077/6	B---	4/64	4/64	-/--
10		Ford 570E	352776	BBA	2077/7	B---	4/04	4/64	-/--
31		Ford 570E	358350	BBA	2148/1	B48	3/65	3/65	-/--
32		Ford 570E	359515	BBA	2148/2	B48	3/65	3/65	-/--
33		Ford 570E	359516	BBA	2148/3	B48	3/65	3/65	-/--
34		Ford 570E	359595	BBA	2148/4	B48	3/65	3/65	-/--
35		Ford 570E	360890	BBA	2148/5	B48	3/65	3/65	-/--
18	TDG 5401	Guy Warrior 2	WTB5071?	Brockhouse		B66F	-/66	-/66	-/--
19	TDG 5402	Guy Warrior 2	WTB5075?	Brockhouse		B66F	-/66	-/66	-/--
24		Guy Warrior 2	WTB5092			B66F	-/66	-/66	-/--
39	TDG 5406	Guy Warrior 2	WTB5094?	AB&C		B66F	-/66	-/66	-/--
13	TDG 5409	Daimler SRC6	36009	TMBB		B66F	6/67	6/67	-/--
40	TDG 5416	Daimler SRC6	36166	TMBB		B66F	6/67	6/67	-/--
41	TDG 5417	Daimler SRC6	36168	TMBB		B66F	6/67	6/67	-/--
11	TDG 5410	Daimler SRC6	36200	TMBB		B66F	7/67	7/67	-/--
1		Mercedes-Benz 352097-20-601163		AB&C		B---	-/70	-/70	-/--
40		Mercedes-Benz 352097-20-601216				B---	-/70	-/70	-/--
41		Mercedes-Benz 352097-20-601198				B---	-/70	-/70	-/--
42		Mercedes-Benz 352097-20-601217				B---	-/70	-/70	-/--
43		Mercedes-Benz 352097-20-601197				B---	-/70	-/70	-/--
44		Mercedes-Benz 352097-20-634618				B---	-/70	-/70	-/--
45		Mercedes-Benz 352097-20-663163				B---	-/70	-/70	-/--
46		Mercedes-Benz 352097-20-663164				B---	-/70	-/70	-/--
47	TDG 8845	Mercedes-Benz 352097-20-666944				B---	-/70	-/70	-/--
48		Mercedes-Benz 352097-20-653456				B---	-/70	-/70	-/--
49		Mercedes-Benz 352097-20-638565				B---	-/70	-/70	-/--
50		Mercedes-Benz 352097-20-663165		TMBB		B---	-/70	-/70	-/--
51		Mercedes-Benz 352097-20-644025		TMBB		B---	-/70	-/70	-/--
52		Mercedes-Benz 352097-20-663162		TMBB		B---	-/70	-/70	-/--
53		Mercedes-Benz 352097-20-663891		TMBB		B---	-/70	-/70	-/--
30		Mercedes-Benz 352097-20-644026		TMBB		B---	-/70	-/70	-/--
		Guy Warrior	WTB6219	BBA	2723/5	B---	8/71	8/71	-/--
		Guy Warrior	WTB6227	BBA	2723/6	B---	8/71	8/71	-/--
		Guy Warrior	WTB6236	BBA	2723/9	B---	8/71	8/71	-/--
		Guy Warrior	WTB6229	BBA	2723/10	B---	8/71	8/71	-/--
65	TDG 10943	Leyland	?	?		B--	-/--	-/--	-/--

Notes:

Fleet numbers 1-10 are recorded as AEC with TMBB bodies. These will have included the six Regals shown above.

TDG 3697 (15) has also been recorded as TDG 3767.

? (8) is shown in Daimler records as new to Excelsior Bus Service, Johannesburg.
TDG 3511, 6671 (22, 23) have also been reported as TDG 666/7.
? (14) renumbered to 23 at an unknown date.
TDG 5401/2/?/6 (18/9, 24, 39) had AEC AV470 engines. 39 is quoted with chassis number WTB5094 but
    this is also claimed by Duffey's Transport, Mafeking.
TDG 5416/7 (40/1) renumbered 5, 14, at an unknown date.

NORTHERN BUS SERVICE, JOHANNESBURG

Northern Bus Service commenced in 1946. It was not a municipal operator but ran urban services in Johannesburg. It was sold to Johannesburg MT in 1956.

1	TJ 34407?	Guy Arab III 5LW	?			B---	6/46	6/46	by-/55
2	TJ 34408	Guy Arab III 5LW	?			B---	7/46	7/46	2/56
3	TJ 306?5	Guy Arab III 5LW	?			B---	10/46	10/46	2/56
4	TJ 6???2	Guy Arab III 5LW	?			B---	10/46	10/46	by-/55
5	TJ 15362	Guy Arab III 5LW	?			B---	1/47	1/47	2/56
6	TJ 6267	Guy Arab III 5LW	?			B---	1/47	1/47	2/56
7	TJ 13701	Guy Arab III 5LW	?			B---	3/47	3/47	by-/55
8	TJ 6846	Guy Arab III 5LW	?			B---	3/47	3/47	2/56
9	TJ 10075	Guy Arab III 5LW	?			B---	3/47	3/47	by-/55
10	TJ ??381	Guy Arab III 5LW	?			B---	3/47	3/47	2/56
11	TJ 11554	Guy Arab III 5LW	?			B---	4/47	4/47	2/56
12	TJ 13908	Guy Arab III 5LW	?	Northern BS		B---	5/47	5/47	2/56
13	TJ 13867	Guy Arab III 5LW	?			B---	6/47	6/47	2/56
14	TJ 13868	Guy Arab III 5LW	?			B---	6/47	6/47	by-/55
15	TJ 10026	Guy Arab III 5LW	?			B---	7/47	7/47	2/56
16	TJ 51383	Guy Arab III 5LW	?			B---	7/47	7/47	by-/55
17	TJ 18913	Guy Arab III 6LW	?	Northern BS		B---	10/47	10/47	2/56
18	TJ 64258	Guy Arab III 6LW	?			B---	9/47	9/47	2/56
19	TJ 34185	Guy Arab III 6LW	?			B---	12/47	12/47	by-/55
20	TJ 9278	Guy Arab III 6LW	?			B---	2/48	2/48	2/56
21	TJ 82525	Guy Arab III 6LW	?			B---	10/48	10/48	2/56
22	TJ 65892	Guy Arab III 6LW	?			B---	8/49	8/49	2/56
23	TJ 35604	Guy Arab III 6LW	?			B---	10/49	10/49	2/56
24	TJ 93405	Guy Arab III 6LW	?			B---	1/50	1/50	2/56
25	TJ 90179	Guy Arab III 6LW	?			B---	2/50	2/50	2/56
30	TJ 33586	Daimler COG6	?	Weymann		H58R	-/39-/40	10/51	2/56
31	TJ 97903	Daimler COG6	?	Weymann		H58R	-/39-/40	6/51	2/56
32	TJ 97904	Daimler COG6	?	Weymann		H58R	-/39-/40	8/51	2/56
33	TJ 97905	Daimler COG6	?	Weymann		H58R	-/39-/40	6/51	2/56
34	TJ 110.012	Daimler COG6	?	Weymann		H58R	-/39-/40	8/52	2/56
35	TJ 110.013	Daimler COG6	?	Weymann		H58R	-/39-/40	10/52	2/56
36	TJ 110.014	Daimler COG6	?	Weymann		H58R	-/39-/40	2/52	2/56
37	TJ 110.015	Daimler COG6	?	Weymann		H58R	-/39-/40	7/52	2/56
38	TJ 14666	Daimler COG6	?	Weymann		H58R	-/39-/40	11/52	2/56
40	TJ 33320	Berliet	?			B---	8/50	8/50	by-/55
41	TJ 121.484	Bussing Tu11	?	Bussing		B---	7/54	7/54	2/56
42	TJ 121.341	Bussing 4500T	?	Bussing		C41D	7/54	7/54	2/56
43	TJ 83413	Leyland ER44	522598	BBA	M673	B51F	8/54	8/54	2/56
44	TJ 125.932	Leyland ER44	521951	BBA	M687	B51F	3/55	3/55	2/56
45	TJ 123.933	Leyland ER44	521952	BBA	M859	B49F	4/55	4/55	2/56
46	TJ 49022	Leyland ER44	521958	BBA	M865	B53F	4/55	4/55	2/56
50	TJ 58156	Daimler G6HS	25050	Swiss Aluminium Co		B64F+16	-/54	-/54	2/56
51	TJ 111.759	Daimler G6HS	25377	Gove		B54F+13	10/54	10/54	2/56
52	TJ 125.931	Daimler D650HS	25396	Swiss Aluminium Co		B51F+24	-/55	-/55	2/56
60	TJ 123.598	Leyland HR44	521588	BBA M709		B45F	12/54	12/54	-/55
61	TJ 123.599	Leyland HR44	521589	BBA M710		B45F	12/54	12/54	-/55

Notes:

TJ 6846, 13867. 64258 (8, 13/8) had bodies rebuilt by Northern Bus Service.
TJ 82525 (21) was rebodied AB&C B--- -/54.
TJ 33586, 97903-5.110.012-5 (30-7) ex Durban Municipality.
TJ 14666 (38) ex Volksrust, new to Durban Municipality.
TJ 58156 (50) also recorded with a Gove body.

Disposals:
TJ 34408, 30675, 15362, 6267, 6846, 77381, 11554 (2, 3, 5, 6, 8, 10/1): Johannesburg MT 453-8/62.
TJ 13908, 13867, 10026, 18913, 64258, 9278, 82525 (12/3/5/7/8, 20/1): Johannesburg MT 459-61/3-6.
TJ 65892, 35604, 93405, 90179, 33586, 97903-5. 110.012-5 (22-5, 30-7): Johannesburg MT 467-78.
TJ 14666, 121.484/341, 83413, 125.932/3, 49022 (38, 40-6): Johannesburg MT 479/83-8.
TJ 58156, 111.759, 125.931, 123.598/9 (50-2, 60/1): Johannesburg MT 480-2/9/90.
TJ 83413, 58156 (43, 50): also recorded as Johannesburg MT 486/1.

ROODEPOORT MUNICIPALITY

Operation commenced in 1947 with five AEC Regals and ceased in 2003 when acquired by Metrobus.

		AEC Regal	O6625588			B---	7/47	7/47	-/--
		AEC Regal	O6625589			B---	7/47	7/47	-/--
		AEC Regal	O6625592			B---	8/47	8/47	-/--
		AEC Regal	O6625593			B---	8/47	8/47	-/--
		AEC Regal	O6625594			B---	8/47	8/47	-/--
6	TU 6047	Bristol LWL6G	77.032	ECW	2394	B39F	5/49	5/49	by12/68
7	TU 6048	Bristol LWL6G	77.029	ECW	2389	B39F	-/49	-/49	by12/68
8	TU 6105	AEC Regal IV	9822E1849	BBA	130/1	B66F	9/55	9/55	by11/68
9	TU 6126	AEC Regal IV	9825E2119	TMBB		B66F	10/56	10/56	by6/72
10	TU 6015	Leyland ERT2/1	560540	AB&C		B66F	4/57	4/57	by12/71
11	TU 6017	AEC Regal IV	9825E2090	TMBB		B66F	5/57	5/57	by12/71
12		Daimler COG5		MCCW		H--/--R	-/--	-/57	-/62
13		Guy Arab III		BMS		B---	-/--	-/57	-/62
14	TU 6043	Guy Arab III		BMS		B---	-/--	-/57	-/61
15	TU 6039	AEC Regal IV	9825E2216	TMBB		B66F	8/58	8/58	by6/73
16	TU 6046	AEC Regal IV	9825E2219	TMBB		B66F	4/58	4/58	by12/73
17	TU 6157	AEC Regal IV	9825E2236	TMBB		B66F	1/59	1/59	by12/71
18	TU 6158	AEC Regal IV	9825E2237	TMBB		B66F	1/59	1/59	by12/73
19	TU 6184	AEC Regal IV	9825E2421	Craftsman		B66F	11/59	11/59	by5/72
20	TU 6185	AEC Regal IV	9825E2419	Craftsman		B66F	12/59	12/59	by5/72
4	TU 6186	AEC Regal IV	9825E2420	Craftsman		B66F	1/60	1/60	by12/68
21	TU 6187	AEC Regal IV	9825E2418	Craftsman		B66F	2/60	2/60	by12/71
22	TU 6188	AEC Regal IV	9825E2417	Craftsman		B66F	3/60	3/60	by5/72
1	TU 6009	AEC Regal IV	9826E2587	TMBB		B66F	8/61	8/61	by12/69
14	TU 6043	AEC Regal IV	9826E2588	TMBB		B66F	8/61	8/61	by12/73
12	TU 6212	Leyland ERT2/1	611690	Brockhouse		B66F	11/62	11/62	by12/76
2	TU 6031	Leyland ERT2/1	622578	TMBB		B66F	2/63	2/63	by12/71
3	TU 6034	Leyland ERT2/1	622579	TMBB		B66F	2/63	2/63	by6/82
13	TU 6213	Leyland ERT2/1	611355	Brockhouse		B66F	4/63	4/63	by3/79
24	TU 6215	Leyland ERT2/1	L21583	TMBB		B66F	1/65	1/65	by5/79
25	TU 6228	AEC Regal VI	U2RA316	TMBB		B66F	10/65	10/65	by5/78
26	TU 6237	AEC Regal VI	U2RA393	TMBB		B66F	9/66	9/66	by7/81
27	TU 6238	AEC Regal VI	U2RA394	TMBB		B66F	9/66	9/66	by4/81
23	TU 6033	AEC Regal VI	U2RA398	TMBB		B66F	8/67	8/67	by12/83
5	TU 6035	AEC Regal VI	U2RA399	TMBB		B66F	8/67	8/67	by12/89
4	TU 6277	Leyland ERT2/1	?	TMBB		B66F	-/69	-/69	by12/93
6	TU 6373	Leyland ERT2/1	?	TMBB		B66F	-/69	-/69	by3/94
7	TU 6374	Leyland ERT2/1	?	TMBB		B66F	-/69	-/69	by12/90
8	TU 6147	Leyland ERT2/1	?	TMBB		B66F	-/69	-/69	by3/96
28	TU 32614	Mercedes-Benz O317K		Craftsman		B66F+20	6/72	6/72	-/--
		317240 20 005157							
29	TU 32615	Mercedes-Benz O317K		Craftsman		B55F+22	6/72	6/72	-/--

No.	Reg.	Chassis	Chassis no.	Body	Body no.	Seating			
9	TU 32634	Mercedes-Benz O317K	317240 20 005151	Craftsman		B62F+16	6/72	6/72	-/--
19	TU 32635	Mercedes-Benz O317K	317240 20 005157	Craftsman		B66F+16	6/72	6/72	-/--
20	TU 32636	Mercedes-Benz O317K	317240 20 005149	Craftsman		B66F	6/72	6/72	-/--
22	TU 32637	Mercedes-Benz O317K	317240 20 005153	Brockhouse		B60F	6/72	6/72	-/--
30	TU 32644	Leyland ERT2/1	?	Brockhouse		B66F	-/72	-/72	by5/96
21	TU 32645	Leyland ERT2/1	?	Brockhouse		B66F	-/72	-/72	by5/96
10	TU 32646	Leyland ERT2/1	?	Brockhouse		B66F	-/72	-/72	by5/96
11	TU 32647	Leyland ERT2/1	?	Brockhouse		B66F	-/72	-/72	by5/96
31	TU 32708	Leyland ERT2/1	?	Brockhouse		B66F	-/72	-/72	-/--
1	TU 32747	Bussing 192E	?	Springfield		B70F	-/72	-/72	by10/90
17	TU 32748	Bussing 192E	?	Springfield		B70F	-/72	-/72	by12/90
2	TU 32756	Mercedes-Benz O317K	317240 24 2000501	Craftsman		B62F+16	-/72	-/72	-/--
12	TU 32755	Mercedes-Benz O317K	317240 24 2000502	Craftsman		B62F+18	-/72	-/72	12/03
15	TU 6039	Leyland ERT2A/1	7105385	Brockhouse		B66F+16	6/73	6/73	by4/96
14	TU 6043	Leyland ERT2/1	?	Brockhouse		B66F	-/74	-/74	by4/96
16	TU 6046	Leyland ERT2/1	?	Brockhouse		B66F	-/74	-/74	by4/96
18	TU 6158	Leyland ERT2/1	?	Brockhouse		B66F	-/74	-/74	by4/96
32	TU 32734	Leyland ERT2/1	?	Brockhouse		B66F	-/74	-/74	-/--
33	TU 6309	Leyland PSU3C/2R	7602153	De Haan		B65F+17	6/77	6/77	5/96
34	TU 6342	Leyland PSU3C/2R	?	De Haan		B66F+16	6/77	6/77	by11/02
35	TU 6343	Leyland PSU3C/2R	?	De Haan		B65F+17	6/77	6/77	-/--
25	TU 6107	Nissan CB20ND	00351	BBL (?)		B65F+16	6/78	6/78	-/--
36	TU 6112	Nissan CB20ND	00361	BBL (?)		B65F+16	6/78	6/78	-/--
13	CBK 728T	Nissan CB20N	00462	De Haan		B64F+16	4/79	4/79	12/03
37	CBK 755T	Nissan CB20N	00463	De Haan		B64F+16	4/79	4/79	3/03
24	CBK 734T	Nissan CB20N	00461	De Haan		B64F+16	6/79	6/79	12/03
38	DJM 286T	Mercedes-Benz OF1617	355098 64 619903	Busmark		B65F+21	4/80	4/80	12/03
39	DKK 164T	Mercedes-Benz OF1617	355098 64 619571	Busmark		B65F+24	5/80	5/80	12/03
40	DKW 989T	Mercedes-Benz OF1617	355098 64 619570	Busmark		B65F+24	5/80	5/80	12/03
41	DLJ 248T	Mercedes-Benz OF1617	355098 64 619569	Busmark		B65F+24	5/80	5/80	12/03
26	FML 508T	Mercedes-Benz OF1621	355098 64 674302	BBL (?)		B65F+22	8/81	8/81	12/03
27	FML 486T	Mercedes-Benz OF1621	355098 64 674303	BBL (?)		B65F+16	4/81	4/81	12/03
42	FMS 178T	Mercedes-Benz OF1621	355098 64 674304	BBL (?)		B55F+17	3/81	3/81	12/03
43	FMS 161T	Mercedes-Benz OF1621	355098 64 674305	BBL (?)		B55F+17	7/81	7/81	12/03
44	GTF 782T	Mercedes-Benz OF1624	397047 64 855652	BBL (?)		B65F+16	8/82	8/82	12/03
45	GZT 065T	Mercedes-Benz OF1624	397047 64 855653	BBL (?)		B65F+22	6/82	6/82	12/03
3	GXC 777T	Mercedes-Benz O305	307001 61 030950	BBA	3917/1	H98F+16	6/82	6/82	12/03
46	HYY 199T	Mercedes-Benz OF1624	397047 64 936636	BBL (?)		B65F+22	7/83	7/83	12/03
47	HYY 202T	Mercedes-Benz OF1624	397047 64 936637	BBL (?)		B65F+22	7/83	7/83	12/03
48	HYY 211T	Mercedes-Benz O305	307001-61-032450	BBA	4051/1	H98F+16	7/83	7/83	12/03
49	HYY 220T	Mercedes-Benz O305	307001-61-032451	BBA	4051/2	H98F+12	7/83	7/83	12/03
50	HYY 221T	Mercedes-Benz O305	307001-61-032723	BBA	4051/3	H98F+12	7/83	7/83	12/03

51	DFP 782T	Leyland O708 (?)	550803	?		B19F	-/80	-/84	--/--
52	JNP 386T	Mercedes-Benz 613 310404 60 587694		Miller		B26F+8	3/84	3/84	12/03
53	JFM 835T	Leyland Victory 2 ADE JVTB 820128		BBL (?)		B60F+16	6/84	6/84	12/03
23	JYN 326T	Leyland Victory 2 ADE JVTR820149		BBL (?)		B59F+16	-/84	-/84	12/03
54	KKC 322T	Mercedes-Benz O305 307001 61 041111		BBA	4194/1	H57/41F+16	4/85	4/85	12/03
55	LDN 696T	Daimler CRG6LX	64582	BBA	2642/23	H58/41F+6	5/72	-/86	-/90
56	LDN 886T	Daimler CRG6LX	64583	BBA	2642/24	H58/41F+6	5/72	-/86	-/90
57	LDN 717T	Daimler CRG6LX	64584	BBA	2642/25	H58/41F+6	5/72	-/86	-/90
58	LDN 702T	Daimler CRG6LX	64585	BBA	2642/26	H58/41F+6	5/72	-/86	-/89
59	LDN 708T	Daimler CRG6LX	64586	BBA	2642/27	H58/41F+6	5/72	-/86	-/90
60	LDN 724T	Daimler CRG6LX	64587	BBA	2642/28	H58/41F+6	5/72	-/86	-/90
61	LDN 730T	Daimler CRG6LX	64588	BBA	2642/29	H58/41F+6	6/72	-/86	-/90
56	MTN 201T	Leyland TRC/3R	8401146	BBL (?)		B58F+27	5/88	5/88	12/03
57	MTN 203T	Leyland TRC/3R	8500247	BBL (?)		B58F+27	5/88	5/88	12/03
58	MTN 206T	Leyland TRC/3R	8400981	BBL (?)		B58F+27	5/88	5/88	12/03
59	FVZ 794T	Mercedes-Benz O305 307001 61 030838		BBA	3926/3	B54F+37	7/82	by-/88	12/03
60	FVZ 795T	Mercedes-Benz O305 307001 61 030874		BBA	3926/4	B54F+37	8/82	by-/88	12/03
61	CGP 778T	Mercedes-Benz O305G 307101 21 007907		?		AB61+62	5/79	by-/88	12/03
62	KJT 190T	Leyland TRCTL11/3R8300704		BBA	4129/1	B61F+16	3/85	3/85	12/03
63	MVF 607T	Leyland TRC/3R	8401048	Santini		B61F+16	10/87	10/87	12/03
64	MRR 324T	Leyland TRC/3R	8400979	Santini		B61F+16	3/88	3/88	12/03
65	NBV 743T	Leyland TRC/3R	8500325	Santini		B66F+16	10/88	10/88	12/03
66	NCC 029T	Leyland TRC/3R	8500326	Santini		B66F+16	10/88	10/88	12/03
67	NDV 559T	Leyland TRC/3R	8500327	Santini		B66F+16	12/88	12/88	12/03
68	MYT 788T	Mercedes-Benz O305 307001 61 049430		BBA	4440/1	H98F+16	9/88	9/88	12/03
69	MYT 787T	Mercedes-Benz O305 307001 61 049460		BBA	4440/2	H98F+16	9/88	9/88	12/03
70	NNY 227T	Leyland TRC/3R 8500328		Santini		B66F+16	8/89	8/89	12/03
71	NTB 944T	Mercedes-Benz O305 307001 26 000081		BBA	4495/1	H98F+16	10/89	10/89	12/03
72	NTB 924T	Mercedes-Benz O305 307001 26 000082		BBA	4495/2	H98F+16	11/89	11/89	12/03
73	NTB 929T	Mercedes-Benz O305 307001 26 000083		BBA	4495/3	H98F+16	11/89	11/89	12/03
74	PKJ 213T	Mercedes-Benz O305 307001 26 000087		BBA	4567/1	H98F+16	11/90	11/90	12/03
75	PJY 978T	Mercedes-Benz O305 307001 26 000088		BBA	4567/2	H98F+16	12/90	12/90	12/03
5	NVS 157T	ERF Trailblazer E6	65269	BBL	1370/1	B50F+12	12/89	12/89	12/03
1	NVN 654T	ERF Trailblazer E6	65268	BBL	?	B50F+12	10/90	10/90	12/03
55	PJH 915T	ERF Trailblazer E6	66616	BBL	?	B65F+16	11/90	11/90	12/03
17	PLP 198T	ERF Super Trailblazer	66617	BBL	?	B65F+16	-/91	-/91	12/03
7	PLP 223T	ERF Super Trailblazer	66618	BBL	1370/2	B65F+16	-/91	-/91	12/03
76	HTG 186T	Mercedes-Benz O305 307012 61 033207		BBA	3952/21	B60F+12	2/83	11/91	12/03
77	HTG 182T	Mercedes-Benz O305 307012 61 032947		BBA	3952/18	B60F+12	2/83	11/91	12/03
78	HTG 177T	Mercedes-Benz O305 307012 61 033178		BBA	3952/27	B60F+12	2/83	11/91	-/--
79	HVT 530T	Mercedes-Benz O305 307012 61 032978		BBA	3952/22	B60F+12	2/83	11/91	12/03
80	HYH 360T	Mercedes-Benz O305 307012 61 035290		BBA	4012/5	B60F+12	7/83	11/91	12/03
81	HYK 395T	Mercedes-Benz O305 307012 61 035259		BBA	4012/3	B60F+12	6/83	11/91	12/03
82	HYK 418T	Mercedes-Benz O305		BBA	4012/2	B60F+12	6/83	11/91	12/03

83	HYK 403T	Mercedes-Benz O305 307012 61 035258	BBA	4012/4	B60F+12	6/83	11/91	-/--
84	HYK 415T	Mercedes-Benz O305 307012 61 035275	BBA	4012/1	B60F+12	6/83	11/91	12/03
85	JWZ 781T	Mercedes-Benz O305 307012 61 035242	BBA	4076/5	B60F+12	6/84	11/91	12/03
86	JWZ 788T	Mercedes-Benz O305 307001 61 038864	BBA	4076/7	B60F+12	6/84	11/91	-/--
87	JWZ 799T	Mercedes-Benz O305 307001 61 038900	BBA	4076/2	B60F+12	6/84	11/91	12/03
88	JWZ 790T	Mercedes-Benz O305 307001 61 038843	BBA	4076/4	B60F+12	6/84	11/91	12/03
89	JXD 188T	Mercedes-Benz O305 307001 61 038863	BBA	4076/3	B60F+12	6/84	11/91	12/03
90	JXN 705T	Mercedes-Benz O305 307001 61 038844	BBA	4076/6	B60F+12	7/84	11/91	12/03
91	JXW 437T	Mercedes-Benz O305 307001 61 038882	BBA	4076/1	B60F+12	6/84	11/91	12/03
92	KLV 652T	Mercedes-Benz O305 307001 61 038825	BBA	4158/2	B60F+12	6/85	11/91	12/03
93	KLV 639T	Mercedes-Benz O305 307001 61 042453	BBA	4158/1	B60F+12	6/85	11/91	12/03
94	KLV 662T	Mercedes-Benz O305 307001 61 042452	BBA	4158/4	B60F+12	6/85	11/91	12/03
4	SHZ 097T	ERF Super Trailblazer 307001 61 042495 72097	BBL	1642/1	B60F+12	3/94	3/94	12/03
6	SJB 408T	ERF Super Trailblazer 72098	BBL	1642/2	B60F+12	3/94	3/94	12/03
8	TWL 747T	Volvo B10M YV31M2F1XT2044570	BBA	4745/1	B49F+25	4/96	4/96	12/03
10	TWL 735T	Volvo B10M YV31M2F1XT2044571	BBA	4745/2	B49F+25	4/96	4/96	12/03
11	TWL 725T	Volvo B10M YV31M2F15T2044770	BBA	4745/4	B49F+25	5/96	5/96	12/03
14	TWL 737T	Volvo B10M YV31M2F19T2044769	BBA	4745/3	B49F+25	4/96	4/96	12/03
15	TXK 401T	Volvo B10M YV31M2F17T2044771	BBA	4745/5	B49F+25	5/96	5/96	12/03
16	TXK 402T	Volvo B10M YV31M2F10T2044773	BBA	4745/9	B49F+25	5/96	5/96	12/03
18	TXK 406T	Volvo B10M YV31M2F16T2044776	BBA	4745/10	B49F+25	5/96	5/96	12/03
20	TXK 398T	Volvo B10M YV31M2F1XT2044775	BBA	4745/7	B49F+25	5/96	5/96	12/03
21	TXK 403T	Volvo B10M YV31M2F13T2044332	BBA	4745/8	B49F+25	5/96	5/96	12/03
30	TXK 399T	Volvo B10M YV31M2F15T2044772	BBA	4745/6	B49F+25	5/96	5/96	12/03

Re-registered:
TU 32646 (10) to LRR 756T c1979.
TU 32748 (17) to LRR 751T c1979.
TU 32756/5 (2, 12) to LRT 270/84T c1979.
TU 6039 (15) to LRX 670T c1979.
TU 32614/5/34/5/7, 6342/3 (28/9, 9, 19, 22, 34/5) to LRR 764/3/2/1/59/68/7T c1979.
TU 6309, 6107/12 (33, 25, 36) to LRX 652/61/59T c1979.
CBK 728/34/55T (13, 24, 37) to FTV 433/7/49GP c1996. 37 to PDS 558GP c2002.
DJM 286T (38) to FTV 451GP c1996.
DKK 164T, DKW 989T, DLJ 248T (39-41) to FVF 226/8/9GP c1996.
FML 508/486T, FMS 178/61T (26/7, 42/3) to CZD 263GP, FTV 438GP, FVF 208GP, CXL 019GP c1996.
GTF 782T, GZT 065T (44/5) to CZD 262GP, FVY 117GP c1996.
GXC 777T (3) to FVF 213GP c1996.
HYY 199/202/11/20/1T (46-50) to CXL 016/5/4/7/8GP c1996.
JNP 386T, JFM 835T, KKC 322T (52-4) to FVF 214GP, FVY 118GP, FTV 452GP c1996.
JYN 326T (23) to CZD 264GP c1996.

MTN 201/3/6T (56-8) to FVF 231/2/4GP c1996.
FVZ 794/5T, CGP 778T (59-61) to FVF 235/6/8GP c1996.
KJT 190T, MVF 607T, MRR 324T (62-4) to FVF 211GP, DNS 942GP, FVF 212GP c1996.
NBV 743T, NCC 029T, NDV 559T (65-7) to DNS 946/9GP, DYC 862GP c1996.
MYT 788/7T, NNY 227T (68-70) to DJJ 293/4GP, CZD 261GP c1996.
NTB 944/24/9T, PKJ 213T, PJY 978T (71-5) to DNS 950-2GP , DRJ 423/4GP c1996.
NVS 157T, NVN 654T, PJH 915T (5, 1, 55) to DYC 860GP, DJJ 292GP, FVY 119FP c1996.
PLP 198/223T (17, 7) to FVY 109FP, DYC 861GP c1996.
HTG 186/2/77T, HVT 530T (76-9) to FCL 457GP, DYC 863/53GP, DRJ 425GP c1996.
HYH 360T, HYK 395/418/03/15T (80-4) to FCL 466/5GP, DYC 855GP, FCL 463/2GP c1996.
JWZ 781/8/99/0T (85-8) to DYV 856GP, FCL 461GP, DYC 857/9GP c1996.
JXD 188T, JXN 705T, JXW 437T (89-91) to DNS 954GP, DYC 858/65GP c1996.
KLV 652/39/62T (92-4) to DNS 955-7GP c1996.
SHZ 097T, SJB 408T (4, 6) to FPN 641/2GP c1996.
TWL 747/35/25/37T (8, 10/1/4) to FTV 429/30/3/4GP c1996.
TXK 401/2/6/398/403/399T (15/6/8, 20/1, 30) to FTV 215/6/8/9/23GP, FVF 225GP c1996.

Notes:

The AEC Regals new in 1947 were numbered 1-5, order unknown. Withdrawal dates were as follows:
> by 1/60: 4, by 8/61: 1, by 2/63: 2/3, by 8/67: 5.

The original 8-10 were possibly 3 Daimler CVG6. If so, they may have been diverted from a JMT order and
> could have included chassis numbers 13558/9. These have also been suggested for
> Petermaritzburg Municipality.

9 (TU 6126) not TU 6125 as recorded previously.
? (12) (Daimler COG) ex Durban Municipality.
?. TU 6043 (13/4) ex ?
TU 6046. 6157 (16/7) not 9825E2229/32 as in 527EO.
TU 6186 (4) does not have a TMBB body as recorded previously.
TU 6238 (27) not TU 6033 as in 527EO & 539EO.
TU 6033 (23) not TU 6215 as recorded previously.
TU 32634/7 (9, 22) rebodied BBL DP66F c1984.
TU 6342/3 (34/5) had chassis numbers 7601665/7, order unknown.
FMS 178/61T (42/3) rebuilt to B52D at an unknown date.
DFP 782T (51) ex ?
LDN 696/886/717/02/8/24/30T (55-61) ex Johannesburg MT 370-6.
FVZ 794/5T (59/60) ex Benoni Municipality.
CGP 778T (61) ex ?
HTG 186/2/77T, HVT 530T, HYH 360T, HYK 395/418/03T (76-83) ex Pretoria Municipality 524-7/32/0/29/31.
HYK 415T, JWZ 781/8/99/0T (84-8) ex Pretoria Municipality 528/41-4 (this corrects the order in WWK3).
JXD 188T, JXN 705T, JXW 437T, KLV 652/39/62T (89-94) ex Pretoria Municipality 545-7/51-3 (this corrects
> the order in WWK3).

Disposals:

TU 32755, CBK 728/34T, DJM 286T, DKK 164T, DKW 989T (12/3, 24, 38-40): Metrobus 312/3/24/38-40.
TU 6309 (33): scrapped.
TU 6342 (34): Schoeman (dealer), Rivonia.
CBK 755T (37): NJ Manake, Westergloor.
DLJ 248T, FML 508T/486, FMS 178T/61, GTF 782T, GZT 065T (41, 26/7, 42-5): Metrobus 341/26/7/42-5.
GXC 777T, HYY 199/202/11/20/1T, JNP 386T, JFM 835T (3, 46-50/2/3): Metrobus 303/46-50/2/3.
KKC 322T (54): Metrobus 354.
LDN 696/886/717/08/24/30T (55-7/9-61): Guide Cape Tours (Pty) Ltd, Cape Town 4, 1, 2, 3, 6, 5 8/91, re-
> registered CA 1594/21/2/763/576/375. 55-7/9 were rebuilt to open top initially, 61 rebuilt later
> to open top.
>
> 60 to Santos Express, Mossel Bay, at an unknown date and re-registered CBS 17503,
> withdrawn 10/07.
LDN 702T (58): scrapped.
MTN 201/3/6T, FVZ 794/5T, CGP 778T, KJT 190T, MVF 607T, MRR 324T (56-64): Metrobus 356-64.
NBV 743T, NCC 029T, NDV 559T, MYT 788/7T (65-70): Metrobus 365-70
NTB 944/24/9T, PKJ 213T, PJY 978T, HTG 186/2T, HVT 530T (71-7/9): Metrobus 371-7/9.
NVS 157T, NVN 654T, PJH 915T (5, 1, 55): Metrobus 305/1/55.
PLP 198/223T (17, 7): Metrobus 317/07.
HYH 360T, HYK 395/418/5T, JWZ 781/99/0T (80-2/4/5/7/8): Metrobus 380-2/4/5/7/8.
JXD 188T, JXN 705T, JXW 437T, KLV 652/39/62T (89-94): Metrobus 389-94.
SHZ 097T, SJB 408T (4, 6): Metrobus 304/6.

TWL 747/35/25/37T, TXK 401/2/6/398/403/399T (8, 10/1/4-6/8, 20/1, 30): Metrobus 308/10/1/4-6/8/20/1/30.

SPRINGS MUNICIPALITY

Springs Municipality sold its non white operations and fleet to PUTCO in 1975. A fleet of 43 buses was reported in 1984 and 45 in 1988. The operation had closed down by 1999 and no vehicles remained to pass over to Ekurhuleni Transport when that was formed in 2000.

		Leyland LTB1	50981				3/30	3/30	-/--
		AEC Ranger	665035				-/32	-/32	-/--
		Albion SpPW67	16207K				2/35	2/35	-/--
		Albion SpPW69	16405H				5/35	5/35	-/--
		Albion SpPW69	16405I				5/35	5/35	-/--
		Albion SpPW69	16412G				2/36	2/36	-/--
		Albion SpPW69	16412H				2/36	2/36	-/--
		Daimler COG5/40	8281				-/36	-/36	-/--
		Daimler COG5/40	8282				-/36	-/36	-/--
		Daimler COG5/40	8342				-/37	-/37	-/--
		Daimler COG5/40	8343				-/37	-/37	-/--
		Daimler COG5/40	8432	Park Royal		B39F	9/38	9/38	-/--
		Daimler COG5/40	8433	Park Royal		B39F	9/38	9/38	-/--
		Daimler COG5/40	8434	Park Royal		B39F	9/38	9/38	-/--
		Daimler COG5/40	8435	Park Royal		B39F	9/38	9/38	-/--
		Daimler COG5/40	8436	Park Royal		B39F	9/38	9/38	-/--
		Daimler COG5/40	8437	Park Royal		B39F	9/38	9/38	-/--
		Daimler COG5/40	8514	Park Royal		B39F	10/39	10/39	-/--
		Daimler COG5/40	8515	Park Royal		B39F	10/39	10/39	-/--
		Daimler COG5/40	8516	Park Royal		B39F	10/39	10/39	-/--
		Daimler COG5/40	8517	Park Royal		B39F	10/39	10/39	-/--
		Leyland OPS1	460492			B---	6/46	6/46	-/--
		Leyland OPS1	460497			B---	8/46	8/46	-/--
		AEC Regal	O6624780	?		B---	5/47	5/47	-/--
		AEC Regal	O6624781	?		B---	6/47	6/47	-/--
2	TS 429	Daimler CVG	?	TMBB		B39F	12/47	12/47	-/--
22	TS 216	Daimler CVG5?	?	Wevell		B39F	-/47?	-/47?	-/--
31	TS 3624	Bristol LWL6G	77.016	ECW	2379	B39F	2/49	2/49	-/--
44	TS 3595	Bristol LWL6G	77.021	ECW	2381	B39F	2/49	2/49	-/--
45	TS 4902	Bristol LWL6G	77.030	ECW	2392	B39F	2/49	2/49	-/--
3	TS 8195	Bristol LWL6G	77.043	ECW	2400	B39F	2/49	2/49	-/--
4	TS 8196	Bristol LWL6G	77.041	ECW	2405	B39F	2/49	2/49	-/--
30	TS 3014	Bristol LWL6G	77.004	ECW	2372	B39F	3/49	3/49	-/--
49	TS 824	Guy Arab III				B--F	c-/49	c-/49	-/--
58	TS 496	Daimler		Wevell		B39F	-/--	-/--	-/--
6	TS 165	Bristol LWL6G	77.024	ECW	2385	B39F	10/50	10/50	-/--
7	TS 585	Bristol LWL6G	77.034	ECW	2395	B39F	10/50	10/50	-/--
8	TS 924	Bristol LWL6G	77.027	ECW	2391	B39F	10/50	10/50	-/--
9	TS 875	Bristol LWL6G	77.033	ECW	2390	B39F	10/50	10/50	-/--
28	TS 718	Bristol LWL6G	77.019	ECW	2384	B39F	10/50	10/50	-/--
29	TS 876	Bristol LWL6G	77.037	ECW	2398	B39F	10/50	10/50	-/--
	TS 5937	Guy Arab IV 6LW	FD71946	TMB		B53F	-/53	-/53	-/--
27	TS 11400	Guy Arab IV 6LW	FD72894	BBA	146/1	FB52F	2/56	2/56	-/--
28	TS 11401	Guy Arab IV 6LW	FD72977	BBA	146/2	FB52F	3/56	3/56	-/--
29	TS 11402	Guy Arab IV 6LW	FD72978	BBA	146/3	FB52F	3/56	3/56	-/--
30	TS 11403	Guy Arab IV 6LW	FD73122	BBA	146/4	FB52F	7/56	7/56	-/--
31	TS 11404	Guy Arab IV 6LW	FD73190	BBA	146/5	FB52F	8/56	8/56	-/--
51	TS 10605?	Guy Arab IV 6LW	FD72431	Blanckenberg		B53F	3/55	3/55	-/--
52	TS 10606	Guy Arab IV 6LW	FD72420	Blanckenberg		B53F	-/55	-/55	-/--
53	TS 10607	Guy Arab IV 6LW	FD72434	Blanckenberg		B53F	4/55	4/55	-/--
54	TS 10610	Guy Arab IV 6LW	FD72445	Blanckenberg		B53F	-/55	-/55	-/--
55	TS 10611	Guy Arab IV 6LW	FD72547	Blanckenberg		B53F	-/55	-/55	-/--
56	TS 10612	Guy Arab IV 6LW	FD72548	Blanckenberg		B53F	-/55	-/55	-/--

57	TS 10613	Guy Arab IV 6LW	FD72546	Blanckenberg		B53F	-/55	-/55	-/--
58	TS 10614	Guy Arab IV 6LW	FD72577	Blanckenberg		B53F	-/55	-/55	-/--
59	TS 10608	Guy Arab IV 6LW	?	Blanckenberg		B53F	-/55	-/55	-/--
60	TS 10609	Guy Arab IV 6LW	?	Blanckenberg		B53F	-/55	-/55	-/--
62	TS 5293	Guy Arab IV 6LW	FD71657	Blanckenberg		B53F	1/57	1/57	9/75
63	TS 10603	Guy Arab IV 6LW	FD72244	Blanckenberg		B53F	10/54	10/54	9/75
64	TS 10604	Guy Arab IV 6LW	FD72013	Blanckenberg		B53F	10/54	10/54	9/75
65	TS 5870	Guy Arab IV 6LW	FD71896	?		B53F	8/53	8/53	9/75
66	TS 1704	Guy Arab IV 6LW	FD71919	TMBB		B53F	7/56	7/56	9/75
70	TS 6065	Guy Arab IV 6LW	FD71655?	Blanckenberg		B53F	3/53	3/53	9/75
		Guy Arab IV 6LW	FD73121	BBA	224/1	B57F	11/56	11/56	-/--
78	TS 11405	Guy Arab IV 6LW	FD73191	BBA	146/6	FB57F	8/56	9/56	9/75
79	TS 11406	Guy Arab IV 6LW	FD73236	BBA	146/7	FB57F	9/56	9/56	-/--
80	TS 11407	Guy Arab IV 6LW	FD73228	BBA	146/8	FB57F	2/57	2/57	9/75
81	TS 13001	Guy Arab IV 6LW	FD73423	BBA	210/1	B52F	4/57	4/57	9/75
82	TS 13002	Guy Arab IV 6LW	FD73424	BBA	210/2	B52F	4/57	4/57	9/75
83	TS 13003	Guy Arab IV 6LW	FD73425	BBA	210/3	B52F	4/57	4/57	9/75
84	TS 13004	Guy Arab IV 6LW	FD73426	BBA	210/4	B52F	3/57	3/57	9/75
85	TS 13005	Guy Arab IV 6LW	FD73427	BBA	210/5	B52F	3/57	3/57	9/75
32	TS 13006	Guy Arab IV 6LW	FD73500	BBA	210/6	B52F	3/57	3/57	-/--
33	TS 13007	Guy Arab IV 6LW	FD73516	BBA	210/7	B52F	10/57	10/57	9/75
34 (?)	TS 13008	Guy Arab IV 6LW	FD73517	BBA	210/8	B52F	4/57	4/57	-/--
		Guy Arab IV 6LW	FD73608	BBA	242/1	B57F	6/57	6/57	-/--
86	TS 13009	Guy Arab IV 6LW	FD73609	BBA	251/1	FB57F	8/57	8/57	
87	TS 13010	Guy Arab IV 6LW	FD73699	BBA	251/2	FB57F	8/57	8/57	9/75
88	TS 13011	Guy Arab IV 6LW	FD73701	BBA	251/3	FB57F	8/57	8/57	-/--
89	TS 13012	Guy Arab IV 6LW	FD73623	BBA	251/4	FB57F	8/57	8/57	9/75
90	TS 13013	Guy Arab IV 6LW	FD73624	BBA	251/5	FB57F	8/57	8/57	-/--
43	TS 13014	Guy Arab IV 6LW	FD73991	?		B--F	-/58	-/58	9/75
36	TS 13015	Guy Arab IV	?	TMBB		FB62F	5/59	5/59	-/--
37	TS 13016	Guy Arab IV	?	TMBB		FB62F	5/59	5/59	-/--
38	TS 13017	Guy Arab IV	?	TMBB		FB62F	5/59	5/59	-/--
39	TS 13018	Guy Arab IV	?	TMBB		FB62F	9/59	9/59	-/--
91	TS 13019	Guy Arab IV	FD74102	Wevell		FB57F	8/59	8/59	9/75
92	TS 13020	Guy Arab IV	FD74108	Wevell		FB57F	8/59	8/59	9/75
93	TS 13021	Guy Arab IV	FD74210	Wevell		FB57F	12/59	12/59	9/75
94	TS 13022	Guy Arab IV	?	Wevell		FB57F	10/59	10/59	-/--
95	TS 13023	Guy Arab IV	FD74191	TMBB		FB57F	9/59	9/59	9/75
96	TS 13026	Guy Arab IV	FD74067	TMBB		FB57F	12/60	12/60	9/75
97	TS 13027	Guy Arab IV	FD74064	TMBB		FB57F	12/60	12/60	9/75
15	TS 13024	Guy Arab IV	?	TMBB		FB52F	12/60	12/60	-/--
16	TS 13025	Guy Arab IV	?	TMBB		FB52F	12/60	12/60	-/--
44	TS 18577	Guy Arab V 6LX	FD76042	TMBB		FB63F	6/65	6/65	9/75
18	TS 18549	Guy Arab V 6LX	?	TMBB		FB63F	8/65	8/65	-/--
40	TS 18551	Guy Arab V 6LX	?	TMBB		FB63F	8/65	8/65	-/--
42	TS 13374	AEC Kudu	?	TMBB		B66F+17	11/65	11/65	-/--
45	TS 18570	Guy Arab V 6LX	FD75989	TMBB		B62F	6/65	6/65	9/75
46	TS 18571	Guy Arab V 6LX	FD75980	TMBB		B65F+18	6/65	6/65	9/75
47	TS 18572	Guy Arab V 6LX	FD75979	TMBB		B52F	6/65	6/65	9/75
49	TS 18439	AEC Kudu	2S4RA100	TMBB		B66F+19	6/65	6/65	9/75
50	TS 18440	AEC Kudu	2S4RA101	TMBB		B66F+19	6/65	6/65	9/75
19	TS 13314	AEC Kudu	?	TMBB		B62F	3/66	3/66	-/--
20	TS 18624	AEC Kudu	?	TMBB		B62F	5/66	5/66	-/--
25	TS 18032	AEC Kudu	?	TMBB		B62F	5/66	5/66	-/--
26	TS 18608	AEC Kudu	?	TMBB		B62F	5/66	5/66	-/--
35	TS 15070	Guy Arab V 6LX	FD75780	TMBB		B62F	5/66	5/66	-/--
61	TS 18717	AEC Kudu	2S2RA310	TMBB		B65F	9/66	9/66	9/75
67	TS 18715	AEC Kudu	2S2RA293	TMBB		B65F	7/66	8/66	9/75
68	TS 18712	AEC Kudu	2S2RA305	TMBB		B65F	8/66	8/66	9/75
69	TS 18669	AEC Kudu	?	TMBB		B65F	7/66	7/66	9/75
71	TS 18668	AEC Kudu	2S2RA290	TMBB		B53F	7/66	7/66	9/75
72	TS 18714	AEC Kudu	2S2RA296	TMBB		B53F	8/66	8/66	9/75
73	TS 18711	AEC Kudu	2S2RA294	TMBB		B53F	8/66	8/66	9/75
74	TS 18667	AEC Kudu	2S2RA292	TMBB		B53F	7/66	7/66	9/75

75	TS 18670	AEC Kudu	2S2RA295	TMBB	B53F	8/66	8/66	9/75
76	TS 18741	AEC Kudu	2S2RA298	TMBB	B65F	9/66	9/66	9/75
77	TS 18713	AEC Kudu	2S2RA304	TMBB	B65F	8/66	8/66	9/75
98	TS 18716	AEC Kudu	2S2RA297	TMBB	B65F	9/66	9/66	9/75
99	TS 18744	AEC Kudu	2S2RA311	TMBB	B65F	10/66	10/66	9/75
100	TS 13065	AEC Kudu	2S2RA248	TMBB	B66F	12/65	12/65	9/75
101	TS 18335	AEC Kudu	2S2RA253?	TMBB	B66F+17	3/66	3/66	9/75
102	TS 13311	AEC Kudu	2S2RA257	TMBB	B66F+17	3/66	3/66	9/75
103	TS 18282	AEC Kudu	2S2RA260	TMBB	B66F+17	4/66	4/66	9/75
104	TS 18743	AEC Kudu	2S2RA314	TMBB	B65F+16	10/66	10/66	9/75
105	TS 18742	AEC Kudu	2S2RA315	TMBB	B65F+16	10/66	10/66	9/75
106	TS 18745	AEC Kudu	2S2RA318	TMBB	B65F+16	2/67	2/67	9/75
1	TS 19030	AEC Kudu	?	TMBB	B62F	6/66	6/66	-/--
17	TS 18804	AEC Kudu	?	TMBB	B63F	2/67	2/67	-/--
23	TS 18812	AEC Kudu	?	TMBB	B63F	2/67	2/67	-/--
33	TS 18813	AEC Kudu	?	TMBB	B65F	2/67	2/67	-/--
21	TS 18843	AEC Kudu	?	TMBB	B63F	2/67	2/67	-/--
116	TS 26523	AEC Kudu	3S2RA705	TMBB (?)	B62F+10	11/70	11/70	9/75
117	TS 26526	AEC Kudu	3S2RA637	TMBB (?)	B62F+10	11/70	11/70	9/75
121	TS 21881	Guy Warrior	WUM5891	TMBB	B65F+16	11/67	11/67	9/75
122	TS 21882	Guy Warrior	WUM5892	TMBB	B65F+16	11/67	11/67	9/75
123	TS 21883	Guy Warrior	WUM5900	TMBB	B65F+16	12/67	12/67	9/75
124	TS 21884	Guy Warrior	WUM5901	TMBB	B65F+16	12/67	12/67	9/75
125	TS 21885	Guy Warrior	WUM5902	TMBB	B65F+16	11/67	11/67	9/75
126	TS 21886	Guy Warrior	WUM5903	TMBB	B65F+16	11/67	11/67	9/75
127	TS 21887	Guy Warrior	WUM5919	TMBB	B65F+16	12/67	12/67	9/75
128	TS 21888	Guy Warrior	WUM5907	TMBB	B65F+16	2/68	2/68	9/75
129	TS 21889	Guy Warrior	WUM5908	TMBB	B65F+16	2/68	2/68	9/75
130	TS 21890	Guy Warrior	WUM5909	TMBB	B65F+16	12/67	12/67	9/75
131	TS 21891	Guy Warrior	WUM5910	TMBB	B65F+16	11/67	11/67	9/75
132	TS 21892	Guy Warrior	WUM5917	TMBB	B65F+16	12/67	12/67	9/75
133	TS 21893	Guy Warrior	WUM5918	TMBB	B65F+16	2/68	2/68	9/75
41	TS 21894	Daimler SRC6	36258	TMBB	B58F	5/68	5/68	-/--
42	TS 21895	Daimler SRC6	36259	TMBB	B58F	6/68	6/68	-/--
43	TS 21896	Daimler SRC6	36260	TMBB	C37FT	6/68	6/68	-/--
44	TS 21897	Daimler SRC6	36261	TMBB	B58F	6/68	6/68	-/--
134	TS 23043	Guy Warrior	WUM5905	TMBB	B65F+16	3/69	3/69	9/75
135	TS 18258	Guy Warrior	WUM5989	TMBB	B65F+16	1/69	1/69	9/75
136	TS 18317	Guy Warrior	WUM5990	TMBB	B65F+16	1/69	1/69	9/75
137	TS 18474	Guy Warrior	WUM5991	TMBB	B65F+16	1/69	1/69	9/75
138	TS 18665	Guy Warrior	WUM5992	TMBB	B65F+16	1/69	1/69	9/75
139	TS 18818	Guy Warrior	WUM6007	TMBB	B65F+16	4/69	4/69	9/75
140	TS 18858	Guy Warrior	WUM6008	TMBB	B65F+16	4/69	4/69	9/75
141	TS 18879	Guy Warrior	WUM6009	TMBB	B65F+16	3/69	3/69	9/75
2	TS 26165	AEC Kudu	?	BBA	B62F+15	8/70	8/70	-/--
3	TS 10520	Mercedes-Benz O302	?	?	B60F+15	5/71	5/71	-/--
4	TS 12130	Mercedes-Benz O302	?	?	B60F+15	5/71	5/71	-/--
5	TS 12774	Mercedes-Benz O302	?	?	B60F+15	6/71	6/71	-/--
6	TS 26166	AEC Kudu	?	BBA	B62F+15	10/70	10/70	-/--
7	TS 26164	AEC Kudu	?	BBA	B62F+15	10/70	10/70	-/--
8	TS 26163	AEC Kudu	?	BBA	B62F+15	11/70	11/70	-/--
9	TS 15150	Mercedes-Benz O302	?	?	B60F+15	6/71	6/71	-/--
10		Mercedes-Benz O302	?	?	B60F+15	-/72	-/72	-/--
11	TS 17292	Mercedes-Benz O302	?	?	B60F+15	5/71	5/71	-/--
12		Mercedes-Benz O302	?	?	B60F+15	-/72	-/72	-/--
13		Mercedes-Benz O302	?	?	B60F+15	-/72	-/72	-/--
50	TS 26525	AEC Kudu	3S2RA633	TMBB	B64F+16	10/70	10/70	9/75
51	TS 29178	Mercedes-Benz	0770668	?	B65F+16	4/72	4/72	9/75
52	TS 26522	AEC Kudu	3S2RA704	TMBB	B64F+16	9/70	9/70	9/75
54	TS 26521	AEC Kudu	3S2RA634	TMBB	B64F+16	9/70	9/70	9/75
55	TS 16306	Mercedes-Benz	0744098	?	B65F+16	-/71	-/71	9/75
56	TS 16316	Mercedes-Benz	0743833	?	B65F+16	-/71	-/71	9/75
57	TS 26527	AEC Kudu	3S2RA632	TMBB	B64F+16	10/70	10/70	9/75
58	TS 26524	AEC Kudu	3S2RA639	TMBB	B64F+16	11/70	11/70	9/75

59	TS 16317	Mercedes-Benz	0744097	?		B65F+16	-/71	-/71	9/75
60	TS 16318	Mercedes-Benz	0743832	?		B65F+16	-/71	-/71	9/75
79	TS 26781	Mercedes-Benz	0744099	?		B65F+16	-/71	-/71	9/75
90	TS 26528	AEC Kudu	3S2RA635	TMBB (?)		B64F+16	11/70	11/70	9/75
118	TS 16392	Mercedes-Benz	0743834	?		B65F+16	-/71	-/71	9/75
119	TS 20628	Mercedes-Benz	0721949	?		B65F+16	-/71	-/71	9/75
120	TS 26233	Mercedes-Benz	0744096	?		B65F+16	-/71	-/71	9/75
142	TS 26865	Mercedes-Benz	0827080	?		B65F+16	-/72	-/72	9/75
143	TS 12101	Mercedes-Benz	0827079	?		B64F+16	-/72	-/72	9/75
144	TS 21980	Mercedes-Benz	0827354	?		B64F+16	-/72	-/72	9/75
145	TS 23460	Mercedes-Benz	0827353	?		B64F+16	-/72	-/72	9/75
146	TS 28131	Mercedes-Benz	0834155	?		B64F+16	-/73	-/73	9/75
147	TS 17604	Bussing	235.0163	Bussing		AB103D+28	12/73	12/73	9/75
148	TS 17556	Bussing	235.0159	Bussing		AB103D+28	12/73	12/73	9/75
149	TS 31696	Mercedes-Benz	0904989	?		B64F+16	-/74	-/74	9/75
150	TS 31697	Bussing	235.0161	Bussing		AB103D+28	2/74	2/74	9/75
151	TS 24830	Bussing	915.0057.0057	Bussing		AB103D+28	12/74	12/74	9/75
24	TS 17514	Bussing President		Bussing		AB103D+26	-/73	-/73	-/--
14		Mercedes-Benz O305	?	?		B60F+15	-/77	-/77	-/--
29		Mercedes-Benz O305	?	?		B60F+15	-/77	-/77	-/--
30	TS 37742	Mercedes-Benz O305	?	?		B60F+15	-/77	-/77	-/--
31		Mercedes-Benz O305	?	?		B60F+15	-/77	-/77	-/--
32	TS 37741	Mercedes-Benz O305	?	?		B60F+15	-/77	-/77	-/--
34		Mercedes-Benz O305	?	?		B60F+15	-/77	-/77	-/--
36		Nissan CB20	?	?		B49F+30	-/78	-/78	-/--
37		Nissan CB20	?	?		B49F+30	-/78	-/78	-/--
38		Nissan CB20	?	?		B49F+30	-/78	-/78	-/--
39		Nissan CB20	?	?		B49F+30	-/78	-/78	-/--
27		Hino	?	?		B60F+17	-/79	-/79	-/--
28		Hino	?	?		B60F+17	-/79	-/79	-/--
		Nissan CB20N	01266	BBA	3696/1	B49F+30	8/80	8/80	-/--
		Nissan CB20N	01267	BBA	3696/2	B49F+30	8/80	8/80	-/--
		Nissan CB20N	01279	BBA	3696/3	B49F+30	8/80	8/80	-/--
18		Nissan CB20	?	?		B49F+30	-/82	-/82	-/--
25		Nissan CB20	?	?		B49F+30	-/82	-/82	-/--
40	BBK 997T	Nissan CB20	?	?		B49F+30	-/82	-/82	-/--
42		Nissan CB20	?	?		B49F+30	-/82	-/82	-/--
17		Dennis Lancet	?	?		B62F+15	-/84	-/84	-/--
19		Dennis Lancet	?	?		B62F+15	-/84	-/84	-/--
20		Dennis Lancet	?	?		B62F+15	-/84	-/84	-/--
26		Dennis Lancet	?	?		B62F+15	-/84	-/84	-/--
44		Mercedes-Benz OF1417	?	?		B62F+11	-/85	-/85	-/--
45		Mercedes-Benz OF1417	?	?		B62F+11	-/85	-/85	-/--
1		Nissan CB20	?	?		B49F+30	-/86	-/86	-/--
22		Nissan CB20	?	?		B49F+30	-/86	-/86	-/--
23		Nissan CB20	?	?		B49F+30	-/86	-/86	-/--
33	KYM 131T	Nissan CB20	?	BBA		B49F+30	-/86	-/86	-/--
21		Mercedes-Benz OF1624	?	?		B64F+11	-/87	-/87	-/--
35		Mercedes-Benz OF1624	?	?		B64F+11	-/87	-/87	-/--

Notes:

Daimler COG5/40 8432-7 had Park Royal body numbers B5223-8, order unknown.
Daimler COG5/40 8514-7 had Park Royal body numbers B5720-3, order unknown.
TS 3624, 3595, 4902, 3014, 718, 876 (31, 44/5, 30, 28/9) renumbered 12-4/1, 5, 10 at unknown dates.
TS 5870, 6065 (65, 70) rebodied TMBB B53F at an unknown date.
Many of the Guy Arab IV have full fronts – perhaps they all do.
TS 6065 is recorded with incorrect chassis number FD71665 which was Western SMT 1014.
? (?) (Guy Arab IV FD73121) chassis no also claimed by CC Bus Service, Bramley 104 and 145, assumed
    in error.
TS 13007 (33) renumbered to 48, then 113.
TS 13014 (43) renumbered to 108, rebodied TMBB FB65F+17 -/65.
TS 18577, 13374, 18570-2, 18439/40 (44/2/5-7/9, 50) renumbered to 109/7/10-2/4/5 at an unknown date.
TS 26165/6/4/3 (2, 6-8) had chassis numbers 3S2RA636/8/44/5, body numbers 2577/1-4, order unknown..
TS 15150, ?, 37741 (9, 13, 32) re-registered LPB 223/6T, LPF 235T c1979.

3 Nissan CB20N (new 1980) had fleet nos 15/6, 41, order unknown.

Disposals:

TS 5293, 10603/4, 5870, 1704, 6065, 11405/7, 13001-5/7 (62-6, 70/8, 80-5, 33): PUTCO 1-7, 48, 8-12, 22.

TS 13010/2/4/9-21/3/6/7, 18577/0-2 (87/9, 43, 91-3/5-7, 44-7): PUTCO 13-4, 21, 15-20/3-6.

TS18439/40 (49, 50): PUTCO 246/7.

TS 18717/5/2, 18669/8, 18714/1, 18667/70, 18741/13/6/44 (61/7-9, 71-7, 98-9): PUTCO 225-37.

TS 13065, 18335, 13311, 18282, 18743/2/5, 26523/6 (100-6/16/7): PUTCO 238-44, 302/3.

TS 21881-93, 23043, 18258, 18317, 18474, 18665, 18818/58/79 (121-41): PUTCO 27-47.

TS 26525, 29178, 26522/1, 16306/16, 26527/4 (50-2/4-8): PUTCO 296, 110, 297/8, 111/2, 299, 300.

TS 16317/8, 26781, 26528, 16392, 20628, 26233 (59, 60, 79, 90, 118-20): PUTCO 113-5, 301, 116-8.

TS 26865, 12101, 21980/3460, 28131, 17604/556, 31696/7, 24830 (142-51): PUTCO 119-23/06/7/24/08/9.